DEVOTIONALS
for the
ANIMAL LOVER'S HEART
...and other faith-building stories

By Messianic Jewish Israeli Canadian Author

HANNAH NESHER

Devotionals for the Animal Lover's Heart

Copyright © 2017, Hannah Nesher
Published by Hannah Nesher
www.voiceforisrael.net

ISBN #
paperback: 978-1-77354-044-3
paperback color version: 978-1-77354-075-7

Cover design by Liat Nesher
www.liatnesher.com

Publication assistance and digital printing in Canada by

PUBLISHING
PageMaster.ca

Dedication

This book is dedicated to Pepper - my faithful, furry shih-tzu friend. Even though 'some people' (I won't mention names) called you a 'grumpy old man'; I loved you from the moment I saw your funny half grey – half white face.

I am so thankful that we were able to rescue you that cold and rainy night; and I don't blame you for being scared of thunderstorms ever since.

You stayed at my side (or by my feet) for so many years through all our many ups and downs. You endured the long plane ride to make aliyah (go up) with us to Israel. Whenever I felt sad, afraid or in pain, your quiet presence brought such comfort to my soul. I will be forever grateful to you Pepper; and you will always hold a special place in my heart.

And to Nina, my Shepherd/Caananite mix, a courageous heroine, who taught me the true meaning of devotion and loyalty. We did not really choose you but you chose us – and I'm so glad you did. You guarded me, my family, and our home with your life; and we owe you such a debt of gratitude.

When others in our mountain-top village had their homes broken into or their cars stolen, no one would ever dare come near our house because you were so ferocious in your love for us (even if it meant that you sent the cable technician running for his life; and that many a night we were kept awake listening to you barking away intruders).

You even stood up against five wild dogs and kept them at bay so that Pepper and I could run to safety. You and Pepper looked so cute together on our walks – like Mutt & Jeff – and life is not the same without you.

This book is also written in memory of my firstborn son, Clayton, and his adorable "monkey dog", Wilson.

I love you and miss you more than words can say...

Thank you

To all creatures great and small who have inspired my stories; and to God who created them all.

To my children: Clayton, Courtney, Timothy, Liat & Avi-ad, who have allowed me to share their stories (and embarrassing 'little kid photos') in order to embellish my writings.

To Marilyn, my 'eagle-eye' proofreader, who worked tirelessly to catch those hidden 'typos'.

To Colette for her excellent skills in graphic design, and website development.

To the Holy Spirit (Ruach Hakodesh) who gives me the inspiration, motivation, strength, and grace to write – and even a gentle nudge when necessary to press on to the finish line.

To my friends and partners in ministry and in life, who lift me up when I fall down, pray for me, and who encourage me to never ever give up.

Table of Contents

CHAPTER ONE

A HOUSE FULL OF RABBITS

A Devotional on New Beginnings

After leaving Israel and returning to 'exile'[1], it seemed natural that my (then) husband, David, would also return to his former occupation as a taxi-driver throughout the long, cold Canadian nights. One morning, he came home with a box and a funny look on his face saying, *"I have a surprise for the children."* It seems that someone had run out of the taxi without paying his fare and left something in the back seat, Ready? – a big, black rabbit!

---

[1] 2004

"*Oye! Just what I needed*", I thought to myself, trying to smile. I could already foresee my likely fate with this new 'blessing' - the kids get the cute bunny and I get the dirty clean up job. I tried to give the rabbit away to my sister's children by taking it to the family Chanukah party and offering it as a gift; but she wouldn't go for it, no matter how much her children begged. (I know, unfair tactics but I was desperate).

My sister is definitely more skilled at setting boundaries than I am; so 'Denver', as we called her, came back home. The children were definitely excited by their new pet, but not as excited as two days later when an unexpected event occurred.

I was upstairs having a shower when I heard screaming and squealing coming from the children downstairs. I quickly jumped out of the shower, wrapped a towel around my dripping wet self and raced down the stairs to see what kind of calamity had befallen us during my three minute shower.

Being in Canada now, I didn't expect to meet a knife-wielding terrorist face to face; but by the volume of the shrieks I knew it must be something equally terrifying.

All I could see, however, were some small, pink creatures wiggling on the living room carpet. My young son, Timothy, stood there with a shocked expression on his face. Aha – I got it – these pinkish wormy looking living things were actually baby bunnies! That must have been why we noticed the mama bunny pulling out her own fur and making a quasi-nest structure in her box the day before.

We seemed to be the surprised 'foster parents' to a litter of baby bunnies. I told my husband that he didn't know what a blessing he was bringing me when he brought the rabbit home. It's kind of like marriage – sometimes we get a whole lot more than what we bargained for eh? ☺

We moved the mother and babies into a large bin in the bathroom where she could find some peace and quiet. By the end of the week, we were left with four surviving baby bunnies. Denver gave birth to six but for some strange reason, she stuffed them all in the back of a box, covered them with straw, and then promptly forgot about them.

By the time I realized what was going on, we found two babies already dead and the rest severely dehydrated. We bottle fed them for a time, removed the box so she couldn't hide them again and gave mother rabbit a sound 'talking to' about her motherly responsibilities.

When David heard about the birth of the baby bunnies, he exclaimed, "*It's prophetic!*" I failed to see the prophetic quality of a bunch of bunnies hopping around my bathroom, but soon, the Holy Spirit revealed to me also that this symbolizes the new thing that He is birthing in and through us which would result in blessing and multiplication for many people. The Lord showed me a few other lessons through this rabbit parable.

1) <u>SURPRISE!</u> The birth of something new in our lives may be sudden and unexpected. I happened to be in the shower when I started hearing the children shouting hysterically, "Baby, baby!" Not knowing what was going on, I ran downstairs wrapped only in a towel. We had better be prepared to be unprepared for the new thing God brings forth. Let's hope we're at least somewhat decently clothed at the time. ☺

2) <u>STRESS!</u> If mother bunny experiences too much stress at the time of birth, she may not be able to

mother them properly. Mother rabbits have even been known to eat their young if severely stressed. It's not hard to see the lesson here. When God is birthing something new in our lives, we need a place of peace and a measure of quiet for the birthing process to be successful.

If we are too stressed; if our environments are too noisy and chaotic, we cannot operate in the anointing to bring forth His new purposes. I knew that I needed to have a break during the day from the constant activity and the stressful demands of mothering little ones. This rubbed against the grain of what I expected of a 'good mother'– always there, always available, always unselfish and ready to sacrifice anything for her children.

Others, especially in home schooling, Messianic circles seem to support this concept of motherhood. I think it's great. Except for one problem – it wasn't working for me. I thought I was going to lose my mind! Which takes us back to the issue of God's grace being sufficient for what He has called us to do.

For other women this is probably ideal. The privilege to be home with our children is one that not everyone can afford; and children certainly do need the security of their parents' love and attention. David Wilkerson said, in speaking to a group in Poland, that *"the reason I am here (as a preacher) today is because my mother provided me with that sense of security by always being home when I got back from school."*

The issue is not whether or not it is acceptable for women with children to do any work or ministry besides fulfilling her family responsibilities at home. I don't mean to create a debate here. The point is that we must be careful not to guide our lives by others' expectations of who we should be and what we should do. We must be who God in His wisdom created us to be, rather than a cheap imitation of someone else.

Imitating others who we see as 'ideal' and therefore trying to be who we are not is very stressful. In all things we must be guided by the Holy Spirit. We must not make even our own children into idols exalted above God's will for our lives. What if Abraham had refused to offer up Isaac on the altar? What if Hannah had refused to turn her Shmuel (Samuel) over to Eli the Cohen (priest) in the temple?

Denver the rabbit has shown me that we must find ways to de-stress our lives and make room for a quiet place with the Lord before we feel like eating our young. ☺

3) DON'T NEGLECT THE GIFT - If we neglect something for too long it may die. I'm sure that mother bunny never intentionally neglected her babies to the point of starving them to death. She probably just had other things on her mind and became distracted by the affairs of rabbit life.

So, too, may we neglect our visions, dreams and giftings because of the busy-ness of our lives, thinking that we'll get back to it when life calms down, when the kids grow up, or when we have more time. But that awaited time of our life may never come; or the Lord may take us home before we expect.

If we delay too long, these giftings that God has placed within us to use for His glory may die from lack of attention. Beware placing something on the back burner for too long –that convenient time may never come; or when it does it may be too late. The Word warns us not to neglect the gift that was placed within us by the laying on of hands. (1 Timothy 4:14)

It is not only our gift that may die, but our whole being may wither and wilt like a plant without water if we refuse to do what God has called us to do.

When I turned my back on serving the Lord with the gifts He had given me, I became very ill and felt like a dry, dead stick. In contrast, when I express my gifts, I feel like Lazarus emerging from the tomb, resurrected from the dead. A little smelly perhaps from being in there so long, but at least alive!

The servant who buried his talent in the dirt and returned to his master only what was originally given him was called a wicked and unfaithful servant. [2] We are expected to put our gifts to use and not bury them, whether in the dirt or in the back of a box covered with straw.

4) <u>DON'T GET RID OF THINGS TOO QUICKLY</u> - The very thing that we may try to get rid of may be the very thing God will use to bless us. When we first came back to Canada, I was so worn out and discouraged; I thought that was the closing of our season in ministry. I sent off a farewell letter to all our faithful friends, saying shalom, and thought that was the end of it. But God had other plans.

We must learn to accept it if we try to quit, throw something away, or dump it on someone else and it doesn't happen. God may be working out His wonderful plan through what we at one time considered a burden.

I need to say shalom for now; I think the bunnies are trying to multiply again! ☺ (By the way, does anyone want a baby bunny or two (or three or four)?)

---

[2] Matthew 25:14-30 ESV - The Parable of the Talents

Denver with her baby bunnies

Closing Prayer:

Dear God, thank You that even those 'unexpected surprises' can end up as blessings because they teach us important lessons. Help us to see Your wonders in everyday life; and to accept that which you bring into our lives – both the welcome ones - and the not so welcome. Help us to care for our young; and to have patience when they drive us beyond our limits. Show us how to maintain a right balance between pursuing our destiny; and being faithful to our responsibilities. May we not bury our talents in the dirt; but rather use them for Your glory. Thank You for a new beginning in our lives.

CHAPTER TWO

TAKE A LESSON FROM THE ANT

A Devotional on Repentance

Aesop's ants: picture by Milo Winter, 1888–1956

"Take a lesson from the ant, you sluggard..."
(Proverbs 6:6)

There are some very small, even tiny things in life that can come out of nowhere, smack us broadside and knock us into a tailspin – like ants. I woke up one morning especially groggy. Seven days of stomach-cramping diarrhea along with no food intake had left me feeling weak and light headed.

But being the dutiful mother and aspiring Proverbs 31 woman, I woke at dawn and stumbled to the kitchen, fully intending on preparing breakfast for the six children (three mine, three not mine) waiting hungrily to be fed, like noisy baby birds squawking in the nest.

I staggered, however, at the gruesome sight before my eyes – ants! Millions – no – bizillions of them – crawling over every countertop, into and out of every drawer, every cupboard, every crack and crevasse. An army of ants even marched across the walls and ceilings.

AAHHHHHHHHHHHHHHHH!!!!!!!!!!!!!!! I screamed with the kind of scream that usually brings kids quickly, probably thinking something like, *'Wow, Mom is really screaming loud this time – better go see what it's about."*

Breakfast was put on perpetual hold while we dealt with the ant crisis. All we could really do was crowd control. Our spray bottles bought us some casualties but the ants were still winning the battle by noon. It was then that the two year old began vomiting. Down my front; down my back, whatever went in came back out again (even water) – with force. I ran him to the bathroom toilet but missed – at least I got him to the sink. Darn! Plugged. Now I have a sink full of vomited pieces of watermelon and other unidentifiable stomach contents in the bathroom.

By now the ants were also put on perpetual holding pattern while I tried to deal with the vomiting baby crisis – not to mention the mounting pile of stinking, vomit-filled laundry that lay heaped in a corner due to the broken washing machine crisis.

"*Move!*", I said to the mountain with faith as tiny as a mustard seed. Nothing moved.

My various emotions at this point ranged from panic to confusion to depression but settled unwaveringly upon one in particular – anger. And where could I direct my anger (since anger towards God for allowing all these trials to come upon me at once is religiously unacceptable, so it seems)? Ah yes, the old familiar target – my husband – a sitting duck.

"*Why is he not helping me? Why is he so unsupportive? Can't he see that I can't cope with all of this alone all the time?...*"

On and on played these negative, judgmental, destructive tapes in my head. I dunked my head in the kitchen sink, full of cold water (also plugged of course). You may have heard the expression, "*You can marry 'em handsome or you can marry 'em handy.*" Well, it seems like I got handsome. ☺

My Jewish Mama's advice in any emotional crisis was always this – "*Go rinse your face in cold water and you'll feel better.*" Some of these childhood things just come back to us at these kinds of moments. Trouble was it didn't work. I didn't feel better at all; I began to cry.

Another child from the neighborhood, an Israeli seven year old little girl named Ofek, came over to play. "*Why not?*", I thought, "*the more the merrier,* right?" Ofek saw me weeping over my kitchen sink and expressed her sincere concern (in Hebrew).

"*Why are you crying Mammy? Whatever is wrong?*" I couldn't answer. I could only cry harder.

"*Liat, Liat! Your Imah (mother) is crying! Come see.* " she said as she pulled my daughter over to 'see Mom cry', clearly distressed at my distress.

It seemed easier to vent in Hebrew so I began to express how overwhelmed I felt and how lonely and alone.

"*No one cares for my life*", I said. "*I work all day from morning till night and no one sees.*" I was seriously getting into this pity party now.

"*I take care of everyone else's kids and no one ever thinks to take care of mine. I never have a break!*"

"*What about your husband?*" Ofek inquires innocently.

"*He doesn't care about me either!*" I respond with a sniffle.

"*Why not?*" she asks - in true feminine fashion.

"*Oh, he cares only for himself. I have been sick and eaten nothing for a week and he doesn't care at all. No one cares...*"

Ofek was truly shocked. I can tell she cares. She may be only seven, but she is my friend now.

"*Are you brogus*?" Ofek asks.

When a Hebrew- speaking child says they are '*brogus*' with you, they mean they are no longer friends; they are mad at you and don't want a relationship with you - friendship has been severed - whether temporarily or permanently.

I think for a moment about how to respond. I know I really should say "*No, we still love each other.*" After all, it would be the '*Christian thing*' to say. But I am mad. And so I speak the unthinkable,

"*Yes, I am brogus with him.*"

Silly to be having this heart to heart conversation with a little girl but she was there and she cared enough to ask.

Somehow, this terrible, horrible, no-good, awful day mercifully passed. My friend Vickie came by. A woman with an answer for everything, she simply would not accept my pitiful whining that I can't take it anymore. "*Oh don't you say that girl! Yes you can, girl!*"

She kept at me like a cheerleader to a flagging team, and held Avi so that I could at least shower off the vomit and put on clean, dry clothes.I felt embarrassed that she, not being a Believer in Yeshua, should see someone who is one of His own, in such a helpless and overwhelmed state. How could I continue to witness to her after all this nonsense? Where was my '*walking in victory and triumph in Yeshua*'? But she had helped me and I was grateful.

HIS MERCIES ARE NEW EVERY MORNING

The next morning I awoke to a new dawn, remembering that His mercies are new every morning; therefore, we are not consumed. But then I saw them – ants! Swarming hordes of the little black demons, they seized upon any tiny crumb that had fallen on the floor or been left on the countertop overnight.

It took me awhile, but I finally managed to get the ants (and the vomit) cleaned up once Vicki revealed the secret ingredient to keeps ants away. [1] But it took me a lot longer to clean up after my angry and self-pitying tirade. More tears, more time and a few good, hot cups of tea helped.

Listening to a beautiful music CD[2] that ministered in a very real way to my soul helped, as did reading a truly honest book that spoke to my heart as a woman.[3] I got honest with the Lord and He eventually revealed to me the lesson He wanted me to learn from the ant invasion. This is basically what He said,

"Hannah, these ants you see represent the demonic realm. Just as the ants are attracted to any crumb of food, so are the demons attracted to even the smallest and most insignificant of sins. Even a crumb of sin will draw hordes and hordes of demons!"

---

[1] Boric acid powder
[2] Songs of Ministry by Dennis Jernigan
[3] Captivating by Stasi & John Eldredge

Just as we had to sweep the ants out the door and then wash every vulnerable surface with bleach, so too do we need to deal with our sins and the demons that are attracted to them in a similar way. We sweep them out the door by repenting of our sins and then do a total cleanse by washing, not with bleach, but with the powerful and precious blood of Yeshua (Jesus).

We cannot afford to be casual anymore about our sins if we want to keep the demonic realm off our back and out of our homes and families. Remember, even the smallest sins will draw hordes of demons just as the smallest crumb draws an army of ants! Every sin that the Holy Spirit and the Word reveals must be dealt with, and ASAP!

I began to understand that if I didn't want to wake up to the gross sight of ants swarming all over my kitchen in the morning, I needed to clean up after supper a lot better than I had been doing in the past. I tend to be 'casual' about my housekeeping (a nice way of saying I can be messy).

My middle son's first attempt at composing a song contained the words, "*Help me Lord, I have a pig-sty for a home....*" Imagine that! Kids say the darndest things, don't they? ☺

It may not actually have been a pig-sty, but maintaining my kitchen at this scrupulously level of cleanliness stretched me way beyond my comfort zone and meant I had to forgo a lot of other things I'd much rather be doing than cleaning. I had to make sure that not even one crumb of food was left on any countertop. Every dish had to be washed. All floors had to be not only swept but also wet mopped with bleach in the water. Often it took me until after midnight to clean up – but it was worth it to wake up and find my kitchen clean, free of pests and ready to cook in.

Do Not Let the Sun Go Down on Your Anger

The Holy Spirit then showed me that in a similar way, the worst manifestation of a demonic invasion happens when the sin is left undealt with overnight. The Word says, **"Do not let the sun go down on your wrath, nor give place to the devil...."** (Ephesians 4:26-27)

I was finally 'getting it'. I can go to bed angry, saying, *"Ah, forget it; it's not worth the effort to get this all cleaned up...and anyways, it wasn't really so bad – what's one little crumb of bitterness and resentment? Where's the harm in a few unkind words spoken?"*

The price we pay is way too high for this kind of casual attitude towards our sin, especially anger but also pride, rebellion, or any other sin. When we allow that anger to remain overnight, not dealing with it through repentance and the cleansing of the blood of the Lamb, we have just invited hordes of demons to take up residence with us. And then we wonder why things are not working out in our lives?!

"Let all bitterness, wrath, anger, clamor, and evil speaking be put away from you with all malice. And be kind to one another, tenderhearted, forgiving one another, even

as God in Messiah forgave you." (Ephesians 4:31-32)

Today I got mad at my husband again and called him a few choice names under my breath. After all, why should today be different than any other day? My husband seemed to have the unique ability, of all the people in the world, to provoke me to absolute wrath-induced insanity. But today was indeed different. Because before I went to sleep, I thought about ants - lots of them – and I repented for my anger and lack of respect, and asked for my husband's forgiveness.

I also asked the Lord's forgiveness - that His blood would cleanse me of this grievous sin. I then was able to sleep soundly with complete peace of mind. And I woke up the next day to a clean kitchen – no ants whatsoever – until I noticed the black pile swarming all over the laundry room...oye! Here we go again....

"Cease from anger, and forsake wrath; do not fret – it only causes harm." (Psalm 37:8)

Closing Prayer:

Dear God, some situations and people can drive us to the point of insanity! But I thank You that even these annoyances and irritations are teaching us to be more patient, loving and kind.

We repent, Lord, for our anger which we know does not accomplish righteousness; and only opens the door for the enemy to cause destruction in our lives.

Help us to release any bitterness we have been holding in our hearts; and to forgive all who (in our eyes) have sinned against us. Thank you for Your forgiveness.

CHAPTER THREE

AVI'S BLANKIE

A Devotional on Faithfulness

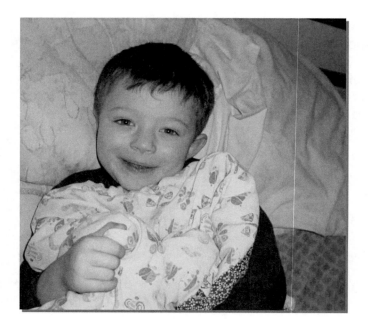

**"Your lovingkindness (chessed), Adonai,
reaches to the Heavens,
Your faithfulness stretches to the skies."**
(Psalms 36:5)

As I tucked my youngest son, Avi, into bed the other
night, I noticed his favorite blankie – now ragged
and torn to shreds at the edges. It seemed that my
futile efforts at hand sewing and patching just

wouldn't suffice anymore. I decided to take it in to a professional seamstress for repair.

After consulting his seamstress, the man returned, sadly shaking his head. *"It's not worth it.",* he said. *"It will cost more to repair this blanket than to buy a new one."* His advice? *"Just throw it in the garbage!"* I glanced over at Avi, sitting in the stroller, clutching at his blankie, looking at me with such trusting eyes. I knew I couldn't do it. So we took the tattered blanket back home.

The next day, I thought I'd try another alterations and repair shop. The woman took it in her hands, held it up to survey the damage and asked, *"What do you want me to do with this?",* as if to say, *"I'm a seamstress, not a miracle worker".* But she too looked at Avi cuddling his precious blankie and in a moment understood its value. She thought for a minute and then, her eyes lit up with an idea. *"How about if I turn inside the whole edge and just sew up the seam all the way around?" "Perfect!"* I exclaimed.

When the blanket was ready, we picked it up and the delight in Avi's eyes was evident. He was so happy to have his blankie back, good as new. The seamstress was well pleased to have been able to help a little boy. On the way home, Avi asked me a question,

"Mommy, why did the one guy say to throw my blankie away because he couldn't fix it but the other lady did fix it?"

I answered, "*Because the man in the one shop didn't understand how special your blankie is, so he didn't want to work so hard and spend so much money to fix it. But the lady in the other shop understood how special your blankie is to you, so she thought of a way to fix it.*"

My own answer led me to a profound thought – that Avi's blanket could be a parable to describe God's love for us. Sometimes we give up on people. They are so difficult, so 'ragged at the edges', so fragmented in their soul that we give up on the relationship. We throw them away and try to find someone new.

Some people are so broken - perhaps dirty, drunk, and drugged – we want to say, "*It's not worth the effort. It would take too much of an investment to bring this person back to any kind of usable condition - too much time; too much money. Best to just throw them on the garbage heap of broken humanity.*"

But this is not God's love; not God's heart. He sees the intrinsic value in every human soul – and so He came up with an answer – He sent His son, Yeshua.

"For God so loved the world (humanity) that He gave His only begotten Son, that whoever believes in Him should not perish but have everlasting life." (John 3:16)

I have been in women's shelters – both as a client and later as a minister of the gospel. I have been witness to the tears of incarcerated women, longing for the children they cannot care for. I have seen people whom society has given up on – hookers and drug addicts, homosexuals and criminals – people who have given up on themselves. And I know that I know that I know that God sent me there to tell them that He has not given up on them. He loves them; He values them; He would do anything to restore them to the abundant life that Yeshua died for them to have.

We can give up on our marriages (too much trouble; I'll get a new spouse); on our children (they're so demanding; I deserve a life); we can even give up on our calling (too difficult, too many obstacles); but God's unchangeable character is to be faithful and long suffering. May we become more like Him as we grow in His love. May we stop judging people that God created and sent Yeshua to die for as hopeless cases, fit only for the garbage dump.

May we walk in the humility of Moses when God threatened to destroy rebellious Israel and make of Moses an even greater and mightier nation.[1] Rather than accept God's offer, Moses prostrated himself before God, praying that God would not discard His people, Israel.

How many in the Church are smugly content to respond in an opposite manner, "*Yes, God, you're right – Israel is a rebellious and stiff necked people. Forget about them and start over again with us. We, the Church, will become Your people, the 'New Israel'. We will be an even greater and mightier nation than the old Israel which is not worthy of You*".

---

[1] Deuteronomy 9:13-14

This 'replacement theology' has run rampant in the Christian Church for too long. It reflects an arrogance completely unlike God's servant Moses. May we prostrate ourselves before the Lord and plead for the salvation of Israel and the Jewish people, to whom we owe a great debt, from whom we have received the Messiah, the Word of God, and a place in the Covenants and promises.[2]

Sometimes we feel so lost and broken, ripped to shreds by the storm winds of life. We have tried numerous patch-up jobs but it's just not working anymore. The thin threads of our own self-effort will not hold up to the trials and tribulations we have endured. This is when we can come to God, not based on our goodness or abilities, but coming boldly to His throne through the new and living way made possible by the blood of Yeshua. We can admit that we can't do it anymore; we can't fix ourselves; we need His help.

A preacher once stood in front of a group of derelicts, took a hundred dollar bill out of his wallet, and asked, "*Who wants this $100?*" Of course everyone put up their hand. He then threw it to the ground, smashed it into the dirt with the sole of his boot, and picked it back up. Holding this dirty, ragged, crumpled hundred dollar bill out to the crowd, once again he asked, "*Who still wants this $100?*" Of course the people again eagerly responded. That bill, damaged as it was, still had value. And so do we.

---

[2] Ephesians 2:11-13

No matter how much we have been dragged through the mud, stepped on by others, crumpled and crushed by life's adversities, we still have great value as people created in the image of the Almighty Elohim. No matter how long we have wallowed in the filth with the swine, we can come to our senses, get up, and run back to our Father in heaven. May we never give up on ourselves; may we never give up on others. There is One who can heal all the brokenness if we will only come to Him.

Prayer: Dear God, we come to You as the healer of the brokenhearted, the One who can mend our wounds. Thank you that You never give up on us. Help us not to give up on other people whom you have created and loved. In Your mercy, please come now and heal us, in the name of Yeshua Hamashiach (the Messiah).

CHAPTER FOUR

BECOMING A REAL DOG

A Devotional on Authenticity

My Dog Pepper

**"God created man in His own image, in the
image of God He created him;
male and female He created them."** (Genesis
1:27)

Dogs know how to just sit at their master's feet.
Sitting at my feet right now as I write[1] is my own
little furry companion. Our children are such a

---

[1] Written in Edmonton, Alberta, Canada 2008

blessing, but this year we have an addition to our family – no, I'm not pregnant again (phew!); our new 'baby' came in the form of a little Shih-Tzu terrier we named Pepper. This little dog has taught me a lot about resting in the Lord, about God's unconditional love; and about just being who God created me to be.

It was not *my* idea to get a dog. My daughter, Liat, at eight years old began to pray each night before bed for a dog - not just any old mutt, but the perfect one for our family. Even though I liked the idea of having a pet, I knew that a dog could be more trouble than it is worth if not properly trained; and this takes time - time that I didn't feel I had to spare.

Plus, I wasn't too sure that I wanted the responsibility of a dog, not having fully recovered yet from the 'rabbit ordeal'. I felt concern for Avi's allergies, remembering how he coughed and sneezed all night long in the Negev when the wind blew the camel and donkey dander into the Bedouin tent where we (tried to) sleep.

I also didn't want to spend the outrageous prices that people charge here in Canada for even a cross breed dog. In Israel, there are so many stray animals that it would be unthinkable to pay hundreds (or even thousands) of dollars for a dog! But Liat, never a quitter, continued to pray.

Late one night, while my husband David was driving his taxi, he spotted a little dog running across an intersection. It was pouring rain and the poor little thing was soaking wet, scared, skinny and obviously in need of some TLC – so he brought him home. Early in the morning I heard the now familiar refrain, *"Honey, wake up! Look who I brought home."* Through bleary eyes, I saw the funniest little face – half grey and half white – the hair on his head perfectly parted down the middle.

This funny fellow had no collar or tags, no identification, tattoo, or microchip. We immediately put in a lost dog report on the internet and tried to find his owner, but to no avail. And so, Pepper became part of our family and he is, indeed, the perfect dog for us – clean, non-shedding, hypoallergenic, quiet, and gentle with children. It broke my heart to see how painfully thin he was - his bones stuck out all over his body. But what was even worse to see in this sweet dog was how he cowered in fear so easily - evidence of likely abuse and mistreatment, probably at the hands of a man. He loves women and children but hates all men (except those in our immediate family whom he accepts as part of the pack).

One of the things I love the most about Pepper is how he always curls up by my feet. Wherever I am, there he is. If I move, he moves. Sometimes (often) I forget he is there and accidentally step on him when I get up, but he is a good forgiver. When David walks into the room, he says, *"Oh look, Pepper is lying at your feet."* I always answer, *"And where else would he be?"*

Pepper makes me think about Mary (Miryam in Hebrew) sitting at the feet of Yeshua and this reminds me of her better choice than Martha. I often look at Pepper curled up at my feet and say, *"Lord, I want to be just like Pepper, just sitting at your feet. Wherever you are, Lord, that is where I want to be. Wherever you go, I want to follow You."*

We rescued Pepper from the dark night - from death and destruction. He was lost; but now he's found; orphaned but now he has a home and family. He was sick and hungry but now he is healed, well fed, and satisfied. The Lord has also rescued us from the Kingdom of darkness - from hell and death. He wants to feed us, care for us and place us in the family of God. He wants us to be healed from all the abuse, neglect and mistreatment we have suffered as well.

It has been incredible to witness the transformation of this little dog. In the beginning, he had real problems! He would become physically ill if we left him, even for a short time. He would never make a sound, not a bark or a growl; he never gave sloppy doggie kisses and he most certainly never played. He just sat there most of the time with what we called his *'grumpy old man'* face. My eldest son babysat him for a weekend and ended up calling us to come home early saying that the dog obviously has 'emotional problems'. But through consistent love and care, little by little, we began to notice changes.

I'll never forget the first time we heard him bark. When a strange man came to our door one day, Pepper growled and barked one tiny squeaky bark. All the children jumped up and down in delight: *"He barked, Mom, did you hear that? Pepper barked! He actually barked!"*

Learning to play was a bigger challenge. He didn't seem to have a clue about how dogs are supposed to behave. A couple of months later, after lots of encouragement, one of the children got him to run after a ball. It didn't take him long to catch on. Now he is ever ready for a game of 'throw and chase'. He even has several chew toys that he has learned to mangle – some of our plastic animals are now missing essential body parts. As Liat put it, Pepper is actually *becoming a real dog*!

I thought about the transforming love of God in our own lives. We can be so damaged by abuse and disappointing (or even tragic) life experiences that all we can do is sit with our own grumpy face on, listless and depressed. But as we are loved and cared for in relationship with healthy, positive people that God brings into our life; as we feed ourselves on the nourishing Word of God and receive His unconditional love, we become more of who God originally created us to be before we got all messed up.

We don't change into someone else; we simply return to our original design. We become more authentically the unique, special, beloved child of God, created in His very image and likeness.[2] In Hebrew, the word used is Tzalmeinu צַלְמֵנוּ (our image), which is the same word used to take a photograph or photocopy צֶלֶם (tzelem). Isn't that amazing? We are a carbon copy, a photograph of our Father, the Almighty God - Creator of the Universe!

God has placed seeds of greatness within us - genius, and incredible creativity; but most of us live well below our potential. It is up to us to develop the gifts that God has placed within us, not just for our sake, but for the blessing of those we share with.

"As each one has received a gift, minister it to one another, as good stewards of the manifold grace of God." (1 Peter 4:10)

We later found out that Pepper's former owner had put a shock collar on him, preventing him from barking without receiving a painful jolt. Likewise, the enemy has tried to silence us, to rob us of our inborn voice. But just like Pepper, we can rediscover

---

[2] Genesis 1:26

who we really are. We can become real and live with authenticity.

By the grace of God we can regain our zest for life in our natural abilities to express our giftings and talents; to play, to enjoy life, to love and be loved in return; to give kisses and hugs; and to express our own, unique 'voice' (even if it starts out as a tiny bark).

<u>Closing Prayer:</u>

Dear God, thank you that You created us in Your beautiful image and likeness – we are fearfully and wonderfully made. You know us so intimately and have a good plan and purpose for each one of us – to give us a hope and a future. We have so many fears and insecurities that hinder us from being all that You have created us to be. Some of us have been used and abused to the point that we don't even know who we are anymore. We are afraid to speak up, or to enjoy our lives. We may even have forgotten how to play. Teach us, O God, Your ways; show us Your paths. Restore us to Your original design; heal us from all the damage that life has inflicted upon us (or that we have inflicted upon ourselves). Send loving people into our lives to help care for us. We want to sit at your feet and worship You again. Where you are is where we want to be.

CHAPTER FIVE

CALLING FROM THE OUTER COURT

A Devotional on Intimacy with God

"For you did not receive the spirit of slavery
to fall back into fear, but you have received
the Spirit of adoption as sons, by whom we
cry, "Abba! Father!" (Romans 8:15)

When we returned from Israel (or should I say rather when we got unceremoniously kicked out of Israel), God was so gracious. He gave us a soft landing. Friends of ours 'just happened' to be going out of town for an extended vacation a day before our arrival. They generously offered us their beautifully furnished and spacious home as a temporary lodging place until we could get our bearings.

As I walked through this luxurious suburban home, enjoying the sensation of squishing my bare toes into the unfamiliar plush, white carpeting (Israeli homes usually have cold, hard, stone floors), I couldn't help but contrast this opulence with our Jerusalem apartment. Compact would be an understatement!

Very few people in Jerusalem live in actual houses – small apartments are the norm due to the outrageously high cost of real estate in the 'Holy City'. Apartments in Israel, however, are not like Canadian ones. Most come with only the four walls – no appliances and usually no closets either. I had almost forgotten what a 'real house' looked like and what it felt like to live in one.

One of my favorite rooms in our Canadian temporary 'house of refuge' was their family room. Big bay windows looked out onto a lovely garden with a fountain and colorful flowers. A fireplace made the room seem cozy and a big comfy rocker-recliner faced the 'entertainment station'. I loved to sit in this room and relax by watching a video or just enjoying some quiet time with my Bible. Double, glass French doors opened onto the second 'family room' where the children could play while I watched them through the doors.

One day as I lounged on the comfy chair that I had now claimed as my own, I heard my four year old daughter, Liat, calling me.

"*MOM!!!!!!!*", she called loudly. I could hear her, even though the doors separating our rooms were shut tight.

"*YES!!!*" I called back to her, equally as loud. But she apparently couldn't hear me.

So she called again, "*MOMMMMMMMM!!!!!!!!!!!!*", louder this time.

And again I called back to her, each time a little more frustrated. Finally, I could see that we were getting nowhere fast, so I reluctantly eased myself off my easy chair and opened the doors to ask what she wanted. It was just to know that I had heard her. It was one of those Mom moments that help us to grow in patience and character (so they say). Why couldn't she just get up and come to me instead of hollering from so far away? I thought.

As I settled back into my chair; however, the Spirit of God spoke to me in the stillness. "*This is what you do,*" He said to my heart.

"*What do I do?*" I asked.

"*You call out to Me from the other room. I hear you and I answer you back but you can't hear My voice because you are hollering from the other room – the outer court."*

He said, *"If you come to me into the inner court, the Holy of Holies, you will be able to hear Me answer you more clearly."*

As I pondered this in my heart, I realized that it was true. So often, I call out to God and although He hears even my thoughts and answers my prayers, I sometimes cannot hear His reassuring voice because I have not taken advantage of the privilege of entering the inner court of my God - a new and living way made possible by the blood sacrifice of Yeshua His son.

 "Therefore, brethren, having boldness to enter the Holiest by the blood of Yeshua, by a new and living way, which He consecrated for us, through the veil, that is, His flesh, ..." (Hebrews 10:19-20)

May we all come boldly to His throne to find mercy and grace to help us in our times of need (which is always). **"Let us therefore come boldly to the throne of grace, that we may obtain mercy and find grace to help in time of need."** (Hebrews 4:16)

 May we stop hollering at Abba from the other room with the doors closed and instead run to Him to be cradled in His loving embrace. May we enter His gates with thanksgiving in our hearts and enter His courts with praise, for the God of Israel inhabits the praises of His people.

Prayer:

Thank you Abba Father that you have made a way for us to enter into the inner court and to boldly approach your throne without fear. Thank you that when Yeshua died on the cross, that the veil separating us from you was torn and we can now find intimacy with you.

Help us overcome our fear or laziness that keeps us hollering to you from the other room. Thank you that You do hear our prayers and You do answer them. Help us to come closer to you through the new and living way of Yeshua Hamashiach (the Messiah) so that we may hear your voice more clearly and know your love as an experiential reality in our lives.

CHAPTER SIX

CHAINS THAT BIND US

A Devotional on Freedom from Bondage

**"And he brought them out from darkness and
the shadow of death,
shattering their chains."** (Psalm 107:14)

I witnessed a most comical sight early one morning
in our village of Neve Oved in the Galilee, while
sitting on my upper porch. The old, spotted Pointer
dog, which seemed a permanent fixture in the field
of weeds across the road, had finally broken
loose! Running here, there and everywhere in his
newly found freedom, I'm sure the dog would have

been enjoying himself immensely had it not been for one most obvious complication – the chain.

Still bound firmly to the collar around his neck, a long, heavy chain followed the dog wherever he trotted, becoming snagged on every rock and crack along the way.

"Never mind", the dog seemed to say, *"I'll just run another way."* And off he would go, backtracking to untangle the chain and then taking an alternate route.

I laughed at the silly dog, but at the same time, clearly saw the spiritual lesson in his antics. The dog had obviously found freedom, but was experiencing great difficulty in enjoying the benefits of such liberty because of having to drag the long chain with him wherever he ran.

We too have been set free. When we received Yeshua as our Messiah and accepted the sacrifice of His very own life in exchange for our own, our redemption price was paid in full. We have been forgiven. The Son of God delivers us from the Kingdom of Darkness, severing those chains which had been binding us to death and destruction.

"He has delivered us from the power of darkness and conveyed us into the kingdom of the Son of His love, in whom we have redemption through His blood, the forgiveness of sins." (Colossians 1:13-14)

He set us free, not because we deserved to be ransomed from the pit, but out of God's great love for us and as a free gift. By grace we have been saved through faith and not our own good works.[1] While we were yet sinners, the Messiah died for us.[2]

"Therefore if the son makes you free, you shall be free indeed." (John 8:36)

That's the good news! So if we're so free, then what is our problem? It seems to me that many of us...okay some of us....alright – I'll just speak for myself then – have the same problem as our friend, Mr. Spotty Pointer. We've broken loose from captivity, but the chains follow us and snag us up time after time after time.

Since I'm writing this at Passover, let's look at the Israelites. We seem to delight in using them as a 'bad example' that heaven forbid we should ever follow! The children of Israel toiled as slaves in Egypt for approximately four hundred years until God supernaturally delivered them with a mighty hand and an outstretched arm.

What was the final step to their salvation? Faith in the blood of the lamb. Although there seemed to be no logical explanation in the natural, each household was commanded to slay a lamb and to place its blood on the doorposts and lintels of their home. When the angel of death approached to kill the firstborn, if it saw the blood of the Lamb, it was not allowed to enter within the household to destroy.

---

[1] Ephesians 2:8
[2] Romans 5:8

"When I see the blood I will 'pass over' you."
(Exodus 12:13)

Whichever Israelite household obeyed the command and by faith applied the blood of the Lamb, that family was saved. That's the good news. So what was the problem? Although physically severed and saved from bondage in Egypt, the Israelites dragged their chains of captivity with them into the midbar (desert), causing them to fall into idolatry, unbelief, rebellion, and negativity. They failed to leave their 'slave mentality' behind in Egypt, but instead carried it with them into their new found freedom.

It was this 'chain' to their past that tripped them up every time and eventually caused them all to perish. Out of the multitudes that God rescued from Egypt, only two men (Joshua and Calev) made it into the Promised Land by choosing to trust God.

Their attitude remained, *"With God's help we can overcome. Kadima! (onward!)"* The rest of the motley crew kept up a cowardly, self-pitying attitude that constantly whined, *"We can't do this. We're probably going to die. Let's go back to Egypt."*

This is serious stuff! I believe the Passover Seder ends too soon. It fails to give the admonition about what happened AFTER the Israelites' deliverance.

"But with most of them God was not well pleased, for their bodies were scattered in the wilderness...these things happened to them as examples and they were written for our admonition." (1 Corinthians 10:5, 11)

We also are saved by our faith in the blood of Yeshua, called the Lamb of God, who was slain to pay the price for our sins, as prophesied by our Hebrew Prophets. We have been set free – rescued, delivered, ransomed - that is an indisputable fact by the Word of God. Then why do we (sorry – I) not walk as if we're free? It's that chain from our captivity we drag around behind us for all to see.

Non-believers can see the chain; let's not fool ourselves. They hear us talk and see how we behave when we're not abiding in our spiritually pious mode at prayer meetings or congregational services. After all, when we're sitting, it's easy to ignore the chain – just stuff it under the pew. But once we start to walk – that's another story.

When trials hit, when pressures build, when relationships trouble us, when supplies run out – what do we do with the chain then? What is our response? Do we have Joshua and Caleb's overcoming attitude or do we whine and complain like the Israelites?

What, really, is the problem? The problem is that although we find spiritual freedom in Yeshua, we bring our slave/victim mentalities from our past into our present lives as Believers. This manifests as doubt, unbelief, negativity, whining, complaining, backbiting, gossiping, self-pity and a host of other 'subtle sins' that yet bind us.

Therefore we have difficulty making any real progress or bearing the abundant fruit that the Father chose us to bear for His Kingdom's sake. Perhaps we get a vision and start walking in one direction – but the chain yanks us back - snag! O.K., we try a different direction – snag!

"Never mind, I guess I didn't really hear from God, I'll just backtrack and take an alternate route..." - snag!

What is the solution? Like our canine friend, we are also running a type of race but rather than being led by our noses, we are running to obtain the prize that is eternal life.[3] The apostle Paul (Shaul), who encountered serious difficulties in his life as a Believer and follower of Adoneinu Yeshua (our Lord Jesus) is well qualified to exhort us in how to run the race.

"Let us lay aside every weight, and the sin which so easily ensnares us, and let us run with endurance the race that is set before us, looking unto Yeshua, the author and finisher of our faith..." (Hebrews 12:1-2)

We must lay aside that heavy chain which is dragging us down, those sins which so easily snag us every time (and each of us probably knows exactly which those are for ourselves), that is making it difficult, if not impossible for us to run, let alone finish, the race set out before us.

Let us not be like Fido, who runs aimlessly, hampered by the chain of his captivity that he drags behind him. It was for freedom that the Messiah has set us free. Now that the chain has been severed, let's

---

[3] 1 Corinthians 9:24

remove the remaining shackles of captivity from around our neck and walk in perfect liberty.

May we truly take hold of the Word of God, leave the past behind, including all its failures and victories, and look forward to the new thing God is bringing forth in our lives. If we hold on to the past, we will become its' prisoner; we will become paralyzed in it, as was Lot 's wife who looked back at Sodom and Gomorrah and was turned into a pillar of salt.

Tears of regret over the past will hold us captive. God is doing a new thing! Halleluyah! Let's walk into the wonderful future God has prepared for us as we enter into this bibilical new year.

"Do not remember the former things, nor consider the things of old. Behold I will do a new thing, now it shall spring forth; shall you not know it?" (Isaiah 43:18-19)

<u>Prayer</u>: Dear Lord, I am reminded of an old hymn I used to sing:

Break through the chains in my life
Tear down the strongholds and the walls!
Deliver me from all bondage and strife
That I may hear when you call and give you my all
Oh Lord my all I give you my all!

O Lord, my soul desires to serve you
To honor you in everything I do
I surrender and lay down my life to you!
Oh Holy Spirit come down and break through!

(Written by Gary McDonald and Tommy Walker © 1995 Integrity's Praise! Music, Integrity's Hosanna! Music)

Yeshua we thank you for setting us free from the Kingdom of Darkness – by Your grace. We ask you now, as our mighty Deliverer to remove from us any remaining chains from our former captivity and teach us how to walk in freedom that you died to give us. Reveal to us the truth that will set us free – search us and know our heart. Try us and examine our thoughts. See if there remain any wicked ways in us and teach us to walk in the everlasting way. We ask this in the name of Yeshua and because of Your awesome grace.

"The Spirit of Adonai יהוה is upon Me, because the Lord has anointed Me

To preach good tidings to the poor; He has sent Me to heal the broken hearted,

To proclaim liberty to the captives,

and the opening of the prison to those who are bound." (Isaiah 61: 1)

CHAPTER SEVEN

CHARLIE & THE RABBI

A Devotional on Setting the Captives Free

"Ruach Adonai (Spirit of the Lord) is upon me, because Adonai has anointed me to bring good news to the afflicted; He has sent me to bind up the brokenhearted, to proclaim liberty to captives and freedom to prisoners;" (Isaiah 61:1, Luke 4:18)

It has been over two months [1] since returning to the Land of Israel and soaking in the sun/Son; basking in the peace and beauty of this little moshav (village). As I walk my dog, Pepper (off leash of

---

[1] Feb/Mar 2010

course – the whole moshav is a dog park to him), I never cease to be filled with joy by the sights and sounds of this beautiful place – elegant palm trees sway in the breeze, exquisite flowers of every color of the rainbow proclaim the reality of a good and awesome Creator. By February, the spring almond trees are in full pink blossom in time for Tu Bishvat (Festival of Trees) and pretty red poppies dot the fields.

Sweet bird songs fill the air and I lift my voice to join with them in praise to the Holy One of Israel. Right at this very moment, a little bird is peeking its pretty head at me through the window where I write. Often I have felt that God has ordered my steps to a foreshadow of Paradise, the Garden of Eden. And yet, even in Eden, there slithered a snake...

It is here that I have recently encountered that same, ancient, religious spirit that Yeshua often battled with while living (and dying) on earth. Yeshua called them 'vipers' and 'whitewashed tombs' (Matthew 12:34 & 23:27). These are people who display a religious exterior but inside have hearts of stone. It is the same spirit of the Pharisee that enforces a legalistic compliance to all the rules of man as well as God's, but has neither mercy nor compassion.

Right next door to the home that we rented lives the chief rabbi of the area. I am certain that many godly and compassionate rabbis live in Israel; but the one next door simply did not seem to be one of them.

The trouble began when a large, loveable, lunk of a Labrador dog showed up in my yard, begging for food but most of all affection. His collar was obviously too tight, his body too thin, and his skin showed through several patches of missing fur. At first I resisted, but then it began to pour rain and my heart took pity on him as he sat whining piteously outside my front, glass door, looking drenched, hungry, and cold.

Over the next few days, 'Charlie', as we named him, became one of the 'Three Canine Musketeers', romping around the yard with my little Shih Tzu, Pepper, and the Landlord's Shepherd, Nina. Together with Liat and Avi, we had a blast together, frolicking in the nearby 'forest' all the day long. When Charlie got tired of running through the streams and puddles, he would come to lean his bulky body against mine and we rested together in perfect peace. Finally it would be time to come home and Charlie would lollygag in the cool of the tall grass in our yard.

One night, I came home to find Charlie missing. I had been away several hours to attend the Messianic Congregation in Jerusalem, and in our absence, Charlie had been returned to his owner – the rabbi next door. I could hear him crying and barking all day long; and when I followed the sound – there I found him – securely chained in the rabbi's yard. I could just barely reach him with my hand and tried to comfort him but he only cried and barked even harder. This alerted the rabbi's attention and he immediately ordered his Arab worker to move the dog out of our reach.

Sadly, he was chained on a short leash at the back of the yard on a slab of concrete full of his feces, swarming with flies; with only a bucket of dirty water and dry pita bread scattered amidst the filth for his food. The yard was like a fortress, surrounded by high fences with locked gates and guarded by Arab workers. Appalled, I called every SPCA and animal rights protection agency in Israel I could find, but apparently, they are desperately short on money and manpower. They did refer me to a man, with whom I communicated almost every day. However, even he admitted that he follows up on complaint calls such as mine on his own time after working an 11 hour day. He said he would try to talk to the rabbi, but did not promise anything. Hundreds of cases even more serious than this one were calling for his attention, he told me. Finally, he stopped returning my calls altogether.

I tried to speak with the rabbi respectfully and kindly, explaining that I was an Animal Health Technician by first vocation, and that a dog especially of this size needs daily exercise and better food. The rabbi became incensed and shouted at me, *"LOH! (NO!)"*

I tried also speaking to the rabbi's grown sons, who also lived on the property, but they said it is their father's dog and they regrettably could not do anything about it.

Frustrated, I began to ask around the moshav discretely about this situation and most everyone cautioned me against becoming involved with his man whom they considered evil and wicked. My son in law also warned me that this rabbi is likely heavy into kabbalah (Jewish mysticism - which can be like a form of witchcraft).

Desperate, I went to the central authority on the moshav and was horrified by what they told me. The man working in the office told me that this 'so-called man of God', used to keep horses. He refused to give them sufficient food or water until finally they became so weak that the jackals came and ate the horses alive. Surely, he said, this dog will die if nothing is done. (No wonder many Israelis want nothing to do with 'religion'.) I began to weep in the office as grief and indignation rose up within me.

"Something must be done to help this dog", I pleaded.

The man in the office looked at me with contempt and said, *"You come from a civilized country, but you are in the Middle East now; things are different here. This is the chief rabbi of the area. He is a former army officer. He has power, position and protectsia* [2]. *No one can or will touch him. There is nothing you can do!"*

His only advice to me was to try passing food under the fence to keep him alive. Unfortunately, the rabbi came upon me passing Charlie some food and water under the fence and he raged at me, threatening to call the police and throw me in jail if he ever saw me near there again.

To be honest, this was my first real encounter with someone that I would consider truly wicked; and I felt not only intimidated, but also frightened for perhaps the first time in my life. This came directly on the heels of my (then) husband, David, being refused entry into Israel at the airport and deported back to Poland [3]; so there was also the sense of being a woman alone and vulnerable with children to care for in a foreign land.

But God reminded me that we are never alone, for He has promised to never leave or forsake us. He helped me to cut off my fears with a swift, sharp two – edged sword, which is His Word. **"I sought the Lord, and He heard me, and delivered me from all my fears."** (Psalms 34:4)

"The Lord is my light and my salvation; Whom shall I fear? The Lord is the strength

---

[2] protection

[3] Due to Israel's refusal to grant him citizenship or even a visa

of my life, of whom shall I be afraid?" (Psalms 27: 1)

"The Lord is my helper; I will not fear, what can (mortal) man do unto me?" (Hebrews 13:6)

I claimed these powerful Scriptures to give me the courage to continue to try and alleviate the suffering of one of God's creatures. I know that there may be some who would say to just leave it alone; it's just a dog. But I felt I had no choice. I could not close and harden my heart while still walking in the love of God.

"If anyone sees someone in need and closes their heart of compassion, how can the love of God be in them?" (1 John 3: 17)

I believe that this primarily applies to people, but also extends to all of God's creatures. The Torah states that **"A righteous man regards the life of his animal, but the tender mercies of the wicked are cruel."** (Proverbs 12:10)

Yeshua prayed for the wicked people who crucified Him, and commanded us to pray for our enemies, so we prayed for this rabbi, my neighbor, that God would exchange his heart of stone for a heart of flesh and put a new Spirit within him;[4] visit him with salvation (Yeshua) and grant him repentance leading to eternal life.

---

[4] Ezekiel 36: 26

We always need prayers for our protection here in the Land where spiritual warfare can be intense. The same day of my encounter with the rabbi, the dog of our neighbor on the other side bit my daughter, Liat. (I know... what a day!) It broke the skin and bruised her leg, but thank God the dog had been vaccinated or it could have been disastrous. Liat had just stepped out of our gate alone for a minute to get some fresh air when the dog suddenly attacked her.

The Lord showed me a powerful word picture of the need to stay within the boundaries of God's protection. The fence represents our obedience. The gate represents our free will. Walking outside the gate represents our sinful desire to stray beyond the boundaries of God's word. In our rebellion, we want to be 'free'; in our pride, we think we will be okay outside the 'restriction' of the fence.

Earlier in the day, I had asked Liat to wear long pants but she chose to stay in her shorts. Had she simply said, "*Yes, Mom.*" and changed into her jeans, the bite would not have been nearly as bad. God is teaching me to walk less in the fear of man but more in the fear of the Lord.

"The angel of the Lord encamps around those who fear Him, and delivers them...Oh, fear the Lord, you His holy ones (K'doshim). Behold the eye of the Lord is on those who fear Him. There is no want to those who fear Him...Come my children and listen to me, I will teach you <u>the fear of the Lord</u>..." (Psalms 34:7-11)

"<u>By humility and fear of the Lord</u> are riches and honor and life." (Proverbs 22:4)

"Charm is deceitful and beauty passing but <u>a woman who fears the Lord,</u> she shall be praised." (Proverbs 31:30)

It takes real humility, especially as a woman in our Feminist - orientated world to walk in the fear of the Lord - in submission and humility - but this is the protective fence that God has set up for our good.

Today when I went out with Pepper and Nina (Three Musketeers minus one) on our daily morning walk, the usual dogs came rushing to their respective fences to growl and bark menacingly until we passed. One particularly fierce dog is both chained and fenced (for which I am truly thankful).

I began to think of how God has all these dangerous demonic forces caged and chained so that even though they may threaten and frighten, they cannot touch us.

I say, *"I am a covenant child of God, covered in the blood of the Lamb; the evil one cannot touch me."*

Halleluyah for God's protective restraint over the forces of darkness that seek to steal, kill and destroy. But it is critical in this hour that we walk in the fear of the Lord and simple obedience, being led by the wisdom of the Holy Spirit (Ru'ach Hakodesh).

"Whoever listens to Me (wisdom) will dwell safely, and will be secure, without fear of evil." (Prov. 1:33)

We are exhorted not to fret or be angry; but allow the Lord to deal with people in His perfect justice and mercy: **"Do not fret because of evildoers, nor be envious of the workers of iniquity, for they shall soon be cut down like the grass, and wither as the green herb."** (Psalm 37:1-2)

Yesterday, my landlords hired the Thailandi workers to cut down all the grass and weeds. This place I moved into has a lovely yard and garden area but for years it was left untended; therefore it had become overgrown with weeds and tall grass.

Outside my window today, I look upon mounds and mounds of cut grass just withering on the ground. My yard stands as a powerful word picture to me today of what the Lord will do to those who resist His grace and mercy to persist in their wickedness.

This man (the chief rabbi) may have great power and authority in this land, but our God is a higher authority. He is El Elyon – God MOST HIGH! Halleluyah!

"I have seen the wicked in great power, spreading himself like a native green tree, yet he passed away, and behold, he was no more, indeed I sought him, but he could not be found." (Psalm 37:35-36)

What are we to do in these situations when confronted with such wickedness? We trust in the Lord and continue to do good. Feed on His faithfulness. Delight ourselves in the Lord and commit our way to Him. Rest in Him and wait patiently for Him to work in the situation. Cease from anger and forsake wrath; do not fret – it only causes harm. (Psalms 37:3-8)

It is not the proud and powerful who will, in the end, inherit the earth and enjoy an abundance of peace (shalom), but rather the meek and humble, those who hope in the Lord. (Psalm 37:11)

And so what became of Charlie? This is where the prayer warriors came in! Animal lovers in the nations joined with me in prayers and petitions to the Lord (with thanksgiving) for Charlie's freedom, safety, and well-being. My daughter, Courtney, along with her mother in law, Batya, and myself committed this whole situation to the Lord with prayer and fasting.

During our time of intercession, the Holy Spirit revealed why He gave me such a burden for this particular dog and why he led me to move into a home next to this rabbi.

This dog stood chained, imprisoned, and mistreated as a symbol for all the Jewish people here in this land and in the nations who are bound and chained by a religious spirit. They are denied the joy of liberty and freedom in the Spirit; they are fed the meager rations of religion rather than the soul satisfying living bread (lechem chayim) that is Yeshua Hamashiach (the Messiah).

They are drinking dirty, stagnant waters of rules and rituals rather than the living waters of the Spirit of God. And they dwell in the midst of their own filth from sin that has not been covered and cleansed through forgiveness in the blood of the Lamb.

They sit day after day after day, oppressed in their suffering, loneliness and sense of alienation from the love of God that is so freely available in the Messiah.

On Shabbat, the Sabbath day, Yeshua entered a synagogue in Nazareth and boldly proclaimed to have fulfilled the words of the Prophet Isaiah,

"The Spirit of the Lord (Ruach Adonai) is upon Me...to proclaim liberty to the captives...to set free those who are oppressed."

(Luke 4:16-18, Isaiah 61:1)

Yeshua reads from scroll of Isaiah in Nazareth synagogue, painting by James Tissot

Therefore, we pray not only for this particular dog; but also for the release of Jewish people caught in the captivity of man-made religion - that they may be delivered into the joy of a personal relationship with the living God through His son, Yeshua (salvation).

NOTE: UPDATE & PRAISE REPORT:

You may be wondering about the end of the story: what ever happened to Charlie & the Rabbi? Well, to make a long story short, I got in touch with an animal rights activist group in Israel through a Yahoo group. They were incensed at the situation and suggested I cut through the chain link fence to get the dog out or even try to charm the Arab worker into letting me into the compound to rescue Charlie.

Neither of these ideas sounded too appealing to me as an Israeli jail is not where I wanted to spend a good portion of the rest of my life. :)

Finally, one woman phoned the rabbi and threatened to plaster it all over the newspapers that the head rabbi of Mateh Yehudah (Tribe of Judah territory) is torturing his dog. Shortly after that phone call, Charlie was set free and came running over to our house. We were able to shove his huge body into my little car and take him to the vet for medical treatment.

'Charlie' was loosed from his chains, received some decent dog food, a cleansing bath and treatment for a terrible skin condition and tick infestation.

Charlie's condition at the time of rescue (2010)

Charlie's 'home' where he was being held captive

This triumphant testimony demonstrates the power that is released when people join together in unity to pray and seek to do good.

Happy Charlie 4 years later in 2014

Charlie often came to visit while enjoying several more years of freedom and decent treatment until, sadly, he passed away in 2015 of natural causes.

Rest in peace Charlie. You deserved better.

Prayer: We thank you, God of Jacob, that you execute justice for the oppressed, give food to the hungry and freedom to the prisoners. Your tender mercies are over all your creations. (Psalms 145:9)

Help us to be courageous in fighting for justice and freedom for any of Your creatures who are oppressed, mistreated or suffering injustice.

Set us free from all religious legalism and bondage; and help us to set others free as well. In Your name.

CHAPTER EIGHT

A DAY AT THE BEACH

A Devotional on Enjoying Life

Liat playing on Hertzliyah beach

The other day, we packed up a picnic lunch, mats for laying on the sand, bathing suits, towels, sunscreen, sun hats, folding chairs, blow up dinghy boat, pails and shovels and containers to keep shells and other interesting stuff we find in the sea, and set off for a day at the beach.

I don't know what took us so long. ☺

It seems that we keep putting off doing fun but 'non-productive' things like this until a more convenient time. The 'to do lists' never end and the day-timer schedules are always packed full of things we 'have to do' like go to the dentist or 'should do' like clean the house. And so beach days often get relegated to something we will do 'one day when we have time ...'

But with Timothy leaving home for university in just a couple of weeks, I came to the realization that our days together are numbered and it's now or never. So...off we went to our favorite beach at Hertzliyah[1], despite the temperatures that soared into the 40's and the jellyfish (meduzzot) warnings.

---

[1] Named after Theodor Hertzl, Father of Zionism

When we arrived, I was surprised to see the beach full of people, many of whom were enjoying the warm waters and gentle waves of the Mediterranean.

Clearly, the same courageous people who do not let the threat of terrorism stop them from riding the buses or sitting at local cafes to drink Espresso are not going to let a few little meduzzot (stinging jellyfish) keep them out of the water.

I decided to join them. Liat, having been stung by a meduzzah at the Rishon L'tziyon beach in the past, was reluctant to enter the water but buoyed by my enthusiasm, she finally relented and joined in the fun. And what fun it was!

We could walk way out into the sea in one area that stayed shallow (between the red flags but far enough away from the black ones). Because the water was so warm, I didn't mind at all being splashed and eventually dumped into the sea by the waves.

After a while, I came to enjoy being moved by the force of the sea and just relaxed into the motion (once I learned to keep my eyes and mouth shut against the onslaught of salty sea water).

I finally realized how long it had been since I just relaxed and enjoyed myself for the sheer pleasure of the experience. It felt like waters of salvation to my parched and weary soul.

The week before we drove to the beach, my car had died in Ein Kerem, a quaint suburb of Jerusalem. Thankfully we got a boost but once we turned the car off, it again wouldn't start. We needed another boost to get it to the garage when they reopened on Sunday. Here in Israel, the weekend is basically Friday afternoon to Saturday night and Sunday is just another working day.

I had assumed the problem was a weak or dead battery, but when checked, the battery was just fine – it was the alternator that was the problem. Now, I don't know enough about cars, engines, or anything remotely mechanical to even begin to discuss this issue technically. But the Holy Spirit showed me a word picture through this situation with my little Seat IBIZA.

Sometimes we feel so low on energy (speaking for myself). I'm not talking about a little fatigue now and again, but to the point of really not being able to function on a fairly regular basis. Like a car with a dead battery (so we think). So we give it a boost – a shot of caffeine, or a herbal energy pill (or both simultaneously) - hoping to jump-start the body enough to get it running again.

But sometimes the problem runs deeper than this and simply giving the body a boost doesn't solve the issue. Once the 'boost' wears off, we need another even stronger boost until even that level of stimulant doesn't quite cut it either.

As far as I was able to understand, when the alternator is not functioning, it is not sending the necessary charge to the battery. So the battery may be fine but it's just not getting the charge it needs.

To all those with any knowledge of mechanics I hope you will forgive me for probable errors in this explanation. ☺ But what the Holy Spirit showed me is still applicable. Our body systems may be functioning, but it is our connection to the charge that is in need of attention.

Just as our bodies need to be fed and cared for with proper nutrition, appropriate exercise, and sufficient sleep, so do we need to 'feed' and care for our soul and spirit. We need to spend time in the Word and prayer and worship. Yes, of course.

But I think we also need to nourish our soul by just spending time in nature, like at the beach, or in the mountains or forest - appreciating the beauty of God's creations. We need to just roll around like a blob in the waves of the sea and laugh when we get tossed on our backside.

We need to lounge in the shade and read a good book just for the sheer pleasure of it – and watch our kids play in the sand.

Avi & Aden (my grandson) playing in the sand at the beach

We need to paint, or listen to music, or dance, or sing or do whatever it is that brings joy to our soul. It seems to me that this is how we fix the problem with the alternator and get the thing 'charging' again. We need to put the 'charge' back in life!

Liat relaxing at the Mediterranean Beach

The thing is that I did, in fact, get mildly stung by a jellyfish (my turn instead of Liat's); and Avi got a sunburn on his back from failing to reapply sunscreen after our picnic lunch. But it was still well worth it!

After awhile, we come to a sober realization in life that we are still sons and daughters of Adam and Eve; and as such share in their banishment from the Garden of Eden (at least while here on earth). Life has its share of tsuris (Yiddish word meaning troubles, sorrows, or trials).

Meduzzot still inhabit the sea and the sun still burns if we're not careful; and yet we can still find joy in life if we will take the time to nurture our souls, as well as our spirit, mind, and body.

The Bible contains a beautiful prayer:

"Beloved, I pray that in all respects you may prosper and be in good health, <u>just as your soul prospers.</u>" (3 John 1:2)

It is essential for our complete health and total well being that we prosper not only in our physical body or in our finances, but also **in our soul**. We can take pleasure, daily, in the goodness of God and enjoy the little pockets of Eden that He has provided here on earth, just waiting patiently for us to come and be refreshed.

"I would have lost heart unless I had believed that I would see the goodness of the Lord in the Land of the living!" (Psalm 27:13)

<u>Prayer</u>: Heavenly Father, we can get so caught up in our work and all the daily duties and responsibilities of life – thinking that these are so so important – while our souls are crying out for even a drop of living water. Help us not to miss the opportunities to enjoy our lives and to actually create times of refreshing and relaxation with our friends and family so that life feels worth living again.

And please God, help us to do this without the typical guilt of feeling 'non-productive'. Life is so short; help us not to waste time on things that don't really matter in the long run. Remind us when we need to take a break just to lounge in the sun or wade in the water; and to enjoy the beauty of Your creation with our loved ones. Heal our bodies and restore our souls.

In Yeshua's name. Amen v'Amen.

Shalom from Israel! Love Hannah ☺

CHAPTER NINE

DO LIKE A DUCK DOES!

A Devotional on Discernment

"He who says he abides in Him ought himself also to walk just as He walked." (1 John 2:6)

Upon reading this delightful little children's story [1] to my children one night, the Lord showed me yet another spiritual truth through animal parables. In the story, several little ducklings follow their mother,

---

[1] <u>Do Like a Duck Does</u>, written by Judy Hindley and illustrated by Ivan Bates (Candlewick Press, 2007)

doing whatever ducks do. The mother duck quacks to her ducklings, *"Do like a duck does! Do like me!"*

It reminds me of the other day, walking along with my own *'ducklings'*. My daughter took on an awkward, ungainly gait, with both arms swinging beside her pre-adolescent body at full stride. *"Look Mom, I'm walking just like you!"* she exclaimed happily. *"I had definitely better get myself checked at the nearest local chiropractor"*, was my first thought. The next was a scary one: "What other qualities and characteristics of mine is she seeking to imitate?"

Could I honestly say to my children, *"Do like me!"*? My hope is that they would imitate generosity, mercy upon the poor, justice, humility, kindness, gentleness, patience, love, and self- control. But these are only marginally present - and then only on a *good* day. What about the *'growing days'*, when self-control flies out the window - along with love, joy, peace, patience, gentleness and all the other fruits of the spirit?

What about the times when we feel like telling everyone to *'take a hike'* (or worse)? What about the times when we do actually allow such words to slip? That is when we need to fall upon the grace and mercy of the Lord to help make up for our faults, failings, and weaknesses. For there are no perfect parents – except our Heavenly Father – and even He had problems with His children! ☺

In Paul's writings in the New Testament, he exhorts us to **"be imitators of God as dear children."** (Ephesians 5:1) In our hearts, we so long to be more and more like Him. We sing, *"Lord, I want to be more like you..."* And we mean it – we really do! Our spirit desires to be conformed into the image of God's Son. But the flesh hates the cross and the carnal mind is perpetually at enmity with God.

Life has a way of making us quite unlike our Lord. We can be grumpy, impatient, and unforgiving; but we can confess these sins and keep paddling along, trusting in God's faithfulness to complete the good work He has started in us, exhorting our own ducklings: *'Do like Yeshua does'*.

 If we are truly following our Savior we need to 'walk as He walked'. **"He who says he abides in Him ought himself also to walk just as He walked."** (1 John 2:6) How did He walk? In sacrificial love; therefore so must we. Love, however, does not mean blind trust. We are to be wise as serpents and gentle as doves.[2]

Creepy Creatures

All is well in the story until Mama Duck notices someone creeping (note the word 'creeping') close behind, following them. Mama challenges this creepy creature, *"Do you think you're a duck?"*

The stranger assures Mama Duck that he is, indeed, *'one of them'* – a big, brown duck. Hmm....Mama notices that this creature seems to lack some essential 'ducky' characteristics. For one thing, he has no feathers, no webbed feet, and no beak. He also possesses some definitely 'un-ducky' ones: four

---

[2] Matthew 10:16

claws on hairy feet, two pointy ears sticking straight up, a long foxy nose and a wicked foxy smile.

Have you ever had this experience? Someone begins to follow us around (perhaps they have their eye on our ducklings); maybe we even run into them at church in the singles group. We ask them if they are a Christian and they assure us that they most definitely are! As a brand new 'baby believer', a man in the church I attended began to follow me. Little did I know that he had his eye on my 'ducklings'.

He claimed to be a Christian – he lifted his hands in church and shouted, *"Glory! Worthy is the Lamb!"* Sounded like a believer.... looked like a believer.... he seemed well off, friendly, and good with children. But I was fooled; I lacked discernment. In reality he had just been released from prison for molesting his adopted daughter. Thank God, I narrowly escaped a disaster by running away to a women's shelter.

The Word says that **"a beautiful woman who lacks discretion is like a pig with a gold ring in its snout."** (Proverbs 11:22)

Not a pretty picture, eh? It seems that there are many attractive, intelligent women and men out there in the Body of Messiah lacking discernment in their relationship choices. How may we discern who is a true Believer and who is a 'fox' in duck's feathers? How can we tell the difference? How can we teach our own children to discern a person's true character before becoming seriously involved? I think that this simple story gives us an astute answer.

Checking out the Fruit

The first step is to do as Mama Duck did and examine obvious outward characteristics. Yeshua said, in reference to discerning false prophets, who come in sheep's clothing but are actually ravenous wolves, **"You will know them by their fruits."** (Matthew 7:16)

This means that if it's an apple tree, it's going to bring forth apples; a banana tree will grow bananas. That much seems obvious. But in relationships, we sometimes don't look closely enough at the branches for the fruit. It's not what they 'say' they are, but what kind of fruit do we see manifesting in their life?

A good tree cannot bring forth bad fruit nor can a bad tree bear good fruit. A fox can claim to be a duck but anyone looking at him can see that he is not what he claims to be. Anyone may claim to be a Believer because they go to church, or because they call Yeshua 'Lord, Lord'; but sitting in church or congregation doesn't make one a true disciple of Yeshua any more than sitting in a garage makes one a car (or sitting in McDonalds makes us a burger). ☺

Yeshua warned us that many people would call Him Adonai (Lord, Lord), but not all will enter the Kingdom of Heaven. To some, even those who have prophesied in Hs name, cast out demons in His name and done many wonders in His name, He will declare to them, "*I never knew you; depart from me, you who practice lawlessness (disobedience to Torah/law)*". Not all those claiming to be believers will enter the Kingdom of Heaven; only those who practice obedience to His commandments (Torah/law). [3]

Of course no one is perfect, but do we see evidence of the fruits of the Spirit in their daily life, as listed in Galatians 5:22-23: love, joy, peace, longsuffering, kindness, goodness, faithfulness, gentleness, and self control? Are these fruits evident outside the church building? Behind closed doors? Or are the fruits of the flesh more evident: adultery, fornication, uncleanness, lewdness, idolatry, sorcery, hatred, contentions, jealousies, outbursts of wrath, selfish ambitions, dissensions, heresies, envy, murders, drunkenness, revelries (partying) and the like?

Anyone can have a bad moment here and there. Perfection is not what these verses refer to – but those who *practice* (habitually) these sins will not inherit the kingdom of God. What kind of habits do we see this person practicing? Do they become

---

[3] Matthew 7:21-23

angry easily? The Bible warns us not to make friends with an angry man lest we learn his ways and set a snare for our soul. (Proverb 22:24-25) Do they regularly become drunk or often cause arguments? These are all red flags. Watch out!

This Mama Duck was no fool; she didn't take this stranger at his word – she put him to the test. She instructed the so-called duck to jump into mud puddles, to eat bugs and beetles, and to do other duck-like things. But the fox not only didn't look like a duck, he also couldn't do the things that ducks do. He didn't like bugs, didn't like muck, and couldn't say quack. And yet the sly fox, his eyes on the prize, continued to affirm, *"I'm a duck! I'm a duck! I'm a duck like you!"*

People may affirm whatever they like, but do they like the things the Lord likes and do the things that believers love to do? Do they hunger for the Word of God? Spend time reading their Bibles and in prayer? Worship and praise? Express a thankful heart? Do they walk in obedience to God's commandments? Are they diligent to continue assembling with other believers? Anyone can 'act' the part for a time, but when people go through some tests, that's when we see their true colors.

 This often takes time; we need to know someone for a reasonable period of time, guarding our heart, before committing to them. The author of '<u>Finding the Love of Your Life</u>, Norman Wright, advises singles to spend at least two years together before marrying. In time, if a person is covering up wickedness in his or her heart, it will eventually emerge and become evident.

"...though his hatred is covered by deceit, his wickedness will be revealed before the assembly." (Proverbs 26:26)

Love may be 'at first sight' but character is revealed over time. The Word of God clearly warns us against these 'wicked foxes' who will try to follow us and even worm their way into our homes in the last days.

*"But know this, that in the last days, perilous times will come. For men will be lovers of themselves (selfish, self-centered), lovers of money (greedy, covetous), boasters, proud, blasphemers, disobedient to parents (disrespectful, dishonoring to parents & elders), unthankful (complainers, whiners), unholy, unloving (harsh, critical, faultfinding), unforgiving (bitter, resentful, holding grudges), slanderers (gossip, speaking against people behind their backs, putting people down), without self-control (over their emotions, appetites), brutal (violent), despisers of good (focusing on negatives), traitors (disloyal), headstrong (stubborn), haughty (proud), lovers of pleasure (hedonistic) rather than lovers of God, having a form of godliness but denying its power. And from such people turn away! For of this sort are those who **creep** into households and make captives of gullible women loaded down with sins, led away by various lusts, always learning and never able to come to the knowledge of the truth."* (2 Timothy 3:1-7)

Beloved people of God, we have to stop being so gullible in the area of relationships and get some Holy Spirit discernment – like Mama Duck!

A recent article that came to me from someone serving in the IDF said this,

"One thing I have been learning in working with the special forces here in Israel is the training we are receiving is reinforcing us over and over not to be gullible and naïve when dealing with the terror tactics of those who want Jihad.. **And therein lies our main Achilles heel with us Western believers, we are just too gullible, nice, gracious, and soft. We like to accept things without testing it first.** <u>We are harmless like doves but not wise like serpents (Matthew 10:16)!"</u>

Even this week, a close brush with a wicked 'fox', really hit close to home - and it hit hard! The church where I had attended asked for anyone with extra room in their vehicle to come forward to give a ride to some people wanting to attend the church picnic. Always the willing 'Mother Theresa', I volunteered; and therefore ended up giving a young man a ride to the lake. He seemed a nice enough fellow, although a little lonely, and I felt sorry for him. And so when he said he so enjoyed himself with us and asked if he could come over to swim in our apartment complex's pool, I agreed.

My friend and I, also a single mother, took our children for a swim in the pool with 'Mr. Fox'. He seemed to be having such a good time with the children as they jumped and played in the pool, but my friend and I both felt that we must be careful not to let our ducklings out of our sight with this friendly, playful fellow. He called a couple more times, pleading to come and 'play' with the children again, saying how lonely he is and what a good time he had, but I felt cautioned not to even take his calls.

A few days later the Police arrested him and confiscated his computer, charging him with child pornography. If anything has drilled it into my heart, mind, and soul, to stop being so 'nice' and gullible and trusting, this has to be it! As believers, we strive to be gentle, meek and mild like Yeshua going to the cross, but we must also get a hold of that warrior spirit inside of us, that Lion of Judah that roars against the wicked.

Mama Duck put this duck imposter to the final test – total submersion in the river. The mother duck and all her ducklings go down into the water, as does the stranger. The difference now becomes clearly evident, for the ducks bob right back up again to the surface, but the fox sinks and almost drowns. He finally gives up his pursuit of the ducklings and slinks back home.

When we are totally submerged in the living water of the Spirit of God, what is the outcome? Do we rise up to new life, or sink down and give up? When we are immersed in the mikvah [4] are we truly 'born again', or do we just backslide and return to our old life of sin, shame and deceit? The final test of whether or not we truly belong to the Lord is summed up in one word – love:

"By this all will know that you are My disciples, if you have love for one another." (John 13:35)

This is how we can truly separate the sheep from the goats (or the ducks from the foxes) – by whether or not we demonstrate our love for one another – not

---

[4] Mikvah – ritual water immersion (baptism)

just in word but in deed. Do we care for the poor, the needy, and the defenseless? Do we speak up for those who have no voice, like the unborn children of the world in danger of abortion? Do we visit those who are sick and in prison? Would we rescue those being led to the slaughter like the Jewish people of Europe in WWII, packed into cattle cars, on their way to die in gas chambers at the hands of Nazis? Whatever we do (or not do) for the least of Yeshua's brethren, we do (or fail to do) for the Lord. [5]

Too often, we are led by our emotions, or deceived about the true nature of people we come into contact with. It is true that we are not to judge, Yeshua said, but then tossing all caution to the wind and accepting everyone who says they are a 'duck' as a duck, is simply foolhardy. Only a fool would believe everything they are told.

 "The simple believes every word, but the prudent considers well his steps." (Proverbs 14:15)

As the old saying goes, 'Talk is cheap.' There are times when we must not believe someone's words.

"He who hates, disguises it with his lips, and lays up deceit within himself; when he speaks kindly, do not believe him, for there are seven abominations in his heart;" (Proverbs 26:24-25)

 I would think that God does expect us to use wisdom and common sense or He wouldn't have

---

[5] Matthew 25:31-46

given us these gifts of discernment. Let us not allow our emotions to override our good sense; but protect our ducklings from the foxes in our midst by examining the fruit in their lives, noticing if they truly walk as Yeshua walked, and observing how they pass or fail to pass the tests that come their way – especially the ultimate test of love.

In the end, Mama Duck says, *"I always knew...that was no duck."* And in the end, if we are equally as wise, so will we - for it is *the little foxes* that spoil the vines. [6]

Prayer: Dear God, continue to transform us more and more into Your image, so that people would see we 'walk the talk'. Help us to be truly gentle as a dove but wise as a serpent. Grant us discernment through the power of the Holy Spirit to recognize the deceivers in our midst in order to see people and situations for what and who they truly are. Amen.

---

[6] Song of Solomon 2:15

CHAPTER TEN

DRAWING DEEP

On Getting Through the Dry Seasons of Life

"Blessed is the one who trusts in the LORD, and whose hope is in Adonai. For he will be like a tree planted by the water, that extends its roots by a stream And will not fear when the heat comes; But its leaves will be green, And it will not be anxious in a year of drought nor cease to yield fruit." (Jeremiah 17:7-8)

It amazes me how the herb garden in the front of my house has stayed green and alive, despite this incredible heat wave we've been experiencing here in

Israel; and in spite of my neglect to water the shrubs and bushes (my bad).

Although we don't live in the Negev anymore, it sure feels like it this summer! The other day, the thermometer in my car read +50 from sitting in the sun all morning. Now that's hot! For some reason, 'water the garden' fell off the grid of my lengthy 'to do' list this past week as lethargy took hold. And yet, when I looked at the garden, there it stood in all its glory, still green and flourishing.

How do they do it? I wondered.

Obviously, since water is essential for life, and since it was not being provided by my own garden hose, the plants must be getting it from another source. Not being a botanist, I can't be 100% sure of this fact, but I am assuming that the trees and plants draw their necessary moisture from deep underground throughout the hot, dry summer.

As I thought about this, I considered my own 'dry and thirsty times', when I don't seem to be getting any 'surface watering'. Nothing too much of anything fun, interesting, exciting, or entertaining is happening to bring times of refreshing to the 'same ole same ole' of life.

We all go through these times, when even the Spirit of God seems to have neglected to water our soul, as the Psalmist wrote:

"My soul thirsts for You; My flesh longs for You, in a dry and thirsty land where there is no water." (Psalm 63:1)

Camel and Bedouin tent in the Negev Desert

We may be going through the motions – still praying, reading our Bibles, and going to congregation (kehilla), but even the worship and the Word seems dry and boring. Our relationships may have lost their sizzle and we may feel as if they've been reduced to mere duty and obligation. We seem to have lost sight of our vision; and the joy of our salvation has dissipated.

What do we do in times like these? How do we stay green and flourishing when the road is long and the way is dry? When we are hot, thirsty and weary? I think we can do just want this hardy Israeli vegetation does - go deep!

We need to draw our joy from a source of living water that lies well below the surface of life:

"With joy you will drink deeply from the fountain of salvation!" (Isaiah 12:3)

The Word of God promises that when our delight is in the Torah of God and when we meditate upon His Torah day and night, then we will be like a tree planted by streams of water. We shall yield luscious fruit in season. Our leaves will not wither; and whatever we do shall prosper. (Psalms 1:2-3) Wow!

The prophet Jeremiah warned us that if we trust in man – the arm of the flesh – and our heart turns away from the Lord, then will be like a dried up tumbleweed - a shrub in the desert – living in the 'parched places of the wilderness'. But we are also comforted us with the promise that as long as we are trusting in Adonai, then we don't need to fear the drought - those dry times of our lives – for we will be refreshed.

God is the fountain of living water. Yeshua invites us to come to Him and drink deeply of that which will satisfy our thirst – and this 'thirst quencher' for our parched soul is none other than the Holy Spirit (Ruach Hakodesh).

While we lived in the Negev region of Israel, the children were delighted when the winter rains turned the sandy desert into a 'play pond.'

"The afflicted and needy are seeking water, but there is none, and their tongue is parched with thirst; I, יהוה, will answer them Myself, As the God of Israel I will not forsake them. I will make rivers flow on barren heights, and springs within the valleys. I will turn the desert into pools of water, and the parched ground into springs." (Isaiah 41:17-18)

We may go through dry seasons of our life where we feel like a parched desert land. I think I may be in one right now as a matter of fact. As we get older, and maybe slow down a bit – kids grow up and we no longer need to run after them at such high speeds - we may begin to lose our zest for life.

Dreams we once had in our youth have not yet come to pass and so we may give up on ever accomplishing the things in our heart we had hoped to do, have, or experience. But it is in the peak heat of the summer, that the grapes begin to come to full and sweet fruition.

The Word of God promises that we will still bear fruit even in our latter years. Just like my hardy shrubs, if we will draw deeply from the fountain of living waters, we will stay fresh and green.

"They will still bear fruit in old age, they will stay fresh and green." (Psalm 92:14)

Shalom from Israel!

Prayer: Dear God, You are the fountain of life with miraculous living water that can quench our parched and thirsty souls. Show us how to draw deeply upon these hidden reserves found in Your Holy Spirit as we walk through the wilderness seasons of life. Our heart longs for you in a dry and thirsty land where there is no water. Satisfy the thirst of our soul as only You can. In Yeshua's name. Amen.

CHAPTER ELEVEN

HAVE A HAPPY DAY

A Devotional on Grace Under Fire

"This is the day the LORD has made; let us rejoice and be glad in it." (Psalm 118:24)

It is my hope that, in sharing with you my daily joys as well as my struggles; you will gain a greater understanding of the reality of living as a Messianic Jew in the Land of Israel. Beyond understanding; however, I hope you will also be encouraged in your relationship with God (Adonai). Shilshom (the day before yesterday), I had such a living example of the grace and kindness of our God that I would like to share this wonderful testimony.

Let me first give you the background: the children have all been chronically sick since we arrived, almost two months ago.[1] Nothing really serious – colds, coughs, ear infections – but enough to keep them out of school (which translates as being home underfoot 24/7). When Avi, my two year old son, began to show signs of having an ear infection again, I considered taking him into the nearest northern city of Tiberius to the pediatrician; but in the end I decided to just take him to the local family doctor in the village.

"*Should be okay.*" I thought, not wanting to go through the hassle and expense of traveling into the city by bus with a cranky toddler and preschooler in tow. The doctor had a look in his ear, seemed unconcerned and sent him home with instructions to use ear drops. I should have known better since my nephew, Tal, currently serving in the Israeli Defense Force, went to a doctor with a broken collarbone and was told that nothing was wrong with him.

By nighttime, we knew that something was terribly wrong. Despite all our prayers, anointing with oil, speaking the Word, rebuking the devil, casting out spirits of sickness, home remedies and anything else we could think of, Avi's condition was obviously worsening. Pus was dripping out of one ear and poor Avi was screaming in pain.

Thank God I had brought some children's pain reliever syrup from Canada, which is the only way we relieved some of his pain. Still, no one got much

---

[1] Our second attempt at aliyah, to Neve Oved, Galilee, Israel 2004,

sleep that night. Avi screamed and screamed and screamed in pain, trying to pull his ears off his head, shouting, *"Go! Go!"* He just wanted to get away from the pain; we felt so helpless, so sorry for the suffering of our little boy. Eventually, our emotions turned to frustration, resentment and anger.

My husband and I turned on each other, playing the blame game. *"Well, if you hadn't....if only you had...."* We began to think and speak like the Israelites, *"We and our children are going to die here. Let's just head back to where we came from. Maybe it was better there. Maybe God is not really with us here...."*

"Eli, Eli, lama azavtani?" I cried out: *"My God, my God, why have you forsaken me?"*

Just this past Shabbat, a woman got up in the congregation and gave a Word from the Lord that really touched my heart. She said, *"Some of you are going through a valley right now: a valley of depression; a valley of marriage problems; a valley of sickness. You think, "Why has God forgotten me?" But I say to you, 'I am the God of the valley and I am walking with you. I will never leave you nor forsake you; I will never leave you nor forsake you; I will NEVER leave you nor forsake you.'"*

This woman could not have known my situation; nor could she have known that when I miraculously came to know Yeshua (Jesus) as my Savior, it was through these very words, *"Jesus will never leave you nor forsake you."* I had been forsaken by the father of my unborn baby, but I came to know

Someone who promised to never abandon me.[2] Now, in the middle of this pain-filled night, where was my Lord, my Savior, my Jewish brother, my Lover, my Husband, my faithful companion, my friend? I was ready to book tickets for myself and the children back to Canada the very next day.

Earlier in the evening, as the frustration of the day, the week, the month, the year and the past seven years built up in my heart, the bitterness overflowed from my mouth. "*Why did I ever get re-married, have more children after the age of forty, move to Israel, move back to Canada, and move back to Israel again? Why am I so stupid? How is it that I am such a fool? I have ruined my life and the situation is hopeless. I don't want to be married. I don't want little children that I have to run after constantly all day long; I just want to be left alone and sleep through the night for once!*"

Later, when Avi was so ill, I desperately sought forgiveness and my heart filled with renewed compassion and love for these little ones who need me so much. Hours earlier they seemed annoying noodnicks (nuisances) that just disturb my peace at every opportunity and whose sole purpose seemed to be keeping me so busy with them that I had no life to call my own. Now, after repenting for this attitude and praying to the Lord, they seemed the most precious gifts that the Lord has ever given me on earth.

---

[2] See Hannah's personal testimony, Grafted In Again, www.voiceforisrael.net/shop

Somehow, God gave me strength to stay up and minister to Avi throughout the night and by 6:00 A.M. I got us both dressed to travel into Tiberius, as I should have done in the first place. I was anxious about making this trip alone with Avi; I didn't know my way around the city. I had never done this before, having just remained sheltered in my little quiet and peaceful village up until now. My husband could not come to help me because he needed to stay home with our little girl, Liat, who was five years old at the time and was also suffering from a cold. All I could do was to affirm the word in Scripture,

"Through my God, we shall do valiantly. It is He who shall tread down our enemies. Help me, Lord, for the help of man is useless. Lead and guide me this day; I fall upon your grace and mercy." [3]

Before leaving the house, I grabbed a mug off the counter and made myself a cup of tea. Groggily, through bleary eyes, I noticed the saying on the mug, **"Have a Happy Day**!" Decorated with joyful happy faces, it stood in sharp contrast to my dark, miserable mood; and yet I felt it was a personal love message to me from the Lord.

The sarcastic thought ran through my head, *"Ya right! How am I supposed to have a happy day when I've been up all night with a screaming baby, my marriage is failing and today I face the battle of having to find my way around an unknown city in a foreign land?"*

---

[3] Psalm 108:12, 13

Somehow I felt that the Lord was going to show me this very thing – how to be joyful in Him despite the trials and tribulations of my circumstances; how to enjoy a peace that passes all understanding in the midst of the storm because my Lord is in the boat. I was about to find out that His grace is sufficient for me and His power made perfect in my weakness.

I hopped a ride in the van with the children and principal of the Messianic believers' school in Tiberius. Picking up the children in the surrounding villages, I was able to get a view of the beautiful countryside and praise God for the Land to which He brought us home. A children's song mysteriously began to drift into my consciousness of its own accord; and I began to hum it,

"Oh happy day, oh happy day, when Jesus washed my sins away. He taught me how to watch and pray; and living joyful every day. Happy day, happy day, when Jesus washed my sins away." [4]

I prayed that Avi would not continue to scream in the van. Miraculously, he was calm and quiet the whole way until we reached our destination when he began to fuss and cry. I asked for directions to the medical clinic which was supposed to be a short walk from where he dropped me off. Unfortunately, when I followed these directions, they led me to a clinic all right, but the wrong one! Oye Vey! (Oh no!)

---

[4] **"Oh Happy Day"** is a 1967 gospel music arrangement of an 18th-century hymn. Recorded by the Edwin Hawkins Singers

Here in Israel, there are several health care companies and we have to go to the branch of the clinic of which we are a member. I paused and said in my heart, "*Lord, I asked you to lead and guide me and now here I am at the wrong clinic so where should I go?*"

Though my husband had told me that a medical clinic did not exist downtown, when I asked the receptionist, she directed me to the right clinic only a few blocks away. I considered going to the Ministry of Interior first, but as I began walking uphill, I heard that small, quiet voice, say, "*No, Hannah, go directly to the clinic.*"

I easily found my way to the clinic, walking Avi in a stroller, humming that little happy song along the way. A doorman at the pharmacy pointed me in the right direction. Not only is it unusual to get correct directions in Israel, but the fact that this man smiled at me and acted in a courteous, friendly and polite manner is exceptional. I felt that he saw, not me, but something in or with me that made him feel happy. We know that 'something' to be the Spirit of God.

By now, Avi began to scream again, so I took him to the washroom. He screamed so loudly that the cleaning woman used a key to open the ladies room to see what must be going on in this little cubicle, causing a child to make such a terrible noise.

I made my way to the reception, asking to see the pediatrician. When I saw the number of other mothers and fathers with their children, many Ethiopian women with babies hanging in slings on their backs, I knew the wait would be a long one. I knew by now that to plead for mercy from the Israeli staff would be futile; so I prayed in my heart again, *"Oh Lord, you see how my little one is suffering. Please cause them to let us ahead in the line."*

I probably need to comment on the concept of the *'tor'* in Israel. This means the line. For some reason, one's position in the line is very important when waiting for something here in Israel. Being a generally impatient lot, everyone guards their possession of a place in the line with a fierce jealousy, for often people will try to get ahead of them if allowed.

I did not have much hope. But all the mothers looked at Avi with much sympathy and compassion, clucking their tongues and saying, *"Misken"* (which means 'poor thing'.) His affliction was obvious, as the pus was running all the way down his neck by now. A da'ati (religious) woman wearing a head covering sat first in line. When the door to the doctor's office opened to admit the next patient, this woman looked at me with kindness and said, *"t'kansi! t'kansi!"* (go in, go in!). She was, out of compassion, letting me ahead of her in line.

All the other mothers nodded, *"t'kansi!"* they all agreed for me to go first. My eyes filled with tears. *"Todah, todah rabah!"* (thank you so much) was all I could say. And 'todah rabah' was all I could say to my heavenly Father whom I know heard my silent prayer for mercy and favor in that moment.

The pediatrician was very gentle, thorough, and sympathetic, immediately prescribing a strong antibiotic for Avi and ear drops, saying that the doctor should have definitely prescribed it the day before. I felt grateful for medical care in Israel and for modern medicine too that would help my little boy to heal. I took my prescription to the pharmacy to be filled and also purchased a herbal syrup for the children that my Israeli-brother-in law suggested might strengthen their immune systems here. [5]

I was shocked when the pharmacist totaled my order at 190 shekels![6] Oye!, I thought, but then I knew by now that medicines and especially herbal remedies are very expensive here. I only had twenty shekels and change left, but then I remembered what had happened the night before. When I pulled a cookbook off the shelf, an envelope fell on the floor. Upon opening it, I discovered $150 shekels inside, which was the amount we owed the landlord for our electrical bill. We had put it aside for when he came to collect it, which he had obviously not yet done. I decided to obey that little nudge that I felt to put that money in my purse, 'just in case'. Thank God I had done so, for I had just enough to pay for the medicines when I counted out all my change as well. Halleluyah!

I left the pharmacy, smiling back at the friendly doorman again and it struck me — how would I get

---

[5] We later discovered that Avi's frequent ear infections and Liat's colds were due to mold in the house, which is common in Northern Israeli homes due to the cold, damp winters and lack of central heating.

[6] 190 shekels is approximately $64 CAD

home? I needed the fare to ride the sheirut (shared mini-bus) back to the village.

I then remembered that I had a check in my wallet that a precious brother and sister in the United States had sent us. But in order to cash it, I would need to get to the money changers. Usually, they need to know you in order to cash your checks, or else they require someone they do know to guarantee the check. My husband had been refused on this basis several times. Again I prayed for God's grace and favor. As I approached the money changer, he looked up from behind the glass and gave me a big smile. Believe me, this does NOT happen often here in this tension filled country. And after being awake all night, feeling pressured and rushing out of the house without a single thought to the state of my face, hair or clothing, it was definitely NOT any physical attribute on my part that attracted him.

 I could only give glory to the Lord, who seemed to want to make people happy this day. I presented my American check, fully expecting to be turned down. But he simply asked for my Israeli identification, phone number and name of my village and handed me over the shekels I needed to get home. Halleluyah! This time I was smiling. I half expected him to say, "*Have a happy day*", as we parted. ☺

Now for the last leg of my journey – I had no idea where to catch the sheirut (communal taxi) back to my village. I walked towards what seemed like the town square where many elderly people sat on benches feeding the pigeons next to a large fountain. I stood at the bus stop and within less than a minute a sheirut pulled up. The door opened and I was greatly relieved when I saw the driver. We immediately recognized each other. He was 'my driver', the one who drives people back and forth from our village to the city.

I had once caught a ride with this driver to and from the grocery store. He seemed very kind, even driving around the village to drop off an elderly 'baba' at her doorstep. He actually stopped the van and got out to help her in with her bags of groceries. Drivers like this are few and far between, of this I'm sure. And here was my friendly, helpful driver, just waiting for me. The Lord led me to be at the exact right place at the exact right time. He helped me in with the stroller and baby and bags and all the way home I sat humming my little song, *"Oh happy day, oh happy day, when Jesus washed my sins away...."*

"Come now, let us settle the matter," says the LORD. "Though your sins are like scarlet, they shall be as white as snow; though they are red as crimson, they shall be like wool." (Isaiah 1:18)

Ironically, my parents had just sent me an e-mail the day before called, "Happy Day". It described all the things that, according to the world, make up a happy day: a hot bath, sunshine, time to ourselves, etc. But the one thing it did not mention is that the happiest day of all is the glorious one when Yeshua washed our sins away. May this be the day of salvation for, not only my family, but for all our loved ones who have not yet experienced the abiding joy of our salvation.

<u>Prayer</u>: Dear Lord, your Word is true that in this world we will have tribulation, but you have also said that we can be of good cheer because you have overcome the world. Thank you that your grace is sufficient for us in whatever situation we find ourselves in when we place our trust fully in Your grace and mercy. Help us to rejoice daily in the greatest miracle of all – that Yeshua (Jesus) has washed all our sins away.

Restore to us the joy of our salvation, and turn our mourning into dancing. Let the weeping that has lasted all night be turned into joy in the morning. May every hand that now hangs down in heaviness be instead lifted up in praise, for you are our glory and the lifter of our heads. May every voice that is now still be lifted up in song. Let every day that we walk with you be a happy day because Your loving kindness is truly better than life. Amen .

"Though the fig tree should not blossom,
> And there be no fruit on the vines,
> *Though* the yield of the olive should fail,
> And the fields produce no food,
> Though the flock should be cut off from the fold,
> And there be no cattle in the stalls,

Yet I will exult in the LORD, I will rejoice in the God of my salvation." (Habakkuk 3:17-18)

CHAPTER TWELVE

HAVE A HAPPY DAY
PART II

A Devotional on Finding Joy in Trials and Tribulations

I would like to continue speaking about the 'happy day' issue. How are we to have happiness and joy in the midst of adversity, trials and tribulation? It's easy enough to say, "*Don't worry, be happy.*"; but how do we stay full of joy when we have fallen into that deep, mucky, miry pit from which we cannot seem to extricate ourselves? How do we keep a merry heart when the pressures and problems of life seem to drag us down into the quicksand of depression? What do we do when we feel like we're drowning?

"Save me, O God! For the waters have come up to my neck[1] I sink in deep mire where there is no standing...I am weary with my crying...my eyes fail while I wait for my God." (Psalm 69:1-3)

Sometimes we feel ourselves sinking into this miry pit; and while our feet are peddling hard, we simply can't seem to get our footing. One Shabbat, I heard a message delivered in the Peniel Congregation in Tiberius that had me wondering how the preacher knew what was going on behind closed doors at our house? Or as we say, "The Holy Spirit has sure been 'reading my mail.'"

Just before we left the house for services, I played the rewind button and everyone in the family heard the same familiar ugly words spew out of my mouth, "*Why do I always have to get up early to get all the kids dressed, cleaned, and fed, lunches packed, diaper bag ready, bottles in place, beds made, ...while you guys sit around? Why does no one ever help me around here to get ready?...*" Blah, blah, blah, complain, gripe, murmur, and whine: "*Poor me, poor me, poor me....*"

My husband gave me a quick, "*Why don't you stop with the poor me mentality?*"

I thought to myself, "*Eize chutzpah!*" (What cheeky nerve!); and my heart grew hard. When someone from the kehilla (congregation) casually asked, "*How are you guys doing?*" I couldn't even manage

---

[1] In the original Hebrew it reads 'nefesh' (soul)

an answer. I had a hard time holding back my tears. I could only continue to pray that God would speak a word to my heart that day by His Spirit.

"But as for me, my prayer is to You, ...O God, in the multitude of Your mercy...Deliver me out of the mire, and let me not sink...Let not the floodwater overflow me, nor let the deep swallow me up. And let not the pit shut its mouth on me." (Psalm 69:13-15)

The message on this day was about - of course – trials. The Hebrew word for trial is *'nisayon'* which comes from the root *'to try' (l'nasot)*. Before we even started, the congregational leader, Daniel, got up and said, "*Let us lift up our eyes this morning to the One who has brought us salvation. Let us not continue to look down, looking at ourselves, but look at Him who has saved us. This should be enough to make us smile.*"

I thought about my previous 'happy day' message but just couldn't seem to dredge up the proper emotions of happiness and gratitude. All I could think about was how I was probably going to have to run after my son in the nursery, and sit with my daughter in the preschoolers class during the service, missing most of the message – again!

"*I never even get to hear the message; this isn't fair, I can't even get a cup of coffee afterwards...*" "*Poor me, poor me,*" went the familiar refrain, and again the tears flowed.

"*This has gone on for too long.*", I thought to myself. "*No one should have to carry such a heavy burden... everyone can see that it is too much for me....woe is me!"* I cried as I carried on and on.

We can scoff at this kind of attitude after the fact, but believe me when I say that my misery and depression, my feelings of being used, abused, overworked, unappreciated, overburdened and unable to reach God were very real and distressing.

Tested by God

The speaker began to talk about trials that we go through in life. Good subject. Sometimes we are tested by God, such as was Abraham with Isaac. Scripture states clearly that God tried or tested Abraham (Genesis 22:1) The Hebrew word used is *'nisah'*, related to *'nisayon'* (test or trial). When Abraham heard from God, he didn't debate with his own human reasoning, he obeyed immediately.

 "So Abraham rose early in the morning...and went to the place of which God had told him." (Genesis 22:3).

Abraham obeyed God because he was a God-fearer. **"For now I know that you fear God, since you have not withheld your son, your only son, from Me."** (Genesis 22:12)

God's purpose in the test was to bless not only Abraham but his descendants as well. **"In your seed all the nations of the earth shall be blessed, because you have obeyed My voice."** (Genesis 22:18)

God's goal is always for our ultimate good and the good of others. God tested the nation of Israel in the wilderness to see what was in their hearts.

"And the people shall go out and gather a certain quota every day, that I may test them, whether they will walk in My Torah or not." (Exodus 16:4)

Failing the Test

Obviously, Israel failed the test; their bodies were scattered throughout the wilderness. They did not please God; and never entered the Promised Land, except for two courageous men who followed God wholeheartedly (Joshua and Calev). Had the Israelites passed the wilderness test, their blessing would have been tremendous – a land flowing with milk and honey!

James talks about nisayonot (Hebrew plural for trials). **"Blessed is the man who endures temptation; for when he has been approved, he will receive the crown of life which the Lord has promised to those who love Him."** (James 1:12)

In Hebrew it reads, "Blessed is the man who holds on and stands in the presence of trials." There is a reward for just holding on and standing firm when going through a trial. Sometimes when we have done all else that we know, there is only one thing left to do – stand!

God's word promises, in discussing the failure of the Israelites in the midbar (wilderness), that **"No test or temptation *(nisayon)* has overtaken you except such as is common to man; but God is faithful, who will not allow you to be temped beyond what you are able, but with the test will also make the way of escape, that you may be able to bear it."** (1 Corinthians 10:13)

Therefore, we cannot claim human weakness as an excuse for when we fail a test; God will not allow us to be tested beyond our human limit of endurance and He will also provide a way of escape.

Temptations from the Enemy

Not all tests and trials, however, are from God. **"Let no one say when he is tempted, "I am tempted by God", for God cannot be tempted by evil, nor does He Himself tempt anyone."** (James 1:13)

It is not God who tempts a man with pornographic magazines; God does not draw woman into illicit relationships through internet chat rooms. We need to discern the difference between a test from God to know our heart, and temptations sent from the pit of hell to entrap us.

Yeshua taught his disciples to pray, **"Lead us not into testing and deliver us from evil."** (Matthew 6:13).

The enemy comes only to steal, kill and destroy, and He will if we cooperate. We must be sensitive to both the Holy Spirit and obedient to the Word of God in order to escape from this kind of temptation/test.

Twisted Tests

There seems to be another kind of test that comes neither from God testing us, nor is it directly a scheme of the enemy; but as a result of our own foolishness, poor choices, or sinful actions.

"But each one is tempted when he is drawn away by his own desires and enticed. Then, when desire has conceived, it gives birth to sin; and sin, when it is full-grown, brings forth death." (James 1:14-15)

There are times when we have been drawn away from the perfect will of God, enticed by our own flesh, our own desires, and this, having matured, brings forth the stench of death. There may come a point in our lives, where we must face the terrible truth that what we are going through is basically our own fault.

"A man perverts or twists his way and then his heart frets against the Lord." (Proverbs 19:3)

We may, in disobedience, enter into a situation that either the Spirit of God or the Word (or both) warned against, and are therefore suffering as a natural consequence. We can only confess our foolishness to the Lord and ask for His mercy:

"O God, You know my foolishness; and my sins are not hidden from You...:" (Psalm 69:5)

The conclusion of this good word at Peniel was the encouragement that, even if we have brought this trial upon ourselves through our own foolishness, disobedience, or sin, we can still appeal for help to our God who is merciful to forgive us when we sincerely repent and ask Him to cleanse us from all unrighteousness. After the message, the leader, Daniel, got up and made a collective appeal to the congregation to repent for our sins that have put us in our current trial and to look to God for help and mercy, even though we don't deserve it.

This is His 'amazing grace' - for while we were yet sinners, Messiah died for us. [2] Just now, my husband brought me a yummy grilled sandwich and specialty coffee. *"Why am I receiving such special treatment?"* I asked, knowing I've been difficult to live with lately (an understatement). His answer was, *"Because Jesus died for you."* ☺

There may be times in our lives when circumstances seem to turn against us. The root may be buried in the past. King David was a man after God's own heart but he sinned with Batsheba and as a result, suffered deeply from family problems:

"Now therefore, the sword shall never depart from your house, because you have despised Me, and have taken the wife of Uriah the Hittite to be your wife." (2 Samuel 12:10)

---

[2] Romans 5:8

David's sin of adultery eventually led to his beloved son, Absalom's rebellion. One of the saddest word pictures in the Bible is one of David and the people who were with him, walking barefoot, heads covered, weeping, as they fled from Absalom. (Ironically, this name in Hebrew is Av- Shalom, which means 'Father of Peace'). Can we imagine the grief of King David over the loss of his kingdom through the treachery of his own son?

"Reproach has broken my heart, and I am full of heaviness; I looked for someone to take pity, but there was none; and for comforters, but I found none...." (Psalm 69:20)

We may feel like this at times – heartbroken, heavy, and without comfort. We may drag ourselves through the day, weeping, walking with head down or covered, not wanting to look anyone in the eye lest they see our humiliation and grief. This may even be a time when others, seeing us in obvious distress, may enjoy 'kicking us while we're down'. Criticisms come; personal attacks and accusations flourish.

Shimei, the son of Gera , came out, cursing David continuously, even throwing stones at him and at all his servants. Shimei leveled accusations at David, "*The Lord has brought upon you all the blood of the house of Saul, in whose place you have reigned; and the Lord has delivered the kingdom into the hand of Absalom your son. So now you are caught in your own evil, because you are a bloodthirsty man!*" (2 Samuel 16:7)

"This is YOUR OWN FAULT!" screams the accuser; *"God is doing this to you and you deserve it because of your sins!"*

Let us look at how King David handled this assault. He did not try to fight back or defend himself, but exalted the omnipotence of the Almighty God. **"So let him curse, because the Lord has said to him, "Curse David." Who then shall say, "Why have you done so?"** (2 Samuel 16:10)

He did not place himself under condemnation, but he accepted the trial for what it was. David believed that, despite how bad the situation looked, God was still in control.

"Let him alone, and let him curse; for so the Lord has ordered him. It may be the Lord will look on my affliction, and that the Lord will repay me with good for his cursing this day." (2 Samuel 16:7-8)

Surrendering in the Trial

David surrendered to the trial and He surrendered to God. He did not complain and did not fall into self pity but trusted God with the outcome of his trial. Joseph, as another great man of God, man of faith, and type of the Messiah, also came to recognize that the Lord reigns and all things are under His command.

He said to his brothers, **"So now it was not you who sent me here, but God; and He has made me a father to Pharaoh, and lord of all his**

house, and a ruler throughout all the land of Egypt ." (Genesis 45:8)

Joseph gained a beautiful understanding that gave him peace —even though people's intentions towards us may be evil and may cause us to suffer, God means these trials to work towards not only our ultimate good, but the good of many.

Joseph said, **"But as for you, you meant evil against me; but God meant it for good, in order to bring it about as it is this day, to save many people alive."** (Genesis 50:20).

When I was betrayed, abandoned, and forsaken by the father of my unborn child, I considered it the worst time of my entire life. And yet, God used this experience, not only for my own salvation and that of my family, but also for the saving of many unborn children from destruction through abortion. God can take the absolute worst circumstance, the most horrible trial that anyone may ever have to endure, and by some redemptive miracle, turn it into something good.

"And we know that all things work together for good to those who love God, to those who are the called according to His purpose." (Romans 8:28)

With these promises, how can we ever be without hope? It may take some time, but with patience and endurance, we will receive the promise of good coming out of our trial. In fact, if nothing else, these trials will teach us patience for the perfecting of our character – we will become more like the Messiah and more compassionate towards a suffering humanity through our own trials. For this reason, we can rejoice, even in the midst of various trials:

"My brethren, count it all joy when you fall into various trials, knowing that the testing of your faith produces patience. But let patience have its perfect work, that you may be perfect and complete, lacking nothing." (James 1:2-4)

I listened to Pastor Daniel as he pleaded with us, *"Repent of complaining; repent of self-pity; Do not say, "Why does no one notice my suffering? Why does no one help me? Look up! "*

For the answer to the problems we face here on earth are to be found in the spiritual realm with God. He has the solutions; there are times and situations when He is the only one who can truly help us.

"I lift my eyes up to the mountains. Where does my help come from? My help comes from Adonai יהוה maker of heaven, Creator of the earth." (Psalm 121:1-2)

God promises blessing for obedience and cursing for disobedience. God wants to bless us: **"Blessed be my Lord (Adoni), who daily loads us with benefits."** (Psalm 68:19)

He wants to load us with benefits, but we must learn to fear Him and walk in obedience.

It is difficult, even painful, to face the truth that we may have brought our problems upon ourselves. But living in denial and covering up the problem or blaming others doesn't help either. We must squarely face the truth and then find the courage in God to go on with our lives, trusting and hoping in His amazing grace and mercy.

"O God, who is like You? You, who have shown me great and severe troubles, shall revive me again ...you shall increase my greatness, and comfort me on every side." (Psalm 71:20-21)

I will lift up mine eyes unto the hills, From whence cometh my help. My help cometh from the Lord, Which made heaven and earth.

Psalm 121:1-2

<u>Prayer:</u> Thank you, Adoni (my Lord), for your amazing grace and mercy we have found in Your son, Yeshua. Thank you that nothing can ever separate me from your love in the Messiah.

I acknowledge that this trial I am suffering may be a result of my sin and disobedience. Please forgive me. I repent of complaining and feeling sorry for myself. Help me to bridle my tongue when I am tempted to fall back into this wrong attitude. I thank you that there is no condemnation for those who are in Messiah, Yeshua, so please help me not to fall into a self-condemning attitude either.

Please help me, as I lift my eyes to You, to walk through this trial as more than a conqueror. Use this circumstance, so that it will work ultimately for good and blessing in the end, not only in my own life, but in the lives of many. I surrender to You as Lord to work through this trial to make me wiser, stronger, more patient, more compassionate, and more like Your son, Yeshua. Please give me a fear of God, (Yarh Elohim) that I may hold on and stand firm in the presence of future trials. Amen.

"Why so downcast, O my soul? And why are you disquieted within me? Hope in God, for I shall yet praise Him for the help of His countenance." (Psalm 42:5)

Oh how I need you, Lord

CHAPTER THIRTEEN

HE CAME TO SET THE CAPTIVES FREE

A Devotional on 'When 'self-help' just isn't enough....'

Pepper in Ramat Raziel park

"He has sent me to bind up the brokenhearted,
to proclaim liberty to captives; and freedom to
prisoners;" (Isaiah 61:1)

The Holy Spirit speaks to us in the most amazing
ways! The other morning, my little Shi-Tzu dog,
Pepper, came home from his morning jaunt around

the moshav (village) acting very strangely. He had this kind of panicked gait; he couldn't really seem to walk properly or to sit down and rest. My normally calm, sweet dog was so agitated; I just had to find out what was wrong.

When I checked it out, I found, to my dismay – how do I put this delicately? I discovered a fair sized wad of 'kackie[1]' stuck to his butt. Yes, really. Pepper has lovely fur – it is more like human hair – it never sheds on clothes or furniture. But it does grow thick in the winter and has a tendency to matt in places.

Unfortunately, one of those places where his hair had matted was in the vicinity of his rear end. So when he tried to 'do his business' (it's challenging to use proper terminology here...) it just plain got stuck in the matt.

I'm quite sure that Pepper did everything he could to shake it off, rub it off and even run it off – but stuck it stayed – and there was not one thing in the world he could do for himself about it. The filthiness and stench followed him everywhere he went.

It occurred to me that we may have a similar situation in our own personal lives. We may have become entangled in some sort of sin to such an extent that we cannot in any way, shape or form, extricate ourselves. The cords of sin can potentially

---

[1] Hebrew slang for feces

ensnare us to such an extent that we may be destroyed if we don't find a way to be set free.

"The evil deeds of the wicked ensnare them; the cords of their sins hold them fast. For lack of discipline they will die, led astray by their own great folly." (Proverbs 5:22-23)

We can try to shake it off, rub it off, or even run away from it through moving to a new location, changing career direction, leaving a relationship or finding a new one, and yet we find that the problem remains.

You've probably heard the saying, *"Wherever you go – there you are."* This is a simple but profound message. When sin has a hold on us, the filth and stench follows us everywhere we go. We are unable to 'walk properly' with the Lord. We run around in a panic, unable to even sit and be still - we are 'rest-less' vagabonds.

It could be an issue with addictions, anger, lust, selfishness, greed, pride, or laziness....the list is endless. We may recognize we have a problem, so we try all kinds of 'self-help' strategies. We attempt, by our own limited human efforts, to get free of bondage, but so often we find that it just isn't enough.

Even the great apostle Paul said, **"For I do not do the good I want to do, but the evil I do not want to do—this I keep on doing."** (Romans 7:19)

What a formula for despair! Paul calls himself a *'wretched man'* and asks where he can find deliverance: **"What a wretched man I am! Who will rescue me from this body that is subject to death? Thanks be to God, who delivers me through Yeshua Hamashiach (the Messiah), Adoneinu (our Lord)."** (Romans 7:24-25)

Here is our answer when 'self-help' just isn't enough. Where can we turn for freedom from the bondage of sin? To the One who was sent by the Father to set us free. Yeshua came to Natzeret where He had been raised and went to the synagogue on Shabbat (as was his custom). He was called up to the Torah and read from the scroll of Isaiah where it was written[2]:

"The Spirit of the LORD *is* upon Me,
Because He has anointed Me
To preach the gospel to *the* poor;
He has sent Me to heal the brokenhearted,
To proclaim liberty to *the* captives
And recovery of sight to *the* blind,
To set at liberty those who are oppressed;
To proclaim the acceptable year of the LORD."
(Luke 4:18-19)

When he sat down, all eyes were fixed on him as Yeshua proclaimed these Scriptures fulfilled in Himself. When we are powerless to help ourselves, Yeshua can set us free from sin, bondage, captivity and oppression.

My precious Pepper could do nothing to help himself; he could only submit himself into my loving care and trust that I would know what to do. It was a

---

[2] Isaiah 61:1

messy job, but someone had to do it after all, and who else but someone who loves him so much.

The truth is, we don't need to get ourselves all cleaned up before coming to Yeshua. We can come just as we are – in all of our filthiness, with all of our stench, desperation and utter helplessness – we can simply surrender our whole self into His loving hands, trusting Him to cleanse us and set us free.

When God promised to bring us back to this Land, He didn't get us all cleaned up and fixed up first. No, He vowed to bring us back first, in our sinful condition, and only then would he cleanse us and set us free.

"'For I will take you out of the nations; I will gather you from all the countries and bring you back into your own land. **I will sprinkle clean water on you, and you will be clean; I will cleanse you from all your impurities and from all your idols.**

I will give you a new heart and put a new spirit in you; I will remove from you your heart of stone and give you a heart of flesh. And I will put my Spirit in you and move you to follow my decrees and be careful to keep my laws.

Then you will live in the land I gave your ancestors; you will be my people, and I will be your God. **<u>I will save you from all your uncleanness.</u>**" (Ezekiel 36:24-29)

God is the only one who can save us from our uncleanness and give us a new heart and put a new spirit in us. All we need to do is to ask. This is what

I'm asking of the Lord – to be cleansed and set free – to be a pure vessel that He can use.

Is there possibly anyone in your life who seems to have a faltering walk with the Lord, running around in a panic, restless, unable to settle down, having no peace, loaded down with the burden of sin and guilt; struggling to be free from the cords that bind them but totally unable to help themselves?

I believe the Lord has placed in our hands the key to help loose them from their sins through fervent intercessory prayer: *"I will give you the keys of the kingdom of heaven; whatever you bind on earth will be bound in heaven, and whatever you loose on earth will be loosed in heaven."* (Matthew 16:19**)**

It might get a bit messy, but hang in there – for the joy that comes from seeing someone set free and restored to wholeness.

<u>Prayer:</u> Yeshua, thank You for Your mercy and grace in setting us free from those things which keep us ensnared in bondage. As we repent, forgive us and also cleanse us from all our unrighteousness and filthiness. Help us then to also go forth and set others free to walk wholeheartedly with You. Amen v'Amen.

CHAPTER FOURTEEN

ENTERTAINING STRANGERS - AND FRIENDS...

A Devotional on Hospitality

Madame Cat

"Let brotherly love continue. Do not forget to entertain strangers, for by so doing some have unwittingly entertained angels."
(Hebrews 13:1-2)

When my daughter, Liat, was three-years old, she had a favorite story book which, unfortunately, I couldn't read since it was written completely in Russian; but you can get the general idea from the pictures. The story is about a grand Madame Cat, who has many friends visiting her home, often for several days at a time. Mr. & Mrs. Goat, Mr. & Mrs. Chicken, and even Mrs. Pig all eat the cat's food; they sing, they dance, they all have a good time. Madame Cat even has their photos on her wall.

She thinks they are her good friends and so she is happy to offer them such gracious and generous hospitality. But one day, something most unfortunate happens. Madame Cat's house burns down. So she and 'Monsieur Cat' set off to find a temporary place to lodge. They first come to the goat's house, but are refused shelter there. Now the weather turns colder and they trek on to the chicken coop; but here they are once again refused. By now it is raining and the cats are getting drenched.

They come to the pig's house and again face the door shut to them. (I think it's because piggie has so many piglets, but I'm just guessing... can't read Russian!) So off the cats trudge, this time in the snow... you get the picture... Oh, of course the story has a happy ending: the cats find two orphaned kittens in a broken down shack who are happy to let them inside. They become a family, fix up the house into a grand palace again and live happily ever after... But why am I telling you this story?

Recently, we had a sort of 'Madame Cat experience'. People we fully expected to extend a hand of hospitality - people who had enjoyed a completely open door policy with us time and time again - refused us when we happened to be in need. In my hurt, anger, and confusion, I started to think more about the issue of hospitality.

While studying the parashot (Hebraic Scripture portions traditionally read and studied in Jewish congregations on the Sabbath)[1], I noticed the importance of hospitality in the lives of both Abraham and Lot. Abraham <u>ran</u> to meet the three men who came to visit him. He offered them his gracious hospitality, preparing for them his very best food and drink. [2] Two of these 'men' turned out to be angels and one was a physical manifestation of the Lord יהוה [3].

What would have happened if Abraham had not been so eager to offer hospitality to these 'men'? Would Sarah still have received the promise of a son? Would Sarah have borne Yitzchak (Isaac), father of Yaacov (Jacob), father of the nation of Israel?

What if Lot had not strongly insisted that the two 'strangers'[4] at the gate of Sodom accept his offer of hospitality? Would Lot and his daughters have been spared from destruction? We will never know the answers to these questions because Abraham and Lot were both men of gracious and generous hospitality. But we may ask ourselves – how many

---

[1] See <u>A Messianic Jewish Commentary</u> by the author, www.voiceforisrael.net

[2] Genesis chapter 18

[3] The four Hebrew letters spelling out the name of God (equivalent of YHVH in English)

[4] The strangers were actually angels (Gen. 19:3)

opportunities or blessings have we missed because of our refusal to 'run' to offer hospitality to strangers?

The book of Hebrews exhorts us, **"Let brotherly love continue. Do not forget to entertain strangers, for by so doing some have unwittingly entertained angels."** (Hebrews 13:1-2)

The Word of God promises that as we give, so shall it be given unto us in good measure. When we bless others, we plant seeds of blessing that will return into our own lives. **"The soul who blesses will be made rich, and he who waters (satisfies, refreshes) will also be watered (satisfied, refreshed) himself."** (Proverbs 11:25)

WHO IS MY NEIGHBOR?

We can become so focused on doctrine and theology that we forget the simple importance of showing mercy - of practicing 'random acts of kindness'. Yeshua stated this to be the heart and fulfillment of the whole Torah. A man, a *'Baal Torah'* in Hebrew (master of the Torah), came to Yeshua asking what he must do to inherit eternal life? [5] Now here would have been the perfect place for Yeshua to say, *"Believe in me as the Son of God and you will live eternally"*, but He didn't.

Instead, Yeshua (in true Jewish fashion) answered a question with a question, *"What is written in the Torah?"*

---

[5] Luke 10:25

The man answered with Yeshua's own teaching on the two greatest commandments: *"You shall love the Lord your God (v'ahavta Adonai Elohecha) with all your heart, with all your soul, with all your strength, and with all your mind," and '(love) your neighbor as yourself*." (Luke 10:27).

Yeshua makes the amazing statement that if we would do this – love God and love people –we would inherit eternal life! He then told a parable to illustrate what it means in a practical sense to 'love our neighbor'. In the story of the Good Samaritan, a man was 'mugged' by thieves and left to die. Two 'religious' men not only ignored the man; they went out of their way to avoid him! Perhaps the Cohen (Jewish priest) and the Levite were rushing to perform their religious duties in the temple.

Why were we refused hospitality by our 'friends'? They were busy at a prayer conference! We can attend all the prayer meetings, conferences, and 'worship watches', and still 'miss it' according to God's standards in the Torah.

It was not a Jewish man who helped the wounded man; it was a Samaritan. Though not even a 'brother in the faith', Yeshua said he was the real 'neighbor' of the three men because of the mercy he showed. The Samaritan showed brotherly love and kindness while 'the religious believers' crossed to the other side of the road.

Yeshua commanded us to love one another, so that people could see we are his disciples, but sadly it is sometimes the ones we label as 'non-believers' who are more merciful than our own brothers and sisters in the Lord. We also experienced this when our van broke down on the highway.

Shimshon HaGibor (Samson the Hero)

En route to Jerusalem while driving an old vehicle, we blew a gasket on the engine; and it looked like it was going to be a looooonnnnng wait. It was late at night in winter, with a cold wind blowing; and we had to stand outside, since the van had filled with fumes. With a new baby and two little children, I was more than a little concerned. No one stopped to help while we waited, and waited... but finally a car pulled up and out bounded a man wearing a kippah[6] and a wide grin.

A hearty voice called out, *"Shalom! Sorry I took so long, but I had to do a full circle to get back to you because of the heavy traffic."* Noticing the children and me, he urged us to get into his nice, warm car. *"But don't press any of the buttons!"* he warned Liat with a twinkle in his eye. While we waited in his car, he and my (then) husband Radek[7], tried to start the van but to no avail.

Looking in the rear view mirror, I could see the man, seemingly angry at the traffic, shouting out the open door of the van and waving his fists. Later, I found out that he was petitioning Elohim on our behalf,

---

[6] Kippah is a traditional men's head covering indicating respect for God's presence which is 'above us'.

[7] Radek was my husband's Polish name which he later changed to David

"Oh God, must I shout louder! ? You know that these people need to get to Jerusalem tonight. We ask you to start this van!"

 Passionate prayers such as this I had not seen in most churches' prayer meetings. . **"The effective, fervent prayer of a righteous man avails much."** (James 5:16)

Suddenly, the engine turned over, starting long enough for Radek to get the van to the side of the highway. The man reminded me of Elijah in his manner of prayer, but this man's name was Shimshon (Samson). Even though we shared with Shimshon that we are disciples of Yeshua, he still seemed overjoyed to be in a position to help us. He asked if we were hungry and could he take us to a restaurant to eat or did we need a place to stay for the night?

He assured us that it was his joy to *'run like Abraham'* to do a mitzvah (good deed). He knew that he would inherit a blessing from the Lord. Yeshua also told us that when the Son of man returns with his angels he will reward each <u>according to his works</u>. [8] (oops, so much for the greasy grace gospel...) Shimshon only asked for one thing in return – that we would *"think good things about the people of Israel."*

What a contrast to the treatment we received at the hands of our *'Christian brethren'* in Jerusalem. After standing out on the highway with a newborn babe and little children in tow for over an hour, were

---

[8] Matthew 16:27

we greeted at the door with shalom and welcome? a hug or kiss? Were we even offered a cup of hot tea to warm up or given any food for our children? I'm sorry to say that we eventually had to ask and were then told to get it ourselves.

Not once during the whole time we were stranded did the host or hostess prepare a meal for us. I felt shocked and humiliated at such a lack of hospitality from other believers to whom we had extended hospitality several times in our home. Was this neglect due to malice? I don't believe so. Some people have simply not learned the art of gracious hospitality, especially towards the household of faith. Perhaps we have failed to teach on the subject. Maybe this is why the Lord allowed us such experiences, in order to share His Word about hospitality, which in the future could have serious significance.

"Be hospitable to one another without grumbling." (1Peter 4:9)

While on a speaking tour in the U.S. and Canada, we found a wide range of hospitality amongst believers. Some even gave up their own bedroom (or made sure we were comfortable); they fixed our favorite foods that we had missed in Israel, and took time out of their busy lives to drive us around. They treated us with honor and respect- making us feel loved and welcomed in their home.

Others 'forgot' to give us food or even bedding. We felt like an intrusion, an annoyance or inconvenience to their lives.

A Greater Exodus – Let My People Go!

Why is gracious hospitality so important? The issue of hospitality goes far deeper than good manners. Many have been predicting a coming persecution of the Jewish people in the nations. The prophet Jeremiah predicted that the days are coming when there would be a greater exodus than even the exodus out of Egypt. This will be when God brings the descendants of the house of Israel out of all their countries of exile. "**And they shall dwell in their own land**." (Jeremiah 23:7-8)

Many have already come back to the Land of Israel by making aliyah. But many more remain in exile. These, God will bring out '**with a mighty hand, with an outstretched arm, and <u>with fury poured out</u>**...' (Ezekiel 20:33-34)

This is the exact same language as is used in the exodus from Egypt (Exodus 6:6). Just as God poured out plagues as judgment upon Egypt in order that Pharaoh would 'let His people go!', so shall our God pour out judgment on the nations to set His people free. In fact, the plagues of the book of Revelation mimic many of the ten plagues: blood, frogs, locust, hail, boils, darkness...

Many are predicting increased persecution upon the Jewish people in the Diaspora. We are already seeing the evidence of increasing anti-Semitism in the nations of the world. When this exodus occurs, the people fleeing may need food, drink, shelter, clothing, and medical help.
Probably a smile, a hug, and an outpouring of the love of God are going to be in great need as well. I

know that many have already caught this vision and are preparing their homes to receive these 'guests'. But others are totally unaware, and ill-equipped to offer gracious hospitality to those who may in the future arrive at their door.

Why does this matter? Yeshua states that our eternal destiny actually depends upon it!

"When the Son of Man comes in His glory, and all the holy angels with Him, then He will sit on the throne of His glory. All the nations will be gathered before Him, and He will separate them one from another, as a shepherd divides his sheep from the goats. And He will set the sheep on His right hand, but the goats on the left. Then the King will say to those on His right hand, 'Come, you blessed of My Father, inherit the kingdom prepared for you from the foundation of the world: for I was hungry and you gave Me food; I was thirsty and you gave Me drink; I was a stranger and you took Me in; I was naked and you clothed Me; I was sick and you visited Me; I was in prison and you came to Me.'" (Matthew 25:31-36).

"The righteous will ask, "Lord, when did we see You hungry or thirsty or naked or sick or imprisoned? The King Yeshua will answer them,

"Assuredly, I say to you, inasmuch as you did it to one of the least of these My brethren, you did it to Me." (Matthew 25:37-40)

Yeshua said He came for the lost sheep of Israel.[9] He is referring to the descendants of Israel as His

---

[9] Matthew 15:24

'brethren'. Every time we offer our help – a hot drink, a meal, whatever the need - to one of Yeshua's brethren, we can consider that we have done it unto the Lord Himself!

Obviously, when we refuse even the least of His brethren, it is as if we have refused the Lord. His word is clear as to the consequences,

"And these will go away into everlasting punishment, but the righteous into eternal life." (Matthew 25:46)

These are sobering words when we consider that many who considered themselves Christians turned their backs – crossed to the other side of the road – rather than help a Jew in the Holocaust who was hungry, thirsty, sick, naked and imprisoned. Are we going to get our minds out of these foolish doctrinal debates over minute matters of the Torah and instead focus on loving God and our neighbor with all our heart, mind, soul and strength? Selah....

Boundaries and Balance

Hospitality seems to be a real issue, especially in Israel. For one thing, the norm is for people to just 'drop in' without calling beforehand or checking if the time is convenient. One is just expected to drop whatever was planned and sit to chat over a cup of coffee or tea and cake. Now this would be lovely if there was nothing needing to be done at home. But when home is also one's workplace this becomes a problem.

I remember wanting desperately to finish the writing of the books on my testimony and the Feasts of the Lord while my little one was in kindergarten during the morning hours. Invariably, someone would 'drop in' to chat and I faced the dilemma of offering hospitality or getting my work done. I even tried putting a notice on the door, *"Caution, enter at your own risk, woman at work!"* But this didn't help matters. People ignored the sign and still walked in.

One needs the wisdom of the Holy Spirit as to where to set healthy, Godly boundaries. We have allowed people into our home who brought strife, division, and terrible trouble. One situation led to near disaster when we took in someone who was on the streets and later learned that he had a 'perverse fondness' for children.

Another time, we let an elderly lady (whom we didn't realize was mentally unbalanced) temporarily stay on our couch in our already overcrowded Jerusalem apartment. One night turned two, which turned into a week, which turned into a month..... and ended up being a very messy situation. My daughter had nowhere to sleep when she came home on weekends from boarding school; and worse than that, the lady began to yell and scream at us for no reason. When we kindly asked her to leave, she ended up cursing us and sending random, ranting 'curse' letters to our address for quite some time.

One other time (yes, we are slow learners), we took in a young Russian woman who had just given birth to a son. Apparently her 'husband' (we were told) was in jail and if she didn't find a place to stay, then social services would apprehend her baby. How could we say no? We gave her a place to stay, arranged (and paid for) the baby's brit millah (circumcision) as well as her dental work.

We tried to show her the love of God; but in the end it turned ugly. After several months, we felt it was time she found a more permanent place to live; but she refused to leave. Her 'husband' in prison turned out to be an Arabic Muslim boyfriend instead; who then began to curse and even threaten us over the phone. Even when we found a home in Israel that takes in women and children, she refused to budge because "It is Russian." Finally, we had to call in the International Christian Embassy to intervene. Phew! Hospitality is not always a simple or easy issue.

At times, our home seemed more like a hostel than a family home, with people coming and going at all hours, sleeping anywhere there was room, and eating everything in sight. It got to the point where our son would cry in frustration when he came home from school because he had nowhere to simply 'be' at home. So boundaries and balance is certainly called for in the issue of hospitality.

People in Israel seem to receive a lot of guests because of the numbers of tourists who come looking for a cheap (ie. free) place to stay, not realizing that most Israelis live in small, crowded apartments.

As someone who has experienced being both guest and hostess many times, here are a few general guidelines to help facilitate a positive experience with hospitality for all concerned:

Hospitality etiquette:

For the host

- Greet your guests with a sincere welcome. For many people, especially those not so outgoing, staying in a strange home is rather unnerving and uncomfortable.
- Children may be upset by the change in surroundings. Try to have some toys or games in the house for guests coming with children.
- Offer a hot or cold drink and something to eat, even just coffee, tea, juice and cake or cookies as soon as the guests arrive and get settled.
- Provide clean towels and bedding. Note: Don't give them all the cast offs and pillows you couldn't even sleep with or a bed that is falling down in the middle or hangs upside down! (Yes, we experienced this ☺) Try to think if you would be comfortable?
- Have plenty of food prepared and extra if people are staying over Shabbat. Find out if there are any food intolerances or allergies. Remember that children sometimes have simpler tastes than the adults and may need plastics. If you happen to be on some strange diet, don't expect your guests to eat likewise.
- Put away your breakables and china if little ones are coming so that the mother doesn't have to be a nervous wreck that junior will break something precious of yours.
- Don't expect that the children of your guests are going to be perfect. They may scream, cry, pout, and even – horrors! – get things dirty. Help the mother (and father) to feel at ease that you understand about kids and this is okay with you.

- Fellowship not only with one another but also include the Lord. Offer to pray for your guests' needs.
- Be kind. If you really don't want guests in your home, they will probably sense this and feel like a nuisance. It may be better to be honest and say it's not the best time for you rather than say yes and then have a bad attitude, making everyone feel uncomfortable.
- Hospitality comes from the word 'hospital'. Remember that sometimes people come because they desperately need a break! You can participate in your guests' recovery.
- Be sensitive if your guests are tired or just need some space and allow them to retire to their rooms; don't talk their ear off for hours on end.
- Expect that you will have some cleanup to do at the end of their visit and accept this as part of hospitality without grumbling or complaining.

For the guests:

- Bring towels and bedding to save the hosts having to do much laundry when you leave.
- Offer to bring food to share, especially if coming repeatedly, for an extended period of time, or with several other people. Let your hosts know in advance if there are special dietary needs or considerations.
- Don't allow your children to tear the house apart, or to help themselves to your personal things such as jewelry (yes, we have had kids do this in full view of their parents).
- If your children do tear the house apart, offer to help tidy it up before you leave instead of leaving all the cleanup to the host & hostess

- If you have a baby, don't leave stinky diapers lying
     around to smell up the whole house. Tie the
     garbage and take it outside to the trash if
     possible.
- Offer to help prepare the food & with the dishes
     after meals.
- Be a blessing. Don't come just to receive, but also
     come expecting to be a blessing to your hosts.
- Fellowship together and pray for specific needs of
     your hosts.
- Clean up as much as possible before you leave.
- Express your gratitude for your host's hospitality
     and possibly give a gift.

Shalom and enjoy the blessing of hospitality!

<u>Prayer</u>: God thank you for the gift of hospitality that
     we can both give and receive. As wandering
     Jews, we have so often depended on the kindness
     of strangers who became friends. Bless each one
     with an outpouring of love and hospitality when
     they are in need too. Help us to truly love our
     neighbor and serve one another as if we are
     serving Yeshua Himself. But also grant us the
     wisdom and discernment to know how to set
     right boundaries - when to open our hearts and
     homes; and when to keep the gates shut. Thank
     you for providing for all of our needs in Messiah
     Yeshua as we journey through this life; and thank
     you for the wonderful place You are preparing for
     us when we truly come home.

CHAPTER FIFTEEN

TEN RULES for how NOT to buy a Used Car in Israel

A 'Devotional' on Dealing with Liars, Cheaters, & Swindlers

Hannah with her first purchased car in Israel

"Behold, I send you forth as sheep in the midst of wolves: be therefore wise as serpents, and harmless as doves." (Matt. 10:16)

It seems to me that we have enough *'how to'* advice out there – everything from 'how to build an ant farm' to 'how to find the love of your life'. I think it's time we had some more 'how NOT to do' things like:

'how not to make a fool out of yourself in public'...'how not to marry a jerk'....the list is endless. It's good to know what to do, but we also need to know what NOT to do. That's why I'm writing this article. You know how some people stand as inspirational examples we can learn from and aspire to emulate? And then there are others - the Samsons of life - that we always use as object lessons to warn our little boys against falling for the wrong woman *just because she's 'hot'*.

Some people just seem destined to teach us what NOT to do in life. I'm very sorry to admit it, but I seem to be one of them. One of my grown kids has said that he uses me as an example – of how NOT to parent his own kids. Ouch! So since I seem to be out here, bumbling along, making all the mistakes, I thought that maybe some way, somewhere, somehow, you could actually benefit from hearing about them. So go ahead and use me as an example of what NOT to do in Israel – like how to NOT buy a used car.

1. The first thing that you must NOT do when buying a car in Israel is this: <u>Do not make your purchase under pressure.</u> Like if you have a teenager (not to mention names) who just got his license (maybe a week ago) and is eager (understatement) to drive and keeps asking you over and over again which ads you called on and gets angry (another

understatement) when you admit you haven't called any – that's called <u>pressure</u>.

Add to that a pre-teen, hugely hormonally imbalanced girl (again - not to mention names...) who is throwing tantrums and marathon crying sessions over having missed SO MANY of her dance classes that she can't possibly catch up to the other girls now and doesn't know the dance anymore and you missed the whole dance performance and her life will never be the same – all because you didn't have a car to drive her – that's also called pressure. You may also want to make sure that you don't need to buy a car during a lengthy school vacation during which all the kids are home...bored....driving you nuts....because they can't go anywhere FUN without a car.

Ok, so you want to make sure you are not buying the car under pressure so you can make a calm, rational, well thought out and thoroughly checked out decision.

And speaking of calm, rational, well thought out and thoroughly checked out decisions, DON'T go to the scheduled meeting to see a car <u>absolutely clueless</u> about buying a used car or about cars in general. Like if you've never even looked at makes and models of cars in a parking lot, maybe you're not ready...ya think? Listen to me – denial is not power! ☺

Don't go to buy a car without doing at least some research about various makes and models of cars, their strengths and weaknesses, consumer ratings, checklists - what to look for in a used car, how to buy a second hand car, what to watch out for, etc. There's a saying (somewhere I'm sure) that if we don't know what we want we'll probably get it. Or something like that. I think you get the picture, right? So google it. Know what you want and you have a better chance of getting it. Right? Of course right. That's better.

So whatever you do – DON'T GO LOOK AT THE CAR ON FRIDAY! Because everything is going to be closing early for Shabbat, so you're going to feel in a major rush just to get this thing done before Shabbat and may make a hasty decision that you may later come to regret. We already know this and you would think this doesn't need to be said but … obviously for some of us this needs to be spelled out. Again.

2.   DON'T go look at the car...under pressure...clueless...on a Friday...<u>with</u>

someone who dumps you. He is supposed to know something about cars but just stands there and says, *"Well, it's your decision, what do you want to do?"* when you ask for their expert advice about this particular car. And DON'T go with this same someone who is going to say they are busy and have things to do before Shabbat on Friday so that they dump you with the owner of the car to deal with it on your own – a clueless person matched with a desperate seller can be a dangerous combination!

3. <u>Don't go with the car whose owner has been the most persistent.</u> If they keep phoning you to remind you of your appointed meeting, like twice daily for a week and three times a day the week before, they may just be desperate to sell the car – and that could be a red flag. Just because the person has phoned you ten times doesn't necessarily mean that this is some kind of 'divine guidance' to the perfect vehicle you've been praying for. It may just mean that the guy is desperate to unload his lemon on some sucker – which he's hoping is you!

4. <u>DON'T believe someone is telling you the truth just because they wear a kippah and</u>

<u>tzitzit</u>[1]. Could be a fake. Also don't believe someone who tells you they are an undercover cop with the Israel police force as well as a paramedic and volunteer ambulance driver. Because by now, you may have this charming, handsome, hero pegged as a real mensch[2] – which he very well may be – or not!

5. If he tells you that the car just passed the test (and even shows you the papers to prove it), <u>DON'T assume that this car has passed a good mechanical check</u>. TAKE IT TO THE DINOMETER[3] AND PAY THE .... 500 sheckels and save yourself thousands of sheckels in repairs later! (ie. Don't be so cheap!)

6. Just because you meet his appropriately religious, head-covered wife, and the two of you hit it off right away, chatting like old friends and even exchanging photos of your kids on your cell phones, that doesn't mean they're not taking you for a ride! Yes, <u>friendly swindlers can smile.</u>

---

[1] Tzitzit – fringes that religiously observant Jewish men wear on their garments

[2] Mensch – a nice Jewish guy

[3] Dinometer – a place that for 500 sheckels will do a comprehensive check of the car you are considering to buy

7. If you've just handed over the thousands of shekels in cash and the smiling seller has just walked away, briskly, his tzitzit swaying in the breeze; and if the car won't shift into drive and for some strange reason this 'mensch' doesn't answer his cell phone anymore, you may begin to suspect that you may be in trouble... big time. And by the way, if you are a well-meaning relative of the bimbo buying a used car from a thief, please make it perfectly clear to her in that loud, shrill, nerve-jarring voice reserved for life-threatening situations, that she HAS to take the car to be checked by a certified mechanic, no matter what papers the seller shows you, BEFORE she has handed over all her money and not after. Thank you very much.

8. Once you realize that your newly purchased car has some serious mechanical problems and that the seller's number is now out of service, <u>DON'T USE YOUR CRIMINAL CONNECTIONS</u> to get a deal on a mechanic. (Again, don't be so cheap!) Just because you happen to be friends with someone in jail (long story...don't ask...), and just because he offers to help you out of your predicament by connecting you with a 'friend' of his on the outside, that doesn't mean you have to accept his most gracious offer. Why not just take my

word for it when I tell you that murderers and thieves are not good people to do business with. Because here's the thing – if they rip you off too – which is a fairly 'normal' thing for thieves to do – (after all, that's what liars and thieves do is steal and lie, right?) – like WHAT are you going to do about it?

Go to the non-existent Israeli Better Business Bureau and lodge a complaint that the mechanic friend of a thief friend of a murderer in jail for life has just ripped you off? Go ahead and try – maybe someone needs a good laugh to make their day! Or the second option is that you could go back to the mechanic friend of the thief friend of the murderer in jail for life friend and complain directly to him of the great injustice he did to you - that he did a really bad repair job, in fact didn't repair the car at all, but only took from you another few thousand shekels. You could DEMAND that he honor his pathetic, puny, three month warranty on the new transmission and motor that he supposedly installed (which he in fact didn't). But can I tell you something? You really don't want to get these people mad!

9. Before they get mad at you and before you find out how badly they ripped you off and while you are still on good terms together,

<u>DON'T go to the Arab neighborhoods as a woman alone.</u> A little piece of trivia that may prove helpful to you from my experience is that in the Arabic culture, they are allowed multiple wives. You may not want to be one of them. OF course, the choice is entirely up to you.

10. So when (you notice I don't say if) the car breaks down on the highway, make sure you <u>wear one of those nifty fluorescent yellow vests</u> when you get out to check why the front of the car is blowing out hot steam from the now kaput engine. And when you call for a tow truck and finally a truck comes, don't assume it is a tow truck. And if two laughing, jolly, men speaking Arabic tell you to get in the car and drive it behind them, really and truly my advice is – DON'T DO IT! Because now, whatever life may have been left in that ailing car on its 'last legs motor' has now most likely been completely snuffed out. And now you have to wait – on the side of the highway wearing your cute fluorescent yellow vest - again – for them to REALLY send a tow truck this time.

Since my experience with finding out how NOT to buy a used car in Israel, I have discovered several websites that give you advice on how TO buy a used car. A little too little too late, I'd say....

But I have one last piece of advice on what NOT to do. Just in case you are one of those people who have to learn everything the hard way, and just in case you don't take my DON'T's seriously and you end up buying a real lemon of a car, then please, please, please DON'T beat yourself up about it over and over again. You made a mistake. If we were perfect, we'd be God. Forgive yourself; forgive the swindlers, liars, and cheaters. Remember that there are still lots and lots of good, honest people in Israel. And press on... in joy and love and hope. Each day is a new beginning.

Shalom from Israel and 'Happy Used Car Buying!' (2011)

CHAPTER SIXTEEN

I HAVE LEARNED TO BE CONTENT

A Devotional on Keeping 'Stuff' in Balance

"I have learned the secret of being content in any and every situation, whether well fed or hungry, whether living in plenty or in want." (Phil. 412)

It all started with an iPod. I have nothing against iPods. I think they can be great; but this thing was getting totally out of hand. First, Liat happened to mention to her Dad in Canada that she would like an iPod of her own. And since she is *'Daddy's little* girl', he of course bought her one – which set off a whole chain reaction in our family – none of it good. Because when Liat's older, teenage brother, Timothy, heard that Liat was getting a brand new top-of-the line, generation 4, touch screen iPod WITH camera, he exclaimed,

"Why is SHE, an 11 year old girl, getting this great iPod, which she will probably lose within 2 weeks, when I have so much more use for it in high school?"

To which Avi, my youngest son (then eight years old, chimed in with his own heart's desire for an iPod. *"All my friends at school have an iPod!"* he proclaimed. And much to my surprise, I found out that this was actually true.

So Avi's kita bet (grade 2) friends began coming over after school to check out the Israeli website for second hand products to search for an 'iPod 4 Touch' for 'poor, deprived Avi'. (Note: These were the *'old days'* before iPads, tablets, and other assorted electronic paraphernalia.)

Every time anyone even mentioned the word 'iPod' in our household, someone would go ballistic. I was experiencing in my family, exactly the situation that James, Yeshua's brother, described centuries ago:

"What causes fights and quarrels among you? Don't they come from your desires that battle within you? You want something but don't get it. You kill and covet, but you cannot

have what you want. You quarrel and fight."
(James 4:1-2)

Which goes to show that 'some things never change'. They may not have had iPods in Yeshua's time, but they still had to deal with the same coveteous human nature that we struggle with today. It shocked and dismayed me to see the amount of strife, bickering and jealousy that this one gift of an iPod had provoked in the other children. And it got me thinking about the whole issue of <u>contentment versus covetousness</u>.

After all, is there anything wrong with wanting things? Certainly God is not displeased with us desiring material things or else Yeshua would never have told us to ask for them! He taught, **"Ask and it will be given to you; seek and you will find; knock and the door will be opened to you. For everyone who asks receives; he who seeks finds, and to him who knocks, the door will be opened."** (Mathew 7:7-8)

In fact, James wrote, **"You have not because you ask not..."** (James 4:2)

Yeshua reassured us that God is a good Father who delights in giving good gifts to those who ask Him. One way that our joy can increase is by seeing God answer our petitions by meeting our needs and granting us the desires of our heart.

"Until now you have not asked for anything in my name. Ask and you will receive and your joy will be complete." (John 16:24)

Yeshua came to give us life and life more abundantly – and I believe that means abundance in every sense of the word, not just materially. It is not just 'stuff' that we can ask God for, but more love, peace and joy; more harmony in our relationships, better health, greater wisdom and understanding, patience; and the ability to walk in the fruit of the Spirit.

We can ask for guidance and direction, the knowledge of God's perfect will; and even just a deeper revelation of Him - to see God's glory. Yeshua told a parable about a persistent widow and an unrighteous judge who gave in to her request just because she wouldn't stop pestering him. This parable teaches us to likewise be persistent in asking and not to give up if we don't receive immediately. [1]

It seems to me that Avi has this perfected to an art-form. When he wants something (especially something electronic), I am sure that he must remind me of his request every few minutes throughout the day! It is the first thing on his lips when he wakes up (even before his eyes are open – honestly!) and it is the last thing he mentions at night before falling off to sleep (probably dreaming about his heart's desire too I'm quite sure!).

---

[1] Luke 18:1-8

Thou Shalt not Covet!

And yet, God also commands us, **"Thou shalt not covet!"** (Exodus 20:17) The Word of God contains several warnings against greed and covetousness. **"Let your conduct be without covetousness, be content with such things as you have."** (Hebrews 13:5)

Greed can lead us into a path of destruction. **"So are the ways of everyone who is greedy for gain; it takes away the life of its owners."** (Proverbs 1:19)

So when does this 'asking' or 'wanting' cross the line into greed, lust, and covetousness? We discussed this as a family and came up with a collective distinction, *"Covetousness is wanting the thing that is not yours to have"*. Something can obviously be 'not ours to have' as written in God's word, as in not coveting your neighbor's wife. She is legally and morally not yours to have.

However, something may be completely lawful, and yet not be God's perfect will for us to have because it is not for our highest good or the time may not yet be right for us to have it. Paul had wisdom in knowing that, **"Everything is permissible for me but not everything is beneficial."** (1 Corinthians 6:12)

If we persist in begging for something that is not God's will for us to have, or stubbornly pursue something that God has said 'no' to, it can bring disaster into our lives; because finally God may regretfully give in to our greed and lust, even knowing the distress and anguish it will cause.

"Because I have called and you refused, I have stretched out my hand and no one regarded, because you disdained all my counsel, and would have none of my rebuke, I also will laugh at your calamity, I will mock when your terror comes, ...and your destruction comes like a whirlwind, when distress and anguish come upon you..." (Proverbs 1:24-27)

We Israelites can be a stubborn, greedy bunch! In the wilderness, the children of Israel lusted after quail, despising God's provision of manna, so that God sent the quail until it came out their mouth and nostrils; "...**and while the meat was still between their teeth, before it was chewed, the wrath of the Lord was aroused against the people and the Lord struck the people with a very great plague.**" (Numbers 11:33)

Just because God gives in to us and fills us with whatever our flesh fancies, this doesn't mean that it will bring us life. "...**they would have none of my counsel and despised my every rebuke therefore they shall eat the fruit of their own ways and be filled to the full with their own fancies...**" (Proverbs 1:31)

Like the Israelites in the wilderness, God may give us what we 'lust exceedingly' for, but it may bring a 'leanness to our soul'.

"They did not wait for His counsel, but lusted exceedingly in the wilderness...and He gave them their request, but sent leanness into their soul." (Psalms 106:13-15)

Sometimes we get what we asked for but it only leaves us dissatisfied and still hungering for something else to fill the void in our soul.

The King you have Chosen for Yourself

Israel didn't ask for an iPod Nano (because everyone else had one); but rather, they asked for a king – because all the other nations had a king and they wanted one too! God wanted to be their only King, but they wanted to be like the other nations, even though God had made Israel to be a 'peculiar people', not like the nations around them.

The elders of Israel approached the Prophet Samuel and demanded, **"Now make us a king to judge us <u>like all the nations</u>."** (1 Samuel 8:5).

Isn't this just like us at times - like a kid that says, *"All the other kids have one, so I want one too!"* But God may have a particular, unique plan for our lives that may not include some of the things that others have. God perceived the people's incessant demands for an earthly king as a rejection of His authority, **"that I should not reign over them."**

 God tried to warn them that they were better off with Him as King. He instructed Samuel to forewarn the people of Israel about how their chosen king would behave; how he would oppress and exploit them. This king, chosen by flesh and not by the Spirit of God, would use his position to take, take, take, rather than behaving as a true King like Yeshua, a servant-leader. David, chosen by God, also demonstrated this kind of righteous leadership; but Saul was in it for whatever he could get.

Samuel warned that if the people refused to heed the rebuke of the Lord and receive His counsel, then they would '**cry out in that day because of your king** ***whom you have chosen for yourselves,*** **and the Lord will not hear you in that day."** (1 Samuel 8:18)

Nevertheless, the people refused to obey the voice of Samuel and insisted on having a king over them, **"that we also may be like all the nations, and that our king may judge us and go out before us and fight our battles."** (1 Samuel 8:19-20)

 And we know the end of the story. Ironically, King Saul did not obey God; he did not lead Israel into victory but through one bitter failure after another; and in the end, he died in a final, bloody defeat along with his son Jonathan, on Mount Gilboa.

Isn't this too much like us when we look to 'man' to meet our needs and fight our battles for us instead of the Lord? Before I came to faith in Yeshua, I continually looked to man to be my 'savior', something which got me into heaps of trouble!

Once I began to read the little book of Psalms, Proverbs and New Testament that a precious counselor gave me at a Crisis Pregnancy Center, one of the first verses that really spoke to me was this,

"It is better to trust in the Lord than to put confidence in man. It is better to trust in the Lord than to put confidence in princes." (Psalms 118: 8-9)

As a new believer, God wanted me to come to know Him as my provider, protector, and 'all in all'; but I was stubborn (and afraid to truly trust God). So I married a 'husband of my own choosing', a man from the church I began attending. This foolish decision cost me my dignity, my self-respect, and almost my life, as this man proved to be physically abusive.

After less than a year, I fled with my children to a woman's emergency shelter and obtained a divorce, but I found out the hard way that putting our confidence in an unfaithful man rather than the Lord can be a very costly mistake indeed![2]

---

[2] See Hannah's personal testimony, Grafted In Again, www.voiceforisrael.net/shop

It may very well be God's will for us to marry, but only He knows a man or woman's heart, therefore we need to diligently seek and listen for God's voice in specific matters. To do anything out of God's will, pursuing the desires of our flesh and refusing to listen to the voice of God's Spirit can result in a lifetime of grief and suffering.

It is absolutely imperative that we submit our desires to the Lord, seek His counsel and even receive His correction if we are to walk in security. **"Whoever listens to me will dwell safely, and will be secure, without fear of evil."** (Proverbs 1:33)

That One Thing

Have you ever noticed that it is sometimes that ONE THING we can't have that we want the most? The Arabs have more than 99% of the land in the Middle East, but they still want this one tiny area called Israel that God says they cannot have. It doesn't belong to them; it is not theirs to have.

God spoke in burning jealousy against the rest of the nations and against all Edom (descendants of Esau), **"who gave My land to themselves as a possession, with wholehearted joy and spiteful minds, in order to plunder its open country..."** (Ezekiel 36:5).

God promised the Land of Israel to the descendants of Abraham, Isaac, and Jacob (Israel) by Divine

Covenant; it is not the Arabs' to have; but they will murder innocent Jewish men, women and children to possess it. The blood of the children of Jacob cries out to God from the ground.

The rabbis give a fascinating correlation between Haman, the Amalekite anti-Semite in the book of Esther, and Adam and Eve in the Garden of Eden. They each wanted *that one thing* that was not theirs to have. God had given Adam and Eve (Chava) liberty to eat of every tree in the garden except for one – the tree of the knowledge of good and evil. But of course, this is the one that the serpent tempted them with – and they succumbed to the temptation to eat what was not theirs to eat - to have what was not theirs to have.

When God saw that Adam now possessed the knowledge of his nakedness and was ashamed, He said, **"Who told you that you were naked? And have you eaten from <u>the kind</u> of tree of which I commanded you that you should not eat?"** (Genesis 3:11)

In Hebrew, the word used here for *'the kind'* are: *'hamin'* which looks like this in Hebrew: המן. These are the same Hebrew letters, hey, mem, nun, המן for the name *'Haman'*.

Haman also wanted the one thing he could not have. All people bowed to him, except for one man – the Jew Mordechai. Haman had the homage of every person except one – but he wanted that one too – and was willing to kill all the Jewish people of Persia if he couldn't have it!

Some people may have everything - but they want this *one thing* so desperately that they would do anything to possess it – even kill for it! Ahab, King of Samaria, experienced this level of covetousness. He wanted a certain vineyard which was already owned by another man, Navot, the Jezreelite.

When Navot refused to sell his vineyard, his inheritance from his fathers, to King Ahab for a vegetable garden, Ahab turned sullen. He lay on his bed, turned his face away, and refused to eat, pouting like a spoiled little brat. His wife, Jezebel, arranged for Navot to be murdered in order that Ahab could take over his field.

They may have thought that they 'got away with murder' but God sees. Through the prophet Elijah, the Lord said to Ahab, **"In the place where dogs licked the blood of Navot, dogs shall lick your blood, even yours."** (1 Kings 21:19)

I don't think we are doing our kids any favors by giving in to all the iPods and 'stuff' they want, no matter how much they pout, whine, and get angry. Children used to getting everything they want can grow up into selfish, spoiled-brat adults that will use every destructive and manipulative tactic in their arsenal to get what their sinful nature wants, no matter who gets hurt in the process. Their motto is,

"I know what I want and I'm going to have it and nobody better get in my way!" Know anyone like that? ☺

We need to be willing, not only to be content with the material things we have, but also with our position in life. Korach and the rebels, Datan and Aviram, allowed selfish ambition to blind their common sense. By stirring up the hearts of the people of Israel to be discontented with Moses' leadership, they initiated a full scale mutiny!

Moses' words reveal the root cause of their rebellion – discontentment with their position in life! Korach, Datan and Aviram were Levites, separated from the rest of the Israelite community to serve the Lord by doing the word of the tabernacle. **"...and are you seeking the priesthood also?"** (Numbers 16:10)

There is sometimes a fine line between setting goals and selfish ambition. We need to respect the authorities God has placed over us and, while striving to be the best we can be, accept our God-appointed position in life. It has been said that often people rise to their level of incompetence. Sometimes we may be coveting a position that we just wouldn't have the grace to handle.

Perhaps, if we're working in a position where we feel incredibly pressured and are even developing stress-related sicknesses, we need to ask ourselves whether it is God who has really promoted us to this high position or if, in fact, we have simply 'exalted ourselves' into a place that God never intended for us to function.

Oh, Lord, may we learn to be contented people!

We need to learn to hear and accept a "No!" Paul says he *learned* to be content whether abasing or abounding. (Phil. 4:11) Being content, while there may still be things that we are hoping to see manifested in our lives, is a quality that can be learned. We can want... and we can ask...while still being content as is.

I believe that when we are thankful for what God has already blessed us with, He is happy to give us our hearts' desires that are in line with His will. **"Delight yourself in the Lord and He will give you the desires of your heart."** (Psalm 37:4)

If we are complaining about what He has already given us, then He knows that we will just complain about the next thing. The key is to focus on how much we have already been blessed; how much we already have received, and not all whatever we feel is missing.

Psalm 23 reads, "The Lord is our Shepherd; I shall not want." But in Hebrew it literally translates: *'nothing is missing.'* No good thing does He withhold from them that walk uprightly, from those who seek Him. If we will submit our every desire to the Lord, being willing to wait for His counsel, patiently waiting for the right way and right time for it to come to pass, always saying, *"If it be Thy will, O God..."* we can be content as we 'wait upon the Lord' to see our heart's desire come to pass.

We can trust that God is good, and that His heart is to give us good gifts, even abundant life – if we will only obey His voice and keep Him first place in our lives. **"Seek first the Kingdom of God and His righteousness and all these things you desire will be added unto you."** (Matthew 6:33)

<u>Closing Prayer</u>: Oh God, help us to be people who are willing to hear 'no' and receive it with grace and a good attitude rather than pouting and plotting. Give us the wisdom when to give in to our children's requests and when to hold firm against their demands. Transform us into a grateful, humble, people who model contentment and thankfulness for all Your many blessings that You bestow upon us daily, by Your grace. And in all of our wanting and asking, help us to discern which desires are from You, and which originate in our selfish, sinful nature.

Deliver us from greed, lust and covetousness in all of its destructive forms. Help us to look to You to meet all of our material, emotional, and spiritual needs - to be our King - to go ahead of us and fight our battles for us. Help us not to put our confidence in man, the arm of the flesh, not even in princes, but always lifting our eyes to the mountains from where our help comes from – from You, Creator of Heaven and Earth. We trust in Your mercy, love and goodness, to give us the desires of our heart, if it be Thy will, in Your perfect way and perfect time.

 And Lord, we want only that which You want for us, only the blessings that come from You, for Your word promises,

 "The blessing of the Lord makes one rich and He adds no sorrow to it." (Proverbs 10:22) Amen.

Written March 2011

Ramat Raziel, Israel

CHAPTER SEVENTEEN

I THINK I CAN

A Devotional on Perseverance

*"**And let us run with perseverance the race marked out for us**." (Hebrews 12:1)*

Out of the blue, my four year old daughter, Liat, said a curious and profound thing to me the other day (as she so often does). She said, *"It was a good thing that it broke down, Mom."* As usual, it takes a bit of finagling to find out what Liat, with her bright, inquisitive mind, is actually thinking about.

"What do you mean, Liat, what broke down?"
"The engine," she replied, "The engine on 'The Little Engine that Could.'"

I was well familiar with this story,[1] having watched it many times with her and her little brother who has early on become interested in the amusement of videos. Well, at least now I had a frame of reference.

"Why was it good that the engine broke down?" I asked, now eager to hear her 'wise beyond her years' answer.

"Well, if the first engine hadn't broken down, then the little engine would never have found out that he really could do it!"

I smiled and let that little piece of wisdom out of the mouth of a babe sink into my heart. Yes, that's true.

Immediately, the biblical picture of Joseph came to mind – thrown into a pit by his brothers, sold into slavery, languishing for years in a prison for a crime he didn't commit, forgotten by those he appealed to for help. And in the end, he comforted his brothers with the revelation that all these things had to happen in the grand scheme of God's plans and purposes so that he would be in the right place at the right time (as much as it looked like the worst place and the worst time), to save many people in Egypt from starvation.

You know the story – how he interpreted Pharaoh's dream and was then exalted in a moment from the dungeon to the highest position of glory in all of Egypt, just under the Pharaoh. Yes, situations can change quickly, suddenly. But the point is that God probably could not have used Joseph if he had not

---

[1] I Think I Can, story by Watty Piper

come to the place of acceptance and forgiveness of those who had hurt and misused him, recognizing the hand of God upon His life.

Even in prison, God was with him, Divine favor was upon him; and in everything he did, God made Joseph prosper. He must have recognized God's hand of favor upon him; and understood that somehow, sometime, some way, God would make everything turn out for good and his great destiny would be fulfilled.

As it is written, ***"And we know that all things work together for good to those who love God, to those who are the called according to His purpose."*** (Romans 8:28)

Joseph said to his brothers, who had been his enemies, "Do not be afraid, for am I in the place of God? But as for you, you meant evil against me; but God meant it for good, in order to bring it about as it is this day, to save many people alive. Now therefore, do not be afraid; I will provide for you and your little ones." And he comforted them and spoke kindly to them." (Genesis 50:19-21)

Joseph understood the secret of handling trials and tribulations, especially those brought about by the evil intentions of others:

Firstly, he knew that it was not his place to take revenge, but to leave the score to God who alone can balance the scales of justice in our lives.

Secondly, he knew the importance of not only forgiving his enemies, but also doing good to them and blessing them.

And thirdly, he had absolute trust and confidence that God could and would turn even the worst situation for the good of many. Joseph never lost hope.

God will do the same in our lives if we keep a right attitude - if we keep the seeds of bitterness from taking root in our heart. When a trial comes into our life, instead of giving in to despair or questioning the goodness of God, let's see it as an opportunity for us to grow, to overcome, and in the end to be promoted. If this seemingly 'bad' circumstance had not come into our life, we would probably never move beyond our current comfort zone.

In the story to which Liat referred, *The Little Engine* saw a problem that no one else was able or willing to help solve; and so he tackled it with an inner faith that said, "*I think I can*." Even though small in strength and size, the little engine made up for it in courage and faith. But we can't forget that there came a point where it seemed that all was lost.

A mighty avalanche had buried the little engine under a mountain of snow, completely stopping the little engine literally in his (railroad) tracks. It looked like the tiny fire of combustion in the heart of the engine had been extinguished forever. It seemed, for a moment, that his mission had failed.

It probably looked this way at the lowest, darkest point in Joseph's life too. Although Joseph knew he was destined for greatness, there must have been moments during those long, lonely years when it looked like he would never see the light of day again. In the natural, it seemed like his life would end in a dark, stinking, dungeon - dying amongst criminals and rats for a crime he didn't commit.

Just like the little engine, there are times when we think the flame has completely died out; but the same power that rose Yeshua from the dead dwells in us. God's power can bring us back to life. Yeshua called forth Lazarus out of the tomb even after he had been dead for four days. There was a stench already!

But Yeshua said, "**I am the resurrection and the life. He who believes in Me, though he may die, he shall live. And whoever lives and believes in Me shall never die.**" (John 11:25-26)

Along the tracks, The Little Engine was often assaulted by booming voices that said, *"You're too little! You'll never make it,"* But the little engine was determined to go on; and so he pressed on through the accusations and voices of doubt and unbelief.

But then "WHAM!" Despite his best efforts he got slammed with an avalanche of snow and ice. It covered the engine and all was still and silent for several moments.

But then we rejoice to see the smallest orange glow of the fire in the engine that hasn't been completely extinguished. Life returns to the engine and – of course the happy ending is that the Little Engine completes his assignment and delivers the toys to the needy children at the other end of the line. But it all started with the problem – the broken down engine – and the need. This weak and insignificant engine with a big heart responded with a childlike faith and persevered through the storm.

Since returning from Israel, I have heard those heavy voices of accusation and doubt. I have felt, at times, that my light has gone out permanently; that the fire in my heart has been completely extinguished. But there is still a warm glow that I can sometimes perceive, and a seed of faith that God can and will turn even this for good.

That is His promise to us who love Him and are called according to His purpose. Everyone goes through challenges, tough times, crises – some more than others, it seems. But what makes all the difference is our attitude. If we can maintain a positive attitude, trusting in the Lord to see us through, then we will break through to victory.

But if we allow the problems to bring us down, to drag us into the pit of hopelessness and despair, then the negativity we generate will only draw more and more problems and negative things into our lives.

We can get into these dark moods of despondency that not only cause discouragement in our own lives, but also drag others down around us. We must beat this 'mood' in order to 'run with perseverance the race set before us.'

Peter Daniels wrote this poem in his book, <u>How to Handle a Major Crisis</u>.

Beat the Mood

There is a 'mood' around today that dulls the mind and spirit

It fools the heart and kills the will and makes you feel 'not with it'

Have you been duped into being less than you really ought to be?

Then learn the way to overcome 'the mood' convincingly,

A heavy cloud of doom and gloom directs the hopeless course,

The road of doubt and tragedy runs downhill from this source;

But darkness can be sent to flight with good thoughts tried and true,

With dreams fulfilled by action and performance carried through.

You can cross the toughest valley, any mountain you can climb,

And obstacles you'll overcome with persistence and with time.

In the end you burst right through because your spirit is within;

You know deep in your heart of hearts you really want to win.

And then towards life's journey's end, approaching sunset time,

You look up glad to recognize the Master's beckoning sign

You beat the mood! You did perform! The race of life you won!

And now you stand with heroes and your destiny has come!

Well done, you beat the mood!

Prayer: Help us, Lord, not to fear or avoid the problems in our lives; but to call upon Your help and strength to overcome the obstacles that block our path. May we fulfill the holy assignments you have given us to help people and meet their needs. Help us to grow stronger through the trials by trusting in your faithfulness. Where the fire in our heart has grown dim, revive us Lord, with Your resurrection power. Help us to forgive our enemies, trusting in you to bring justice in Your perfect way and time. Help us not to lose heart along the way; but to persevere with the "*I think I can*" attitude of the Little Engine that Could. In Yeshua's name. Amen.

CHAPTER EIGHTEEN

I WILL CHANGE YOUR NAME

A Devotional on Transformation

"You'll get a brand-new name straight from the mouth of GOD." (Isaiah 62:2 Message)

The Book of Numbers, (Bamidbar), begins with the Lord commanding Moses to take a census of the people of Israel who had come out of Egypt. The Hebrew word for desert - *'midbar'* מדבר – shares the same root as *'m'daber'* מדבר – which means 'speak'.

It is in the wilderness times that God can and often does speak to us a 'word in due season'. My hope is that this writing will speak to each and every heart through the Holy Spirit (Ruach Hakodesh).

In Hebrew, names carry significant meanings. For instance, *'Eli-tzur'* means *'My God (Eli) is a rock (Tzur).'* Of the proper names listed in this census, several contain the Divine name of El (God). The name Tzur (Rock), is frequently used for God as in Tzur Yisrael (Rock of Israel) or Rock of Ages, as well as El Shaddai, which appears three times in the list of names. This name is usually translated into English as 'Almighty' but it actually comes from the Hebrew root for a woman's breast. Shaddai is the feminine, maternal aspect of God's nature that nourishes, comforts, and provides for Her children.

Each male eligible to go to war found his position in his family by his father's house. I began to think about names and their significance; and inwardly, I wondered about all the children growing up today without fathers. So many children today (including my own) are growing up in homes where the father is absent. Where would they be listed? What would be their place in the census?

Even today in the synagogue, when a man is called to read from the Torah, he is always called by his father's name: _____ ben (son of) _____. This is why, in the Hebraic culture in which Yeshua (Jesus) lived, they called out to him, *"Yeshua, ben David, t'rachem alai!"* *"Yeshua, son of David, have mercy on me!"*

By acknowledging Yeshua as a son of David, they declared him the Messiah who would sit on the throne of His father David according to the Word of the Prophets. [1]

If the father's identity of a Jewish man is not known, he will be called by his name, _____, ben Avraham, Yitzchak and Yaacov (son of Abraham, Isaac and Jacob); signifying that he is a still a covenant child of God through our forefathers.

What about the girls? First of all, girls and women are not called up to read from the Torah in an Orthodox synagogue. But on the occasion of a Bat Mitzvah, or in conservative or reform synagogues which encourage female participation, a girl or woman is also called by her father's house. She will be called by her given Hebrew name _____ bat (daughter of) her father. Rarely will she be called daughter of her mother. This is just Jewish tradition.

Name Confusion

I currently live with a great deal of confusion regarding my name, largely due to the chaos and instability which has characterized my life in the past. First of all, like most Jewish children living in exile, my parents gave me an English name (well, ok, a Scottish name); but I was also officially named in

---

[1] Isaiah 9:6-7

the synagogue with a Hebrew name according to Jewish tradition. Perhaps this accounts for some of the later confusion regarding names.

When I went to a bi-lingual Hebrew school, I would be called my English name for half the day and my Hebrew name for the other half. But my last name was solid - my father's name - a name with a good reputation. Proverbs 22:1 says that a good name is worth more than riches. I had that name. I also liked it because it started with an A so that meant I was always at the head and not the tail end in school lists and line ups.

But when I married at the age of nineteen, my name changed to my husband's and I moved to the back of the line, so to speak. ☺ That marriage lasted seven years and ended in divorce, so I decided to change back to my maiden name (I always did like the front of the line).

Ten years later, living in the world, I became pregnant by a Japanese man who abandoned me and our unborn child, leaving my son without a name; without a father's house. So he took my father's name and we lived nearby to my father's family.

This crisis pregnancy led to my salvation; however, as a 'baby believer' in Yeshua as my Messiah, I foolishly married a man in the church I began to attend. He turned out to be abusive – a real wolf in sheep's clothing. After less than a year, I escaped to a woman's shelter; but for a short time, my name had been changed again and I had to again go through the process of changing it back to my maiden name.

By the time I re-married (are you getting dizzy yet? I know I am), I decided just to keep the maiden name. It was too much trouble to keep getting used to new names and changing all my documents. But my parents, still Orthodox Jews, asked me not to use their name on any of my writing, since they strongly disagreed with my faith in Yeshua the Messiah. To them, my faith became such a source of shame and embarrassment to my family that I almost became cut off from my father's house. Rumors are that they held a funeral for me and even sat shivah[2].

Therefore, for writing purposes, I used my husband's last name. When we moved to Israel, the issues became further confused as the children were born. We ended up hyphenating the name of our daughter and due to bureaucratic red tape, our youngest son ended up with just his father's name.

After the Israeli government denied my Polish-born husband a visa, we were forced to return to Canada, feeling defeated and lost. Our dream had been to live in the land of Israel and to raise our children there and we felt we had failed. We didn't know how

---

[2] Sitting shivah is a Jewish custom by which, after the death of someone in their immediate family, the mourners sit in the house for a period of seven days while friends and relatives bring comfort.

to live like 'normal people' in exile anymore and our hearts continually longed to go home.

My (then) husband one day decided that enough was enough with the name thing – each of us carried a different name – the situation was ridiculous. So he trekked us all down to the registry, chose the Hebrew equivalent of my maiden name and with a few stamps and signatures, we all became 'Nesher' (which means 'eagle' in Hebrew). The children all grew up with this name and we began to feel comfortable with it – until the marriage dissolved.

Another failure, another defeat; and another heart-breaking decision brought more chaos. After a few years, the children and I ended up returning to Israel where they refused to recognize the legal name change done in Canada; therefore it was back to the maiden name again. Oh boy.....

Can you see why I wrestle with simple a question that really should have a simple answer - but in my case it doesn't: '*What is your name*'?

What is your name?

In Hebrew, we don't ask, *"What is your name?"* We ask (translated literally), *"How are you called?"* We named my youngest daughter, *Liat*, from Isaiah 43:1, **"I have called you by name, <u>you are mine</u>."** (Lee-atah)[3]

---

[3] Lee-at (Liat) is the feminine form of this phrase "You are mine"

I keep wondering, if God calls me by name, what is it? In the end, the book of Revelations tells us that God is going to give those who overcome a new name, a secret name written on a white stone, which only those who receive it will know.[4] I can

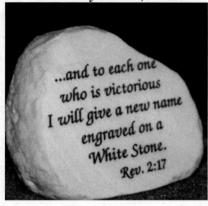

hardly wait to find out what I will be called!

As we journey through life's trenches (and sometimes its sewers) we may receive names for ourselves that are false, negative or destructive.

Perhaps as a child, you were taunted with a derogatory name by some cruel children and it stuck. Maybe something like: *"Fatty, fatty two by four – can't get through the kitchen door."* Oh yes…. :(

Other people may label us with words that pierce like a sword. In that brief but abusive marriage, my (then) husband said, *"I feel sorry for your children that they have you for their mother."* So I received the *'Bad Mother'* label. Besides the bad mother label, I also received (from a later marriage) *'bad cook, bad housekeeper, bad driver,* and worst of all *'rebellious wife."* Oye!

---

[4] Revelation 2:17

These labels are not overcome so easily. My father told me as a little girl that I had no common sense so another label stuck to me that read, '*dumb, foolish, or idiot*'. I lived up to that negative assessment.

What have people said to you or about you? In my mind, I see a person walking around as an adult - fearfully and wonderfully made by God - but with all these labels struck all over their body. These labels carry names like, "*Loser, failure, stupid, fat, ugly, bad, dirty, not good enough, unloved, and unlovable.*" These negative labels cover over the magnificence of who we were created to be.

The word of God says that He created us just a little lower than '*Elohim*' (a name for God). Wow! (Psalm 8:5) Obviously the translators couldn't handle this powerful truth so they falsely translated it as '*angels*' instead of Elohim. We were made in the image of the Almighty and have His nature as our true selves. But this beauty has been marred by all the false names we call ourselves.

Change of Name = Change of Destiny

I see in the Bible many instances of name changes that affect that person's entire destiny. God began with Av-ram and Sarai, whose names mean '*Exalted Father*' and '*My Prince*'. Together, they carried a Divine destiny which they could not fulfill because they were barren. All that God did was to add His own Divinity to their names and they became fruitful.

God's name is often abbreviated as the Hebrew letter 'hey' ה. When God added His own Divine name, ה to both Avram and Sarai, they became 'Avraham' and 'Sarah'. Avraham literally translates as the *father of a multitude of goyim (Gentiles)*. Many little children in church today sing, "*Father Abraham has many sons, many sons has father Abraham. I am one of them and so are you....*"

All those who are of faith in Messiah now belong to our Father Abraham's house. By himself, Avram could do nothing; but Avraham (with God), became the father of a multitude of nations/Gentiles.[5]

The very physical nature of Sarai changed after her name included God's Divine name. In Hebrew, the letter hey ה with the vowel 'ah' also functions to feminize a word. When God added His feminine nature to Sarai, she became Sarah. Her previously barren womb came to life and she became fruitful and bore a son, Isaac (Yitzchak), which means laughter). Those things which are birthed by God, with God, in His perfect timing bring great joy!

God did not change Avram's name in order to make him a King or Monarch but to make him a father (Abba). God also changed Jacob's name to make him a father. The change of name of Isaac's son, from Yaacov (Jacob) to Yisrael (Israel), after wrestling

---

[5] Galatians 3:7,29

with God, also brought him into his divine destiny as the father of the twelve tribes of Israel. Yaacov means a 'twisted deceiver'. It comes from 'ekev' – the heel of the foot; but Yisrael means a 'prince of God' – he became the head and not the tail – above and not beneath.

Abba Father

Faithful fathers are so desperately needed in today's world. Any man who believes that his job, his position, his career, ministry or financial status is what really counts has totally missed the heart of God, which is to father. I weep at the evident longing in so many sons and daughters' hearts to be fathered when their own fathers are absent – or too busy and consumed with work to train up their children in the ways of God. Only one of the functions of a father is to physically provide for the material needs of his wife and children. But the role of a father is so much more!

Just yesterday I visited the widow of a Japanese man who died while his wife was pregnant with their unborn son. Today that boy, Yiru-El, is the same age as my son, Avi-ad. I was so blessed to attend their Bar Mitzvahs where men of God from the kehilla (congregation) stood up (in their own father's absence) to give the father's blessing upon these young men as they entered adulthood.

Many boys (and girls) are growing up without fathers today. But God promises to be husband to the widow and father to the fatherless. Thank God we can all have a place of belonging in our Heavenly Father's house! And God promises to heal the curse of fatherlessness on our Land – to turn the hearts of the fathers back to their children and the children back to their fathers.[6] Halleluyah!

One of the things that surprised me about Israeli culture is how involved the fathers are in the lives of their children. There were four fathers (and me) who came on the recent school field trip. It is often a father who writes out the birthday invitations and makes the phone calls to invite the children. It's the father who picks up the sick child from school. I'm not used to it, but I delight in it and thank God and thank all the faithful fathers!

Perhaps some men have also received a label of *'failure as a father, inadequate, or not good enough, incapable'*...and so have just given up. For all those who still struggle with unresolved 'father wounds' and issues – there is hope! We have an Abba Father who longs to father us - to be everything that our earthly father was unwilling or incapable of being to us.

Yeshua prayed to His Father and taught us to pray likewise, "Avinu shebashamayim" "Our Father, who art in Heaven...." (Matthew 6:9)

---

[6] Malachi 4:6

To all the adult 'little girls (and boys)' still searching for the unconditional love of a father, still seeking for a place of belonging in their father's house, thus says the Lord,

"Listen, O daughter, consider and incline your ear; forget your own people also, and your father's house; So the King will greatly desire your beauty; because He is your Lord, worship Him." (Psalm 45:10-11)

God is our Father who desires us, no matter how much we have been rejected by our own people, our own family or friends.

Names the Angels call us

Sometimes the way we have come to see ourselves - after all the battles, all the sins, all the failures and messes and disappointments of our life - is not the way God sees us at all! The names we call ourselves are not the names the angels call us. Gideon called himself the *'least of his father's house'* but the angel called him a *'mighty man of valor'* (mighty soldier man). (Judges 6:12).

The word he used to describe himself in Hebrew is not so much 'least' but *'tza'ir'*, which means 'youngest'. Gideon thought he was too young to be used by God; sometimes we think we are either too young or too old. But God sees the heart.

David was so young (tza'ir) and insignificant in his father's eyes that he didn't even consider his youngest son, David, when the prophet Shmuel came to choose and anoint the next King of Israel. David's own father called him *'insignificant, not worthy, invisible'* perhaps; but God called him *'anointed, worthy, man of destiny, King of Israel!'*

Perhaps we see ourselves as *'tza'ir'*, the youngest, most inexperienced, the least, not even worthy of consideration in other people's eyes – even our own father's! But Yeshua taught us that '**he who is the greatest among you, let him be as the youngest (tza'ir)...**" (Luke 22:26)

To be 'tza'ir' – the youngest, or least, is not a liability in God's Kingdom. For He deliberately chooses the weak and the foolish to confound the wise.[7] We may take heart in the revelation that the way we see ourselves is often not the way God sees us.

The angel of the Lord called Gideon a 'mighty soldier' (*chayil*). This is the same word used in Proverbs 31 to describe a woman of valor (*eshet chayil*). I suspect that most of us, men and women, feel desperately far removed from the label of *'mighty soldier-man or warrior-woman'*. Most likely we feel more like *Mephiboshet*, who called himself a *'dead dog'* (2 Samuel 9:8); but King David

---

[7] 1 Corinthians 1:27

saw him as belonging to his father Jonathan's house; therefore a Covenant Royal Son.

The Israelite spies saw themselves as grasshoppers; but Joshua and Calev saw God's unlimited power available to help them overcome. The spies labeled themselves '*not able*' but Joshua and Calev refused this label and instead chose the names '*well able*' and '*overcomer*'.

We must also refuse these negative labels. I believe with all my heart that some of us are still walking around with our sticky labels, carrying the names that others have labeled us with; or that we have chosen to label ourselves. But God wants to change our name in order for us to fulfill our Divine destiny.

I love to sing a song on my harp especially for women in prisons, shelters and every place where broken-hearted, wounded women gather.

The song is called *'I will Change Your Name.'* [8]

I sing these lyrics prophetically over the women and I believe the Holy Spirit would want to sing these words over each one of us now:

"I will change your name; you shall no longer be called,

"Wounded, Outcast, Lonely and Afraid"

I will change your name; your new name shall be:

"Confidence, joyfulness, Overcoming One,

Faithfulness, Friend of God, One who seeks My face."

---

[8] Song available on music CD, Av Harachamim (Father of Mercies), sung by the author and her daughter, Liat, www.voiceforisrael.net

Called by a New Name

I once sang this song at a Shavuot (Pentecost) gathering in the Galilee. A woman later came to me and with great weeping explained that the Lord had directed her to come to this assembly where she had endured two hours of worship songs and dances and preaching until she wondered why she had ever come. But at the very end, when the Lord ministered to her heart through this song, <u>I will change Your Name</u>, she knew this to be the reason why she had come.

What do we call ourselves? Zion calls herself an outcast; someone for whom no one cares. But God says, **"You shall be <u>called by a new name</u>, which the mouth of the Lord will name." "You shall no longer be termed 'Forsaken (Azuvah), nor shall your land any more be termed Desolate (Shmamah), but you shall be called Hephzibah (My delight is in Her) and your land Beulah (married) for the Lord delights in you, and your land shall be married."** (Isaiah 62:2-4)

Yes, God promises to do this for Israel, but I believe this is a word in due season for us as well. God wants to give each of us a new name. Recently, I went for prayer for inner healing and deliverance. From emotional woundings suffered in my life, I still carried within me a name called '*abandoned*'. At the end of the prayer session, and without any prior knowledge of the nature of this article, the prayer counselor said, *"Oh, I almost forgot – we must give*

you a new name! What will your new name be?"
My new name became *'accepted.'*

This confirmed to me that God truly wants to change
our names – our very identities. We need this
desperately. There are some among us, even
perhaps sitting beside us in our churches and
congregations, who feel utterly forsaken and
desolate; lonely, abandoned and afraid. In their
heart of hearts, they call themselves *'Azuvah'*
(abandoned), *'Sh'mamah'* (desolate); but God wants
to remove these labels that we have carried around
for so long and give us a new name: *'Hephtzibah'*
and *'Beulah'* – *'My Delight is in Her'* and *'Married'*.

For many of us, like He did with Hosea's wife (and
like he did with me), God had to hedge us in with
thorns and wall us in; take all our lovers – our
idolatrous relationships - away from us. He does
this not to harm us; but in order to allure us, to bring
us into a wilderness and speak comfort to us there.

And what is it that the Lord speaks to us in this
wilderness place? It is that, not only does He want
to change our name; but He also wants us to change
His name! **""It will come about in that day,"
declares Yehovah, "that you will call Me 'Ishi'**
(my man) **and will no longer call Me 'Ba'ali'**
(my Lord/master).""** (Hosea 2:16)

This is actually a hidden Hebrew word play. 'Ishi'
translates as 'my man' – a term of endearment for
one's husband; whereas Ba'al is not only the Hebrew

word for husband, but is also used for Lord, master, and even the name of a false God. Elijah battled and defeated the prophets of Ba'al. (1 Kings 18)

God wants us to come to Him out of a place of love and devotion instead of domination and fear. He wants to woo us back into an intimate, eternal covenant relationship with Himself - the only One who can truly bring us life.

"I will betroth you to Me forever; Yes, I will betroth you to Me in righteousness and justice, in loving-kindness and mercy, I will betroth you to Me in faithfulness, and you shall know יהוה." (Hosea 2:19-20)

This 'marriage relationship' with our Bridegroom extends far and beyond any earthly relationship; past 'until death shall us part', for nothing can ever separate us from the love of God that is in Messiah Yeshua. (Romans 8:31-39)

It has been many years now since I've been 'saved' (over two decades); but I am just now coming to realize that God wants to do so much more than just save us from hell. He sent Yeshua to heal us. Of all the Scriptures He could have chosen to reveal His primary mission as the Messiah, He chose the verses from Isaiah 61:

"The Spirit of the Lord God is upon Me, because the Lord has anointed Me to preach good tidings to the poor; He has sent me to heal the broken hearted, to proclaim liberty to the captives, and the opening of the prison to those who are bound...to comfort all who mourn, to console those who mourn in Zion, to give them beauty for ashes, the oil of joy for mourning, the garment of praise for the spirit of heaviness; that they may be called trees of righteousness, the planting of the Lord, that He may be glorified." (Isaiah 61:1-3)

No matter how deep the wounds, how desolate the brokenness, God is our healer. I just opened to a devotional this morning that read, *"God can heal a broken heart but He has to have all the pieces."* [9]

The Master Craftsman wants to put the pieces back together according to His design rather than have us trying to find all the fragments and Crazy Glue them

---

[9] God's Little Devotional Book for Women, Honor Books, Inc.

into something that works. First of all, it just doesn't. And second of all, how can we ever recover the pieces of our heart that have been entrusted to another and discarded into the nearest trash can?

Can we trust God to transform our brokenness into something of beauty and value? Can we give him our ashes, our mourning, our heaviness and depression and exchange all of these for the new name that He wants to give us? I want to believe that we can; that He is able, for God is faithful to His word:

"You shall be a Crown of beauty and a Royal diadem in the hand of your God." (Isaiah 62:3)

Prayer: Dear God, for so long I felt forsaken, desolate and abandoned. But then You came into my life and promised You would never leave me nor forsake me. There are times when I still struggle with the old negative labels; but I want to receive my new name from You.

Please take all these ashes and make something beautiful out of my life. Take my mourning and give me the oil of joy. Thank you for the new identity I have in You; and that You truly delight in me. It is an honor to call you 'Ishi' instead of 'Ba'ali'; and to know that Your banner over me is always love. Amen v'Amen.

CHAPTER NINETEEN
KOTZIM (THORNS)
A Devotional on Prickly Trials

"Cursed is the ground ...Thorns and thistles (kotzim) it shall bring forth for you..." (Gen. 3:18)

Thorns and thistles, or '*kotzim*' as we call them in Hebrew, seem to be an unfortunate fact of life this side of Eden. In Israel, we seem to have more than our fair share in this dry land where cacti and other prickly plants abound. As anyone is aware who has read the account of Creation and the fall of mankind, thorns and thistles in this world are a result of God's curse upon the earth.

I believe that the thorns and thistles that Adam was forced to deal with day in and day out were not just physical ones. For if the curse merely applied to the ground, then anyone not involved in agriculture would be exempt. No, it seems to me that the kotzim Adam encountered on a daily basis outside the Garden of Eden are the same ones that men and women face even today: the painful thorns of shame, guilt, failure, frustration and futility.

I wonder if every time Adam and Eve looked at one another, they battled blame, bitterness, regret and resentment. I don't think a day of my life passes without me having to process at least one of more (or all) of these prickly 'kotzim'.

Many of us still carry imbedded thorns. What happens if we get a sliver and don't remove it? Of course it become inflamed and infected. I hate removing my kids' slivers; but it has to be done. It is necessary. We need to bring our infected kotzim to Yeshua and ask Him to remove them, even if it hurts.

And then again, there are times when the Lord, in His wisdom, allows for a thorn in the flesh to remain. The apostle Paul called it a '*messenger from Satan*', and pleaded with the Lord three times for it to be removed. But God did not answer Paul's prayer as he hoped. God didn't remove the thorn; He only promised to give him the grace to handle it.

"My grace is sufficient for you, for my strength is made perfect in weakness."
(2 Corinthians 12:7-9)

Paul came to understand that because of the great revelations he had received, God allowed this thorn in the flesh to remain so that Paul would not become proud: **"lest I be exalted above measure."** God knows exactly what we need when we need it; and He has ways of keeping us humble!

Many times, he keeps us walking in humility by allowing kotzim to remain in our lives that we desperately want removed. And we want them removed like yesterday! But sometimes these very things (or people) that bug and bother and annoy and irritate and frustrate us to the nth degree, may

actually be the tool that God uses to bring healing.

The place where we moved back to in Israel was lovely; but the yard had been badly neglected by its previous tenants and stood seriously overgrown with kotzim (thorns).

This can become a potentially dangerous situation since snakes and scorpions love to hide in fields of thorns. When I began to clear the yard, I often came across a plant that gave a nasty sting. My landlords informed me that people have used this plant as a 'natural cure' for arthritis and many other human ailments. Some people (crazy, I know....) intentionally swipe themselves with this stinging nettle, believing that in the sting will come healing.

It may be the same for us. May we submit to the stings of the kotzim in our lives, that we may find healing from strongholds of pride and other sins that betray our soul's purpose on this earth.

"Blows that hurt cleanse away evil, as do stripes the inner depths of the heart." (Proverbs 20:30)

One day, while walking with my two younger children and the dogs down the back alley, I noticed the beauty of the flowers sitting atop the thorns and thistles lining the gravel pathway. To me, these flowers proclaimed *'El Harachamin'* (God of mercies)

Even upon the thorn bushes, he places a crown of beauty; for even in His terrible judgments, God remembers to bestow mercy and grace.

God simply could not give us kotzim without flowers - evidence that even though He may punish, He is still a good God, - gracious, kind, slow to anger and abundant in mercy. Great is His faithfulness.

YESHUA TOOK THE KOTZIM

This truth became suddenly clear to me when I considered that Yeshua wore a crown of kotzim (thorns) upon His head as they carried Him away to judgment, even death on a cross.

"So then Pilate took Yeshua and scourged Him, and the soldiers twisted a crown of kotzim (thorns) and put it on His head, and they put on Him a purple robe. Then they said, *"Hail, King of the Jews!"* and they struck Him with their hands." (John 19:1-3)

If the kotzim are a sign of God's judgment and even the curse, then Yeshua - wearing a crown of kotzim — physically demonstrated how the Messiah took upon Himself the curse that we all deserve. He actually took the 'sign of the curse' - the Kotzim - upon His own head.

"The Messiah has redeemed us from the curse of the Torah, <u>having become a curse for us</u> (for it is written, *'cursed is everyone who hangs on a tree'*), that the blessing of Abraham might come upon the Gentiles in Messiah Yeshua... " (Galatians 3:13-14)

In the ancient system of sacrifices under the Old Covenant, the Cohen Hagadol (High Priest) would, only once a year on the Day of Atonement (Yom Kippur), physically lay his hands *upon the head* of a live goat, called *'Azazel'*, and confess all the sins of Israel upon this 'scapegoat' who would be banished into the wilderness – never to return.

The Cohen Hagadol laying the sins of Israel upon the azazel

This is what Yeshua has done for us. He who knew no sin became sin for us in order that we may become the righteousness of God in Him.[1] The crown of Kotzim upon His head is our proof.

Pricks, Jabs and Irritations

Even though Yeshua took the penalty for our sins, we don't have to live very long in this fallen world, however, to find out that kotzim still exist. Life can still hurt. We still need to walk each and every day with potential kotzim - annoyances that prick at our peace; and irritations that jab at our joy.

Even today, I anticipated a wonderfully quiet, peaceful day of blissful writing while the children studied at school. Instead, the neighbors have chosen this very time to begin renovations on their home and all I can hear are the nerve -jarring sounds

---

[1] 2 Corinthians 5:21

of buzz saws, hammers, and other unidentified (but loud) tools.

Ah yes, kotzim....Yesterday I felt like I had fallen headlong into a briar patch – one kotz after another pricked and jabbed at me until the pain felt unbearable. Nothing major, you understand – no deadly disaster or crazy crisis – just these nasty kotzim - manifesting as kids whining, complaining and bickering until you think you're going to lose your ever lovin' mind!

Or the kotzim of petty trials like insufficient shekels in my wallet; trying to find a bank machine in unfamiliar turf; and finally finding it but it's out of order. Driving around in heavy traffic looking for another one...impatient Israeli drivers honking incessantly...kids hot, tired, hungry and cranky.... finally – yes! Another bank machine!

But no parking...

I spot one space but it's reserved for the handicapped. The ATM is no more than a few feet away so I decide to risk it. Leaving the kids in the air-conditioned car, I sprinted for the machine, sweating profusely in the hot summer sun.

"*Service temporarily unavailable*" the machine read. I'm tempted to curse but know that I should be saying, "*Praise the Lord*" instead (even with gritted teeth).

Out of the corner of my eye, I see the mishtarah (Israeli police). A policeman on a motorcycle drives up and parks right next to my vehicle, radioing something over his walkie talkie. Oye! I race to the car, schvitzing (sweating), tripping, crying, "*Slicha, slicha, slicha, (sorry, sorry, sorry)....*"

I had visions of my kids being taken away into foster care because their mother left them locked in an air-conditioned vehicle while parked in a handicapped parking spot no less.

In my panic and distress, I couldn't even remember a word of Hebrew; I just kept begging for mercy. My bank card still remained in the non-functional ATM machine. He looked at me with that look reserved for the pathetic of this world, and simply said, "*Lechi - Go and get your card.*"

I pulled off onto a side road and just wept until I had no more strength to weep. The only good part to this story is that the kids, seeing their Mom was about to have a nervous breakdown, stopped their shtuyot (nonsense) in the backseat to comfort me.

I kept saying, "*Todah Elohim, Todah Elohim, Thank you God, thank you God.*" I don't know what I was thanking Him for; but I thought I had better practice what I preach and set a good example for the kids.

Other good things then happened. I went back to the household sale where I had purchased a framed poster (since I couldn't get the shekels to pay her for it) and this turned out to be such a blessing. The woman, Wendy, saw my state of distress; and not only gave me a hug, she also prayed for me to know God's peace. Then she ended up giving me the poster I wanted as a gift, along with a couple extra items thrown in for the kids that they had wanted as well. Several years later, this woman edited my huge volume of Messianic Jewish commentaries on the Torah portions (Parashot)[2] - for free! Amazing! God is so good! He brought such great blessing out of such painful kotzim that day.

When someone outside began to yell at me for how I had parked on the sidewalk (a common practice in Israel where parking is scarce), it didn't even phase me a bit! I had such peace (shalom).

Written on the poster sitting beside me on the front seat were the Hebrew words, שמע ישראל [Shma Yisrael (Hear O Israel)].

That evening, I felt so grateful to join the Messianic Congregation where I felt refreshed, renewed and encouraged in God's presence, in worship, and the Word.

Here is how the speaker began his message, "Shma Yisrael – Hear O Israel....." He extorted us to be people who listen for and hear God's voice.

2

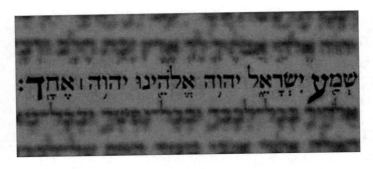

Lev Shome'ah – A Heart that Hears

Solomon, as a young king of Israel prayed for wisdom; but in the original Hebrew, he literally asked for a *'heart that hears' (lev shome'ah)*. God pleaded with His people, Israel, to listen to Him, **"Hear, {Sh'ma } O My people, and I will admonish you! O Israel, if you will listen to Me!"** (Psalm 81:8)

God laments over the fact that His people will not listen to Him or walk in His ways, for if they did, He would give them victory over their enemies, feed them, provide for them, and satisfy them completely. (Psalms 81:11-16)

Herein seems to lie the challenge for us as God's people living in a world full of kotzim. We need to hear clearly from the Holy Spirit – to know if these thorns are a result of dullness of hearing on our part; or simply a result of living outside Eden?

Is our pain due to a refusal to listen to God and walk in His ways? Are we being opposed by the Almighty Himself because our ways are perverse to Him – like Balaam who was sent by King Balak to curse Israel?

Or are we like Jonah, suffering claustrophobia inside the belly of a whale because we are simply headed in a direction away from and in opposition to God's will?

"Thorns and snares (kotzim) are in the way of the perverse; He who guards his soul will be far from them." (Proverbs 22:5)

Could it be that we are dealing with so many painful issues in our lives because of our own sins of laziness and passivity? **"The way of the lazy man is like a hedge of thorns (kotzim); but the way of the upright is a highway."** (Prov. 15:19)

The Word tells us that if we walk past the field of a lazy man, we will see it overgrown with kotzim.[3] If we are lazy or passive, refusing to take responsibility for the little things that come up in our lives, they can eventually become huge, unmanageable, overgrown fields of kotzim that leave us feeling overwhelmed and exhausted with the task ahead.

Or are these kotzim '*messengers from Satan*' being allowed by God in order to refine us and teach us to walk in a greater humility? This is where we need discernment. We need to stop talking to God and listen. *'Sh'ma Yisrael'*. Hear O Israel.

Let us be someone with a heart that listens – lev shomeah – that we may discern truth from error, right from wrong, and good from evil.

---

[3] Prov. 24:30

What does God have to say about our kotzim?

Is He saying, *"Don't worry My child, My grace is sufficient for you. I know what I'm doing. Just trust me in this trial or tribulation; even when you don't understand why I allow this to continue when it obviously causes you such distress and suffering."*

Or on the contrary, is He saying, *"Hey, sluggard, get up early, get out there and start thwacking down some of those nasty weeds!"*

Perhaps some of our questions will remain unanswered, at least until we can ask our Redeemer personally when we meet him face to face. May we not be overly concerned with things too high and complex for us.

Some situations are beyond our limited ability to comprehend all the 'why's of life especially those painful things which have happened in the past; or are still today causing us to cry out to God for mercy.

The one thing God asks of us is that we continue to believe, to trust Him, and to forgive the kotzim of life – even those inflicted upon us by others.

A quote from <u>God's little Devotional Book for Women</u> [4] says, *"Some people complain that God put thorns on roses, while others praise Him for putting roses among thorns."*

---

[4] Honor Books

Those of us who believe in God's Holy Word know
that at the end of the story, those who enter the
Kingdom of the New Jerusalem will find a beautiful
garden completely free of kotzim.

**"God Himself will be with them and be their God.
And God will wipe away every tear from their
eyes; there shall be no more death, nor sorrow,
nor crying. There shall be no more pain, for the
former things have passed away."** (Rev. 21:3-4)

I don't know if I can even imagine such a world! But
this is our hope – eternity with our God to serve Him
in a place where all curses have simply ceased to
exist.

**"For there shall be no more curse, but the throne
of God and of the Lamb shall be in it, and His
servants shall serve Him."** (Rev. 22:3).

Amen. Halleluyah! Even so, come Adonai Yeshua....

Closing Prayer: Thank you Abba Father, that despite the irritating, annoying and sometimes even unbearably painful kotzim of life, you are still a good, good Father and we can trust You to get us through with joy and peace (shalom). Whether it's a 'kotz' as trivial as dropping our cell phone in the toilet (yes... been there, done that, got the T-shirt), or lost keys, or something more serious like a loss of our health, a relationship or a financial fiasco - thank you that Your grace is always sufficient for us; and that You will never give us more than we can handle.

Give us a listening heart like You gave to Melech Shlomoh (King Solomon) – a lev shomeah – that we may judge rightly even in difficult or perplexing situations. We long for that glorious day when there will be no more curses, no more kotzim – and only roses without thorns. Amen.

CHAPTER TWENTY

LETTING GO

A Devotional on Making Room for the 'New Thing'

Liat 12 years old

"Do not call to mind the former things, or ponder things of the past. Behold, I will do something new, now it will spring forth; will you not be aware of it? I will even make a roadway in the wilderness, rivers in the desert." (Isaiah 43:18-19)

You would think it would be easy to find a simple bathing suit in Israel. Not so, apparently...

Since coming back to Israel more than two years ago,[1] Liat has grown from a sweet, little, ten year old girl to a lovely young lady of *'twelve-going-on-eighteen'*. Obviously the bathing suit she brought with her from Canada no longer fits.

So a'shoppping we did go - all over the city of Jerusalem it seems. Up and down the commercial streets of Hillel and Jaffa where clothing shops abound. But no bathing suit found there for Liat.

So we tried the mall. Surely there we would find a nice new bathing suit. We found entire stores devoted to swimsuits but after trying on dozens, we still found none suitable. The problem, it seemed, was one of modesty. Wanting to uphold a certain standard of feminine decency, Liat did not want a bikini, but (thankfully) preferred a one piece.

Since most younger girls in Israel wear bikinis, the only one piece suits we could find were designed in style and size for the figures and taste of us *'older women'* – styles which certainly didn't suit Liat's keen fashion sense! ☺

My patience with this search for the elusive swim suit was admittedly wearing thin. But Liat was not

---

[1] We returned to Israel in December 2009 after spending several years back in Canada

about to give up on something so essential to the upcoming summer pool and beach season. After a few tearful sessions, I agreed to look elsewhere.

Getting a brainwave, I thought that perhaps we had been looking in the wrong places. Maybe at a sports store we'd be more likely to find a one piece Speedo that fit and upheld our standards, while still appealing to Liat. So off we went; but no...

After trying on what seemed to be every style and size in the store, we again went home dejected (her more than me) by our failure to buy a simple swim suit. Later in the evening, I checked in Liat's drawers and found her old, worn out bathing suit.

"What is this still doing here?" I asked. It no longer fit. The chlorine had rendered it practically see-through in all the wrong places. And she was definitely not ever going to wear it again – not even in an emergency. So why were we keeping it?

Just in case.

Isn't that the way with us sometimes? There is something (or someone) in our life that is completely inappropriate. Maybe at one time it served as a blessing; but now it most definitely no longer fits. We've grown up.

Maybe we've grown to a place where we just don't *'fit together'* anymore as we used to. And yet we hold on. Just in case. Just in case we never find another one, a better one. We think we will hang on to what we have until we have something better.

But this is not how life works. We must first be willing to let go of the old in order to make room for the new. Many of us are eager for a *new thing* to happen in our lives; but before we can embrace the new, we must release the old – that which no longer fits, which is no longer appealing or appropriate to the person we have grown to become.

I once tried to insert a video into the VCR (yes, this was before the days of DVD's and electronic movie downloads). No matter how hard I pushed and shoved, that video just wouldn't go into the VCR.

Finally, I had enough sense to check and found that the video we were watching previously was still filling the space; therefore there was no room for the new one. I had to first eject the old video before I could insert the new one. Obviously.

Of course this is obvious with videos and VCR's and yet so often we are trying to do the same thing with our lives. We're pushing and shoving, but the new thing just won't work – no matter how hard we strive in the flesh. We must first make room for it by ejecting the old.

Sometimes it is the old, negative thinking patterns that we need to 'eject'; or it may be a victim mentality – an attitude of bitterness and resentment that we need to release from our heart before the love and joy and blessings of life can enter.

Yeshua said we can't put new wine in old wineskins. **"Neither do men pour new wine into old wineskins. If they do, the skins will burst, the wine will spill, and the wineskins will be ruined. Instead, they pour new wine into new wineskins, and both are preserved."** (Matthew 9:17)

Similarly, we can't sew a piece of unshrunk cloth onto an old garment: **"No one sews a patch of unshrunk cloth on an old garment. If he does, the new piece will pull away from the old, and a worse tear will result."** (Mark 2:21)

It's this attempt to mix the old with the new that can be problematic. We want the new stuff; but don't want to risk getting rid of the old. It is the old 'junk' in our inner man that we must release before we can be filled with new love, peace and joy. We can't drag the pain and disappointments of the past into our present or it will poison our future. We must simply let go and let God.

The other day I noticed a truly disgusting smell coming from my kitchen cupboards. I looked and looked but didn't see anything until finally I pulled out a full bag of potatoes. From the front it looked just fine; but upon closer inspection, the bag contained a few rotting, putrid potatoes that were spoiling the whole sack.

Once I removed the rotten potatoes, the horrible smell disappeared as well. We may think that we have dealt with all the *'rotten stuff'* in our hearts – anger, resentment, bitterness and unforgiveness – and yet its unmistakable stench shows up wherever we find ourselves. We need to cleanse out that rottenness and let it go.

Sometimes the Lord gives us opportunities to 'play out' in the natural what He wants to teach us spiritually. This month I will be moving to a new home in the moshav (village) which is about half the size of where we now live. It means I will, by necessity, be giving away or throwing out a lot of stuff. This is hard for a recovering hoarder.

Letting go can be difficult at times, because we are people who collect things and want to hold onto them. Insecurity can cause us to accumulate more than what is good and can create excessive clutter. I once found a broken mirror that my daughter had pulled out of the garbage. She wanted to keep it 'just in case'.

There is a great animated movie we watched called Up which contains this profound message about letting go. The old man has held onto a whole house full of his 'stuff' from the life he shared in the past with his beloved wife before she died. He is sentimentally attached to all his possessions.

Finally, in a crisis, he is forced to make a choice between hanging on to all his 'stuff'; or letting go – and finding life.

Yeshua said, "**He who holds onto his life will lose it and he who loses his life for my sake will find it**." (Matthew 10:39)

He asks us a profound question, "**What does it profit a man to gain the whole world and to lose his soul**." (Mark 8:36)

When we need to let go of something physical that we are attached to, or a relationship that has been important to us in the past; instead of thinking of it as a loss, we may consider that we are giving it to the Lord – planting it as a seed in His Kingdom.

When we look at letting go in this way, we no longer have to mourn the loss. We know that nature abhors a vacuum; and that whatever we give over to the Lord, in faith and trust in His goodness, He will replace with something even better!

Liat finally took that step of faith and agreed to give away her old bathing suit. Into the give-away bag it went! Later, that same day, Timothy came home and said, "*I don't know what you guys are talking about. I was just in a store that had rows and rows of bathing suits.*" "*One piece bathing suits?*" YES!

Liat enjoying the pool in her new swim suit

(Timothy must have thought we were either daft or totally incompetent in the art of shopping since it was the first store he had walked into).

The very next morning, after letting go of the old bathing suit, we walked into this store and found that Timothy's observation was correct. Rows and rows of one piece swim suits in beautiful styles and colors in Liat's size. She tried on a couple and picked out a beautiful bathing suit she loves and fits her perfectly.

I want to encourage you (as well as myself), not to be afraid to let go of that which is no longer working, no longer appropriate, and no longer a 'good fit' for where we are now in this journey of life.

God promises that instead of our former shame, we shall receive double![2] If we will let go of our ashes, those things that have been burned into nothingness, He will give us beauty. If we will be willing to let go of our mourning, depression and heaviness, He will give us the oil of joy and a spirit of praise![3]

"No, dear brothers and sisters, I have not achieved it, but I focus on this one thing: Forgetting the past and looking forward to what lies ahead," (Philippians 3:13)

Now, I have this old bathing suit that is showing transparent patches in all the wrong places. But I've grown so comfortable with it – and what if I can't find another one I like? I may just hang on to it for a bit longer.... or then again, maybe not. ☺

Prayer: Abba Father, You know how difficult it is at times to 'let go and let God'. Help us to find the courage within to release the old in order to make room for the wonderful 'new thing' that You have in store for us. We trust that You are good – and You know exactly what we need.

Help us to hold our possessions loosely in our hands; that they may not hold us tightly in bondage. We are willing to give up whatever You ask of us; knowing that we are sowing into Your Kingdom and that You always return a double portion of blessing. Amen.

---

[2] Isaiah 61:7
[3] Isaiah 61:3

CHAPTER TWENTY-ONE

LIVING AS A SUKKAH

A Devotional on Playing it Safe

**"God has not given us a spirit of fear and timidity,
but of power and love and a sound mind."**
(2 Timothy 1:7)

Reading a bedtime story to my daughter, Liat, the other day got me thinking about the whole issue of fear and how it limits our lives. In this cute little story, several ducklings hatch out of their eggs and follow their mother to the small pond.

Mother duck warns her young ones about the ever-present danger of the fox, a brownish creature with dark, beady eyes and a furry tail, who lives in the forest and would like nothing better than a meal of succulent young duck.

Eventually, the ducklings and their mother flew over to a larger pond nearby; but one duckling decided that she would never fly, but only walk. She made a decision to *play it safe*. Because of her self-imposed limitation, this duckling could not join her mother and the rest of the family unless she walked through the forest.

As she ventured into the forest, it was not long before she ran smack dab into – you guessed it – a brownish creature with dark, beady eyes and a furry tail. The fox slyly lured the duckling towards its den, hiding its evil intentions; but just in time, the duckling realized the danger she had placed herself in, and took off flying into the air. Soon, the silly duckling was reunited with her mother and brothers and sisters in true safety and fellowship.

Just a silly story, yes, but how many of us live like this duckling? We have somewhere, somehow, for some reason, made a decision to *'play it safe'*. Instead of *'rising up on eagle's wings'* in boldness, faith, and courage, we are walking wearily through dark, scary forests and running smack dab into the enemy of our souls.

It's time that we recognize those dark, beady eyes and furry tail; and wake up to the danger we have brought upon ourselves by our feeble attempts to stay 'safe'. In seeking security and safety by our own human efforts, we are actually playing right into the hands of the enemy.

There is, in actuality, only one true place of shelter and refuge from all the scary things of life. That safe place is in the secret place of El Elyon (Most High God), abiding under the shadow of El Shaddai (The Almighty).

He will cover you with his feathers, and under his wings you will find refuge
Psalm 91:4

"I will say of the Lord, "He is my refuge and my fortress, My God, in Him I will trust.
Surely He shall deliver you from the snare of the fowler and from the perilous pestilence.
He shall cover you with His feathers, and under His wings you shall take refuge;" (Psalm 91: 2-4)

יֹסֵךְ לָךְ וְתַחַת־כְּנָפָיו תֶּחְסֶה צִנָּה וְסֹחֵרָה אֲמִתּוֹ
תהלים צא:4

He will cover you with his feathers, and under his wings you will find refuge.
Psalm 91:4.

"If God be for us, then who can be against us?" (Romans 8:31) "The LORD is my light and my salvation-- whom shall I fear? The LORD is the stronghold of my life-- of whom shall I be afraid?" (Psalm 27:1)

Bird Flu and other Terrors

I was visiting my elderly aunties one day at the seniors' home where they used to live [1] and the conversation soon turned to the dreaded 'bird flu' that everyone said would be coming with vengeance as a plague. I mentioned this above verse from the Psalms (Tehillim) —assuring them that God would deliver us from this kind of pestilence as long as we trust in Him and stay under His shelter.

They were amazed and wanted to know if this was, indeed, written in the "*Jewish Bible*"! All I had on me was a Bible with small print, but they insisted on looking for themselves and trying to read this verse. It is surprising that most Jewish people (including myself before I came to faith in Messiah Yeshua) do not know our own Scriptures.

God promises not only to deliver us from plagues such as the bird flu, but also from terrorism and enemy attack, by day or by night, and even from destruction that comes upon us at noon. So whether we are being assaulted morning, noon, or night, God is going to be there as the Protector of our soul.

The Psalmist makes a bold claim, "**Because you have made the Lord, who is my refuge, even the Most High (Elyon), your dwelling place, no evil shall befall you...For He shall give His angels charge over you, to keep you in all your ways.**" (Psalm 91: 9-11)

We must remember that angels encamp around us!

---

[1] One auntie received the Lord before passing away and the other has moved to a different seniors home in another city.

God does not promise us a life free of trouble, but He will be with us in that trouble zone. He will show us how to walk through it to safety; He will deliver us.

But what does it mean to dwell in the secret place, in the shadow of the Almighty, under the shelter of His wings? I believe it means resting in God and giving up our own feeble, human efforts at securing our own safety and security.

We can do things one of two ways:
either trusting in our own ways and leaning on our own understanding; or trusting in the Lord's ways - which will sometimes totally defy human logic:

"Trust in the Lord with all Your heart and lean not on your own understanding. In all your ways acknowledge Him and He will bring it to pass." (Proverbs 3:5-6)

Sukkot (Feast of Tabernacles or Booths) is a time in which God commanded Israel to live in a temporary shelter called a 'sukkah' for seven days. During this week of Sukkot, we rejoice in the goodness and provision of God, remembering His faithfulness during our wilderness wanderings.

One year, the Holy Spirit gave me a precious new revelation. He said, *"I want you to live as a sukkah."*

I wondered about the meaning of this strange word. How do we live like a sukkah? What are the unique characteristics of these little booths that we build for the week of the Feast of Tabernacles and tear down when the seven days are over?

A sukkah (booth/tabernacle) built by children of Makor Hatikvah Messianic school, Jerusalem, Israel

A sukkah is both temporary and fragile – it is relatively defenseless. So, too, does God want us to tear down the heavy, impenetrable walls that we have built up around our hearts, by our own human reactions to fear, hurt, pain, and betrayal. Instead, He wants to be our defense and our refuge – our fortress and high tower.

Instead of taking vengeance for sins committed against us by others, we can allow Him to be the one to take vengeance on our behalf – in His perfect way and time, not ours.

"Never take your own revenge, beloved, but leave room for the wrath of God, for it is written, "VENGEANCE IS MINE, I WILL REPAY," says the Lord." (Romans 12:19, Leviticus 19:18)

Forgiveness, refusing to hold a grudge, returning good for evil - these are all ways of living as a sukkah. We allow ourselves to be relatively defenseless in the natural - open to the elements - but in the Spirit, we are hiding ourselves in the cleft of the rock; and trusting in His protection.

O the cleft of the Rock,
Where my soul may hide.

If we have been hurt in a relationship, living as a sukkah means forgiving and opening ourselves up to reconciliation again. If we have been beaten down by life and been thrown into a pit, it means getting up again, picking up our mats, and to continue walking with God in faith.

Reckless sukkah living means trusting God enough to fly again – to rise up on wings as an eagle, rather than squawking about in the proverbial chicken coop along with the other prisoners of fear, doubt and overcaution.

In the Sukkah, one can see the stars through the branches of the roof. We catch a glimpse of a heavenly vision – the same stars that our Father Abraham gazed at when God promised to cut covenant with him.

הָיָה דְבַר יְהוָה אֶל אַבְרָם בַּמַּחֲזֶה.
וַיּוֹצֵא אֹתוֹ הַחוּצָה וַיֹּאמֶר הַבֶּט נָא
הַשָּׁמַיְמָה וּסְפֹר הַכּוֹכָבִים אִם תּוּכַל לִסְפֹּר
אֹתָם. וַיֹּאמֶר לוֹ כֹּה יִהְיֶה זַרְעֶךָ.

The word of God came to Abram in a dream.
God took him outside and said, "Look
up at heaven and count the stars.
if you can count them all. That's how many
children and grandchildren you will have."

By living in a sukkah, we are reminded that this world is not our home; we are only strangers and aliens, pilgrims just passing through on our journey to eternity. With this perspective, we can gain the courage to live in obedience to whatever God calls us to do, instead of living our lives as  hamsters running frantically around the endless, meaningless wheels of existence.

When we first moved to Israel, our then youngest son (Timothy) was five years old. One day on a crowded bus, he shouted, *"Mom, look! There is a soldier and he's wearing a kippah!"*[2]

We soon grew accustomed to rubbing shoulders with armed guards and soldiers on the streets packing Uzis and other assorted weapons.

It became a daily event to be stopped by bomb threats, and to have every bag checked at the entrance to every place of business. On busses, everyone is always alert to suspicious behavior, to bags left unattended. The ever-present danger of the enemy surrounds and permeates daily life in Israel. One never knows if the person walking next to you on the street is going to pull a knife and stab you; or if the motorist coming down the street will use his vehicle as a lethal weapon to mow you down.

And yet, in response to the many questions we would receive about whether or not we were 'afraid' to live in Israel, I would have to answer *"No, we do not fear."* I'm not really even sure why this was so; somehow we just felt safe there.

One time, our daughter Courtney was out, walking along a street where ten minutes later, a bomb hit. Our younger daughter should have been standing at a bus stop where a bomb hit but the school let them out an hour later that day so it missed her. Halleluyah!

---

[2] Kippah – skullcap – head covering worn by religiously observant Jewish men to demonstrate respect to God.

When my eldest Courtney planned to get married in Jerusalem at an outdoor venue, a terrible storm suddenly blew up, along with strong winds and rain that destroyed all their preparations. Even the tent covering for which they had paid a fortune, was destroyed in the tempest. Courtney felt devastated, thinking that the whole wedding would have to be cancelled. But miraculously, they found an alternative location (with security) and within a couple hours, moved the entire wedding indoors.

It was a wonderful simcha [3] that went off without a hitch with one exception. While we were downtown getting our hair and makeup done at the salon, we heard a loud blast go off nearby. Soon, the radios began broadcasting that a suicide bomber had just blown himself up downtown. Thank God, there were no casualties. The hair stylist began to shout, in typical Israeli form, *"Shut that radio off! There are brides in here. They don't want to hear about bombs today!"*

Later, we heard from one of the wedding guests who had connections with the Israeli Police and secret service, that they had been tracking this bomber for days. He had been positioned at the site of Courtney and Emanuel's outdoor wedding, which happened to overlook some Arabic villages across the hills.

Apparently, when he saw that the storm had blown everything down and the guests were not arriving, he instead took the bus downtown where he detonated his deadly bomb.

---

[3] simcha – joy, joyous occasion

Bride and Groom at an Orthodox Jewish wedding

"A sound shall be heard in the cities of Judah and in the streets of Jerusalem. A sound of joy and the sound of gladness; the sound of the bridegroom and the sound of the Bride."
(Jeremiah 33:10-11)

The whole wedding demonstrated a prophetic picture of the soon coming reunion between our lovely Bridegroom and His beautiful Bride - a virgin without spot or wrinkle (yes, that's us ☺).

What is the point of this story?! Is it just to praise God for His protection? No, it is to say, "*Trust God even in the storms of life.*" We never know if this 'storm' that devastates us; that we think in our limited human perception is the ruin of our life and happiness, may actually be the thing God is using to save us.

I never experienced the fear in Israel that I have felt in exile – not a physical fear of terrorism – but the fear of wasting my life in a meaningless existence. There is a vague fear of wandering in the wilderness until I die - my carcass lying there as evidence that God was not pleased with me in the end because of my unbelief.

I have heard that the number one fear of most people is not the fear of spiders or public speaking or poverty, or anything of that sort. The numero uno fear of human beings is that of failing to live up to our God-given potential. When we live our lives in the fear of stepping out, of doing that thing that is in our hearts to do; when we try to *play it safe*, the enemy can have a 'hey dey' with us!

Look at what happened when David stayed home instead of going out with his men on the battlefield – he fell into sin with Batsheva. This is what happens when we get lazy and passive – when we lose our offensive edge. We give the enemy a foothold.

He can then torment us with so much fear, guilt, and condemnation that we refuse to engage in life and we fall short of our divine destiny. How sad. How many lives are wasted because people choose to play it safe? How many excuses do we use to live lives devoid of passion, purpose, joy and peace?

God is calling to us in this hour: "The Spirit and the Bride say 'Come!'" (Revelation 22:17). The shofar [4] has blown long and hard and loud on the Feast of

---

[4] ram's horn

Trumpets, [5] shouting: *"Wake up! Wake up out of your slumber!"* We must stop being so busy and become fruitful.

We must be determined to break free from the rat race and live out of our passion and purpose. The time is short. Now is the time to serve God with all of our hearts with joy and gladness — to live with an eternal perspective.

We must work while there is yet light. Win souls. Fulfill the ministry that has been entrusted to us. Stir up the gifts that God has placed within us and even dig them up if we have buried them in the dirt. We don't want to face God and have him call us a wicked and unfaithful servant. If we refuse to use the gifts and talents God has given us, then we are actually robbing the people of the blessing God intended for them to receive through us!

How many of us are working at jobs we hate, living lives that we despise; just out of fear of trying something new, fear of change, fear of the unknown, or fear of failure? The list of potential fears seems endless.

Not only is our sense of personal fulfillment and fruitfulness at stake, however; but we may be endangering our very lives by this kind of cowardly living. For if the Holy Spirit is calling to us, giving us direction about what we must do to survive the coming chaos; and if we refuse this counsel, we may suffer dire consequences for ourselves and our loved ones.

---

[5] Yom Zikaron Tru'ah

There is no softer pillow to rest our heads on at night than the sweet assurance of knowing ourselves to be in the center of God's perfect will and timing.

The wisest man who ever lived, King Solomon, wrote about this in the book of Proverbs, **"Whoever listens to me (wisdom) will dwell safely, and will be secure, without fear of evil."** (Proverbs 1:33)

Wisdom is calling aloud in this hour – are we listening? Noah moved *with godly fear* to build an ark for the saving of his entire household from the flood and was therefore included in the register of the great people of faith in the Bible. (Hebrews 11:7)

This is a good fear, a godly fear; but there is another kind of fear – cowardice – that can really put our lives in danger. Cowards will not enter the Kingdom of God; only those of good courage will overcome and inherit a place in the Kingdom as sons and daughters of the Most High (Elyon).

"He who overcomes shall inherit all things, and I will be his God and he shall be My son. But the cowardly, unbelieving, abominable, murderers, sexually immoral, sorcerers, idolaters, and all liars, shall have their part in the lake which burns with fire and brimstone, which is the second death." (Revelations 21:7-8)

This spirit of fear is not from God; since perfect love casts out all fear. Let us fully embrace the fear of the Lord, which is the beginning of all wisdom, but reject this human fear that robs us of our destiny and inheritance.

When I think of living as a sukkah, I see David, striding forth to meet Goliath, unencumbered by any element of Saul's heavy armor. While just a youth, David faced a mighty, fearsome giant with only five smooth stones; but knowing that he also carried with him the power of the name of Yehovah Tzeva'ot יְהוָה צְבָאוֹת – Captain of the armies of Israel.

"David said to the Philistine, "You come against me with sword and spear and javelin, but I come against you in the name of the LORD Almighty, the God of the armies of Israel, whom you have defied." (1 Samuel 17:45)

Our weapons of warfare are not the sword and spear and javelin of the Philistines; but are mighty spiritual weapons to defeat every enemy. So let us be strong and of good courage; for our God has promised, **"I will be with you. I will never leave you nor forsake you."** (Deuteronomy 31:6)

"So do not fear, for I am with you; do not be dismayed, for I am your God. I will strengthen you and help you; I will uphold you with my righteous right hand."

Isaiah 41:10

ישעיה מא:

10 אַל־תִּירָא כִּי עִמְּךָ־אָנִי אַל־תִּשְׁתָּע כִּי־אֲנִי אֱלֹהֶיךָ אִמַּצְתִּיךָ אַף־עֲזַרְתִּיךָ אַף־תְּמַכְתִּיךָ בִּימִין צִדְקִי׃

"Do all that is in your heart, for God is with you."
(1 Chronicles 17:2)

Prayer: Dear God, thank you that we face our enemies and all the challenges of life, not with our own carnal weapons; but with spiritual weapons of warfare which are mighty to pull down every stronghold.[6]

Help us remember that we are not to hide behind some man-made burdensome armor; but to clothe ourselves in the armor that You have given us: the helmet of salvation, breastplate of righteousness, belt of truth, shield of faith, shoes of peace and the sword of the Spirit – which is Your Word.[7]

Let us not be as those who shrink back in fear; but instead, choosing to live as a sukkah - defenseless and fragile in the natural - but supernaturally protected in the 'secret place' by the mighty shelter and refuge of El Elyon.

May we, by Your merciful grace, overcome all fear, laziness, and passivity that positions us directly into the pathways of the enemy. Help us, Lord to get back on the offensive for Your Kingdom and do great and mighty exploits in Your name. Amen.

"Finally, be strong in Adonai and in the power of His might." (Ephesians 6:10)

---

[6] 2 Corinthians 10:4
[7] Ephesians 6:10-18

CHAPTER TWENTY-TWO

LIVING IN AN ICE AGE

Assorted life lessons from pre-historic mammoths, tigers, squirrels, sloths, caterpillars, worms and eagles

It has been quite an adjustment to leave Israel so suddenly and now to find ourselves immersed in the vast Canadian 'deep freeze'. Currently, I hear (since I haven't stepped a foot out my door in the last several days), that (taking into account a wind-chill factor), the temperature has dropped to a brutal -48 degrees. Yes, that is <u>minus</u> 48!

At this point, I don't think it even matters anymore if that's Celsius or Fahrenheit. Feels like living in an ice age!

Liat is pining for - of all things – the fresh, juicy watermelons and mangoes that she enjoyed feasting upon in Israel. The other day she declared a hunger strike until I could produce them. [1] My apologies to Canadians, but our imported mangoes and watermelons just don't cut it after we've tasted them fresh off the trees and vines. Sigh...

One of the challenges I find with family life here is the boredom of the children in the wintertime who spend more time indoors than what we were used to spending. The warm, sunny climate in Israel encouraged lots of outdoor play. I have reluctantly given in to allowing the children to watch more videos than I would ideally choose. Even Avi, still a baby, has become accustomed to sitting and watching his Gospel Bible Songs videos. (Actually they're pretty good, but after the 100th time, it gets a little old...)

Laying Down our Lives for our Friends

I rarely watch with them (what mother with little ones has time for this?) but recently a particular movie caught my attention. It's called – can you guess? Ice Age. Perhaps some of you have seen it. Does anyone besides me find this movie hilarious or has my sense of humor just become warped by this cold weather?

---

[1] January 2004 (Liat was age 4 & Avi a toddler)

Whenever Liat watches it, she laughs at Sid the sloth, saying, *"That's just like me, I talk all the time!"* We laugh too, recognizing how close to the truth that statement is. ☺

Ice Age is more than just a cheap chuckle, however; if we chip away beneath the surface of the glacier (pardon the poor pun). The story line develops into beautiful truths that Yeshua taught us in His word.

At the end of the movie, the saber-toothed tiger – a former enemy who was bent on evil – learns about the power of sacrificial love. When the huge mammoth risks his life to save the tiger's, he looks in amazement and asks, *"Why would you do such a crazy thing for me?"*

Underlying his question is the sentiment, *"Why ... for someone as hopelessly wicked as me?"*

It reminds me of a moment when my Israeli brother-in-law - an atheistic, hardened, ex-IDF soldier - described the love and acceptance he felt from the people in a Jewish-Israeli religious organization devoted to loving people back to God and His Torah. With tears streaming down his face, he said, *"Can you believe it? ...even someone like me?"*

I fell to my knees later that night in repentance that this man, so in need of the love of God, did not sense such a love coming from us.

Yeshua showed us an example of sacrificial love by laying down His life for all of mankind – even those hopelessly lost in sin and bondage.

Yeshua said this, **"Greater love has no one than this, than to lay down one's life for his friends."** (John 15:13)

In His word, Yeshua commands us to love one another. We must be willing to lay down our rights, our needs, and our demanding self-centeredness for the sake of love. Easier said than done, I know. It sometimes seems even easier to love people 'out there' somewhere across the world than those in our own families, neighborhoods and congregations or fellowships.

The Word of God says that **"While we were yet sinners, Messiah died for us."** (Romans 5:8)

Sometimes we forget that truth; and therefore when we mess up (again), we wonder how God can still love us. But God's love is unconditional. He loves us so much that He sent His only beloved son to die for us – to save us from our sins.

To the tiger's question of why the mammoth risked his life for him, the mammoth simply replied, *"That's what we do in a herd."* We must also become willing to 'lay down our lives' for the sake of 'the herd'.

Returning Good for Evil

The end of the movie also brought home to my simple mind that understands best in word pictures the power of returning good for evil. A scripture that I pasted to my wall for a season was this,

"...not returning evil for evil or reviling for reviling, but on the contrary blessing, knowing that you were called to this, that you may inherit a blessing." (1Peter 3:9)

The reason I glued this scripture to the wall was because somehow it seemed like I was always getting the short end of the stick or the raw end of the deal at home. I know this isn't true in reality, but in my mind, this became my perception – that people in my family were just not treating me right (Hrmph!!).

My challenge, then, was to return a blessing, something I found (find?) exceedingly difficult, even in the trivial, petty issues of daily life. I think most of us could learn a lesson from the mammoth.

Although the humans had killed the mammoth's only son, in the end the 'tough on the exterior & tender on the interior' mammoth went to great lengths to return the human's baby son alive back to his father.

He received death but returned life. So too, did we crucify God's only son by our sin; but in return we have received eternal life.

"For God so loved the world that He gave His only begotten son that whoever believes in Him should not perish but have eternal life." (John 3:16)

May we also become willing to overcome evil with sacrificial goodness.

Squirley Troubles

For those of you who haven't watched the movie, Ice Age begins with Scrat, a pre-historic squirrel, desperately clutching his precious acorn. He anchors it securely in the ground where he thinks it will be safe. He rests – for only a split second – until he hears - CRACK!

The camera focuses on the squirrel's comical face whose expression remains unchanged except for a slight eye tic that gives away his anxiety.

Then the entire ice structure begins to split, sending ice spears showering down menacingly close to the poor squirrel who is now running for his life. Oops, he drops the acorn; he chases it, he stumbles, he falls – bump, thump, ouch!! (that hurt). Finally, he lands and recovers his prize (or so he thinks....) ☺.

Just when the pitiful squirrel thinks he has made it and the coast is clear – SQUASH! The foot of a pre-historic animal lands squarely upon Scrat's now flattened body.

Some days (or is it weeks/months/years?) I think I know just how this creature feels — clutching tightly what I hold most dear to my heart and thinking it secure; but finding it all falling away from me as I chase after it to no avail, suffering bruises, bumps and scrapes along the way.

Feeling definitely bedraggled and frustrated, with never a moment to rest, I may think that I finally have things back under control and am home-free; when suddenly I am flattened by someone's big, clumsy, heavy foot. I may appear to be coping but if someone was to look closely, they might detect a slight eye twitch.☺

In reviewing the stress quotient that we lived under in Israel with the constant threat of death through terrorist attacks, I now believe that this cannot nearly compare to the level of stress that mothers endure who choose to stay home with their children. These are the real heroines (and there are many heroic fathers out there too!).

As we would say in Hebrew, '*Kol Hakavod*'. This literally means, '*all the glory*', but is used as a slang to say, "*Good for you*." Take heart, your service is not in vain. Being a mother and father is one of the greatest callings on the face of the earth. But it does have its moments...

Probably most of us would agree with the reality that life usually consists of one problem (oh alright, we can call them 'challenges' if you prefer) after another. Not every problem (oops – challenge) is huge, life-threatening or disastrous; but it is true that, as Job's friend said, **"Yet man is born to trouble, as the sparks fly upward."** (Job 5:7)

Trouble is a part of life from which we cannot escape; or, as my mother would say from a Yiddish expression, *"Everyone has their own tsuris (sorrows or troubles)."* If we allow our focus to dwell too long upon these 'tsuris', we can become depressed or even bitter. Instead, we need to shift our focus onto trusting in God's good plan and purpose for our lives, even through these trials and difficulties.

From my life in the frying pan these days I have needed to remind myself of an important truth: God is more interested in my character than my comfort. My eldest daughter, Courtney, came for a brief visit in January [2] from where she lived at that time in sunny Southern California. She spoke of how much she enjoys living there with her handsome husband, Emanuel, enjoying romantic walks on the beach and taking the little boy she baby sits to the beach and parks nearby.

A part of me wished I could have flown back with her to enjoy a little of that sun and surf myself, instead of it taking so much time and energy to get all the children dressed in and out of snow suits, mitts, scarves, hats and boots several times each day. But God uses these uncomfortable circumstances to help us grow in the fruit of the Spirit and to be conformed

---

[2] January 2004 at which time my daughter lived in California before returning to Israel.

to the image of His Son. **"For whom He foreknew, He also predestined to be conformed to the image of His Son..."** (Romans 8:29)

God's Patchkie Stick

Not all of our tsuris (troubles) can be blamed on the devil. Elohim as Abba (Dad) may also use 'correction' (a nicer word than what we would be tempted to call it) to show us an area of our lives where we are either in rebellion or just out of line with His perfect will. The Word tells us that if we love our children we will not let them get away with everything but will correct them with a rod. Liat called the rod a 'patchkie stick'.

When it seem like the bumps of life are getting pretty rough, we are not to despise the patchkie stick of the Lord, for He corrects us only out of perfect love.

"Behold, happy (ashrei in Hebrew means blessed/rich) **is the man whom God corrects; Therefore do not despise the chastening of the Almighty."** (Job 5:17)

Here the name used in Hebrew is Shaddai, which comes from a root word referring to a woman's breast. Using Shaddai shows the maternal, nurturing, gentle side of Elohim. I don't know about you, but when I had gotten into any kind of trouble as a child, I always went to my Mom, knowing that compared to Dad's tendency towards harshness, she was a real softie.

Liat instinctively knew that Mommy's patchkies were not nearly to be feared as much Dad's. Using the name Shaddai is a beautiful reminder to us that even when Elohim finds it necessary to correct us, the chastening is tempered with a tender mama's mercy. Some of our circumstances may cause great pain, but if we continue to trust in Him through our trials, He will bring emotional, spiritual and physical healing from the hurt caused by this chastening.

"For He bruises, but He binds up; He wounds, but His hands make whole." (Job 5:18)

Transformation

Sometimes I feel like I should say, *"do as I write, not as I do,"* for although I encourage people to have a good attitude in times of testing, I find myself all too easily becoming discouraged, depressed or even angry at difficult situations in my life. I become frustrated with negative qualities I see in myself or in someone I'm in relationship with, especially when no matter what I do or how hard I try, it just doesn't seem to change or improve. Can anyone relate?

Yes, some burdens we must just *'give to* God' and let the Holy Spirit work in His timing, but there are other things that we know are not the will of God and yet they will not budge no matter how much we pray about it. This is when I think we have to get radical – we have to fast!

I might be the last person to suggest giving up food – we're talking Jewish mother here. ☺ But there comes a time, I believe, in most people's lives when we become so desperate for change that we are willing to give up anything – even our physical sustenance – if it will make a difference.

Yeshua told His perplexed disciples who couldn't figure out why things just weren't working for them that some things are "**able to come forth with nothing except with prayer <u>and fasting</u>.**" (Mark 9:29)

So I encourage you, if you are desperate for a breakthrough in your life, if you really need to hear from God, if your prayers alone don't seem to be cutting it, try going on a fast. It doesn't have to be a total Esther or Yom Kippur (Day of Atonement) type fast with no food or water. It can be fasting on juices or even a Daniel type fast with only vegetables & healthy foods and drinks.

It might mean fasting from your favorite food for a period of time or a drink like coffee or tea or pop or a sugar and junk food fast. A fast humbles us before God and says, "*I'm serious here. I desperately need your help more than anything else in my life.*"

God began to speak to me about going on a fast shortly after Chanukah. I resisted and delayed until the New Year but finally began a forty day journey of discovery and hopefully transformation through fasting and prayer. We desperately need to hear from God about the right direction for our family.

Ezra proclaimed a fast for the same purpose: "**Then I proclaimed a fast there at the river of Ahava** (meaning love in Hebrew)**, that we might humble ourselves before our God, to seek from Him the right way for us and our little ones and all our possessions.**" (Ezra 8:21)

We are trusting that at the end of this fast we will have clearly heard the voice of God saying, "Go this way, and don't turn to the right or the left." Fasting helps bring direction to our lives.

Cleansing the Temple

Another benefit of fasting is the physical cleansing that it brings to the body. It's interesting that the Holy Spirit directed me to fast around the time of Chanukah. From the book of the Maccabees, we know that after recovering control of the Temple, the first thing they needed to do before resuming holy activities in it was to get out the junk. They had to remove anything that had come into the Temple to defile it such as the idols and evidence of pagan sacrifices.

We often make a spiritual parallel to our lives and seek to cleanse ourselves of all paganism or idolatry but what about physically? Our bodies are called the temple of the Holy Spirit. (1Cor. 6:19) At one point in my life I was quite the health food fanatic but over the years, I have relaxed in this area (probably too relaxed) and have poured a lot of junk into my body that is definitely not appropriate for a holy Temple!

Before we can be holy as He is holy, we may need to get that junk out first for the body, soul, mind, heart and spirit are all intricately connected. We cannot ignore or abuse one aspect of our beings without negatively affecting all the rest.

Feeling Kinda Wormy

I heard an interesting fact about the transformation of a caterpillar to a butterfly that helped confirm to me the necessity of a fast to personal growth, change, and maturity. After the caterpillar has lived for a season as a wormy looking creature, it changes into what is termed a pupa. As a pupa it remains very still and does not eat until the time it emerges as a butterfly.

 So too may we feel, deep within ourselves, an instinctual divine instruction to become very still; to cease our frenetic movements that are really getting us nowhere and to even cease our intake of food. Beside my bed, I kept a delicate, glass box that a friend gave me while in Israel. It is one of the few possessions of mine that survived the move. On the lid was written, **"Be still and know that I am God."** (Psalm 46:10)

During this season of apparent inactivity, we may feel that nothing is happening but when the ordained time of stillness and fasting is ended, we may emerge totally transformed into the creature of grace and beauty that He has always had in mind. So if you've been feeling 'kinda wormy' lately and vaguely itchy or uncomfortable within yourself – don't lose heart - get set for transformation. His will is to mold and make us into the image of His beloved Son, Yeshua the Messiah.

 "But we all, with unveiled face, beholding as in a mirror the glory of Adonai, are being transformed into the same image from glory to glory, just as by the Spirit of Adonai." (2 Cor. 3:18)

He will not give up, even when we are tempted to throw in the towel; He is faithful to complete the good work He has begun in each one of us.

Eli - Lama? (My God - Why?)

The balance to accepting trouble as a necessary aspect of our spiritual growth is that, it seems to me, life should be more than just a *'grit your teeth and hang on till heaven'* type of experience. God's word promises that He will not give us more than we can bear without providing a way of escape.

So if life seems more than we can bear; if everything is going wrong and nothing going right, it seems to me a legitimate question to ask of the Holy Spirit, "HEY! WHAT GIVES??" I don't think God is offended by honest questioning. After all, Moses did the same when God sent him on a commission to deliver the children of Israel from bondage in Egypt. When at first, it seemed to only make matters worse, Moses returned directly to God and said,

"Adonai, lama (why?) have You brought trouble on this people? Why is it You have sent me? For since I came to Pharaoh to speak in Your name, he has done evil to this people; neither have You delivered Your people at all." (Exodus 5:22-23)

I find this almost shocking – Moses, the most humble man on the face of the earth, challenging the God of the universe on His promises! But Adonai doesn't skip a beat. He simply says, *"Now see what I will do."* (Exodus 6:1)

Sometimes the timing is just not right. It may be the darkness just before dawn breaks. Sometimes we need to wait on the Lord a little longer to see His promises fulfilled in our lives. Even Abraham, through patience and faith inherited the promises. (Hebrews 6:15)

But this may or may not be the reason for our trouble. It may be that we have somehow 'missed God'. Thank goodness that we have not been left as orphans after the death of Yeshua to try and figure things out for ourselves. He has left us the Holy Spirit who will lead and guide us into all truth and help us find our way on the path. I think the Bible demonstrates that it's okay to go to Him in our anguish and ask, 'Lama?" Even Yeshua asked, when dying on the cross, *"Eli, eli, lama azavtani" My God, my God, why have you forsaken me?"* (Mark 15:34)

Never Forsaken

At times, we may feel that God has forsaken us. As Job experienced, it sometimes seems as if every which way that we look for Him, we cannot find Him. It is a very lonely place. It feels like we have, lately, been going through such a painful time. Perhaps others can relate. I heard someone say that there are moments when, even upon this earth, we can experience a taste of heaven.

Feeling forsaken by God, in contrast, must be just a glimpse of the desolation and despair we would feel if cast into a pit of utter darkness - of eternal separation from the light, love, and warmth of the Almighty – the source of life itself. Of course when we are in Messiah, the truth is that nothing can separate us from the love of God that is in Yeshua. (Romans 8:38-39)

When a gentle woman met me in the bathroom of a hotel in one of the lowest times of my life, the life-giving words she spoke were these, *"Jesus loves you and He will never leave you nor forsake you."* I clung to this promise throughout my time of trouble as I came to trust in Yeshua as my Messiah and Savior. I have hung on to this promise ever since.

But recently, weeping, face down on my kitchen floor, in all of my depression, confusion and feelings of being forsaken, I cried out to Eli, my God, and asked, "Lama?" Why God, have you promised to restore us in our family, our marriage, our finances, our health, in peace and in joy – and yet You haven't delivered us at all? In fact, things seemed to have only gotten worse! The Holy Spirit reminded me that although God may hide His face from us it is only for a tiny moment.

"For a little moment (regah katan) I have forsaken you, but with great mercies I will gather you. With a little wrath I hid My face from you for a moment; but with everlasting kindness I will have mercy on you," says your Redeemer (goalech) YHVH יהוה" (Isaiah 54:7-9 HEB).

Even Zion felt that Adonai had forsaken her. Probably many in Zion feel this way today with the news of continued bombings and terrorist attacks. **"But Zion has said, *"God has forsaken me and Adonai has forgotten me."*** (Isaiah 49:14)

God answers Zion that even if a mother could forget and forsake the infant nursing at her breast (inconceivable, right?) yet He will not forget Tziyon. (Isaiah 49:15)

The day will come when Zion, rather than seemingly forsaken and hated, will be an eternal excellence, a joy of many generations. (Isaiah 60:15) Then they will know their 'moshiach' (Messiah), Redeemer and Savior. No longer will Zion be forsaken and the land desolate but it will be called, "Heftzi-bah" (which means **'My delight is in her'**) and Beulah (married). (Isaiah 62:4)

We may endure periods of our lives when we feel forsaken, lost, and alone, but God is faithful to His Word. He will never leave us or forsake us. He may, though, hide His face for a brief moment to call our attention to something in our lives out of alignment with His will.

A Divine Homing Device

As some of you may already know, our family name, Nesher, means 'eagle' in Hebrew. An interesting fact about eagles is that God designed them with a unique characteristic. At birth, a special fluid develops in the baby eaglets eyes that acts as a kind of homing device. Once the young eagles begin to fly, should they ever veer off course, this fluid causes a low level pain in the eyes to signal the need to adjust their direction. We have definitely been experiencing this continual 'low level'(and sometimes not so low-level) pain in our life, signaling that we have in some way veered slightly (or a lot) off course.

I bare you on eagle's wings,
and brought you unto myself.
Exodus 19:4

Through this time of fasting and praying, we believe
that we now understand where we 'missed God' after
leaving Israel. We know that in these end times, it is
becoming more and more critical that we hear from
the Holy Spirit and receive direction. Lives may
depend upon our obedience to God's will and timing.

God promises to guide us and show us the way we
should go: **"I will instruct you and teach you in
the way you should go; I will guide you with My
eye."** (Psalm 32:8)

The Holy Spirit gave me an illustration of this
through a small incident that has become etched in
my memory. Timothy had decided to go skating
across the street from my parents' house. I left the
two smaller children inside the house with my Mom
and walked Timothy across the street.

A beautiful ray of sunshine streaming across an
inviting looking bench beckoned me to stay and

watch him skate for awhile, but instead I decided to head right back to the house to check on the other children and warm up.

As I walked away, I began to lose my peace. My mother had a nice cup of hot chocolate prepared and I looked forward to having a visit with her, but inside myself I felt disturbed and said, "*I need to go back and check on Timothy.*" But my Mom urged me to drink my hot chocolate first and then walk back.

Against the direction of the Holy Spirit, I gave in to the temptation of comfort, warmth, to passivity, (laziness?) and to others' expectations. As I sat there sipping from my cup, Timothy suddenly burst through the door, exclaiming,

"*You wouldn't believe what happened! A kid got hit with a hockey stick right in the mouth and there was blood all over the ice and no one even had a Kleenex or cell phone to help him!*"

I knew instantly that the ramifications of my disobedience were a child's pain and fear. Because I chose comfort, I chose to listen to someone else, I chose not to listen to the small voice of the Holy Spirit, I was not in the right place at the right time to help this boy. I can't tell you how deeply grieved I felt by this incident. It seems like I felt worse over this 'small' sin than by even the awful sins that I had committed before coming to know the Lord. Why was this?

I questioned the Holy Spirit and knew that He was showing me the seriousness of the issue of our obedience. As we move closer and closer to the coming of the New World Order, the failure of the North American economic system and the probable chaos, violence and famine that will grip many nations, we had better be in the right place at the right time or we may tragically miss our assignment.

Joseph was in the right place at the right time, even though it must not have seemed so for many long, lonely years of injustice. But in God's timing, Joseph was exalted to a position and given the wisdom to save many people's lives.

Esther also was raised to a royal position 'for such a time as this'. So too, must each one of us seek the Holy Spirit for our positioning to fulfill our God-given assignment.

We cannot do everything, despite the great need we see all around us. Only God can be everywhere at once. But for each of us, He has a specific assignment.

Yeshua glorified His father by completing His assignment:

"I glorified you on earth by completing down to the last detail what you assigned me to do." (John 17:4 MSG)

May each of us be able to say the same when we stand before His throne in judgment.

Listening to the Donkeys

How do we know where we are supposed to be positioned? It may be easier to know when we are NOT positioned correctly than when we are. God used a donkey to speak to Balaam; and to prevent him from walking in a way that was contrary to God's will.[3]

In every situation, when we are walking in God's ways and heeding the voice of His Holy Spirit, we should be able to walk in a peace that passes understanding.

God promised Israel that He would lead them in the way they should go; but only when they would listen to Him would they have peace.

"Oh, that you had heeded My commandments! Then your peace would have been like a river..."
(Isaiah 48:18)

---

[3] Numbers 22:32

One of the clearest signals that we are off track somehow is that we lose our peace and joy. We feel weak and powerless because the joy of the Lord is our strength. Without it, the inner turmoil drains us of energy and we feel about as lively as a wet rag. The Kingdom of God is righteousness peace and joy in the Holy Spirit. The apostles were able to sing praise even in dingy prisons while facing imminent executions.

So why do we sometimes find it so tough? Were these apostles some kind of super spirituals? I believe that their joy and peace resulted from their knowledge that they were faithfully serving the Almighty according to His perfect will. His Word then promises that His grace will be sufficient for us and His power made perfect in our weaknesses. [4] His favor will surround us like a shield. If then, we don't seem to have grace for even the simplest of tasks, we again need to ask 'why'? If we are experiencing continual frustration, confusion, and strife; then obviously we are operating in the flesh.

Child of Flesh

Ishmael, child of the flesh (born of man's will rather than Divine will), was prophesied to be a wild man whose hand would be against every man and every man's hand against his.[5] This is the chief characteristic of the flesh - strife! If this evil force dominates our lives, then it may be time to seek God for His agenda rather than continuing to ask Him to

---

[4] 2 Corinthians 12:9
[5] Genesis 16:12

bless ours. We must bow down before Him and say, *"Not my will but Thine be done."* (Luke 22:42)

It is within this context of surrender that God can begin to reveal His plans and purposes for our lives. After all, how kind would it really be if He just let us continue coasting along on our merry way, riding upon His grace, if the way we are walking is in opposition to His will? God troubled the wheels of the Egyptians so that they knew that, in fighting against Israel, they fought against God.

God sent a donkey to block Balaam's path when he was also going in the wrong direction. So why do we think that all our obstacles and frustrations in life are from the devil?? If we are blocked, maybe we need to listen to some of the 'donkeys' in our lives that have been trying to tell us something. Perhaps it's time to take a step back and seek for God's direction for our lives.

Closing prayer: Abba Father, thank you that you are still with us in the midst of all our troubles. You loved us while we were yet sinners and you still love us even now. You sent Your son, Yeshua, to give His up His very own life as a sacrificial offering – to give us life and life more abundantly.

Help us to hear Your Voice as we walk this journey of life. Guide us with Your eye and show us the way we should go. Send a donkey, if necessary, to block our path if we are walking in any way that is contrary to Your perfect will. Cause our hearts to heed Your correction; and set our feet back on that narrow path that leads to life eternal. In Yeshua's name. Amen.

CHAPTER TWENTY-THREE

ME TARZAN

A Devotional on Identity

My youngest son, Avi, woke up mercifully early this one morning - unlike most mornings when I had to scoop him up, fast asleep, out of a warm, cozy bed, plop him into his stroller, stuff a breakfast bar in his hand and hurry him off to pre-school. But not this morning. Nope, this morning he actually had time to wake up, eat a banana at his leisure, and watch a little of his favorite cartoon video – Tarzan – before I again hurried him off to pre-school.

As I walked home, an idea began to form in my mind – the thought that I myself am like Tarzan in a way. No, I don't live in the jungle or swing from trees, nor do I have a full grown bear, Black Panther, and other assorted wild animals as my closest friends. Okay, maybe I should really be comparing myself to Jane, but let's just go with the flow and leave it Tarzan for now, okay?

At the beginning of the movie, Tarzan's real parents are killed and he is adopted by a kindly mother gorilla. But his father, the head gorilla of the pack (do gorillas travel in packs?) does not accept this human baby as 'one of them'. As the child grows, he begins to notice that he is different than the others. He hears the teasing; some accuse him openly of not being a true gorilla. He suffers from rejection and even self-hatred. He doesn't know who (or what) he is and feels that perhaps it would be better if he just hadn't been born.

But there is a destiny on Tarzan's life. Although he eventually meets up with 'his own kind', other humans, he cannot forget the family he grew up in. He cannot abandon his mother who showed him such love and kindness, or those who were like brothers and sisters to him. Eventually, Tarzan becomes aware of the danger to the gorillas from the enemy and returns to the jungle to save them. It is only then that Tarzan finds his father's acceptance.

How does the story of Tarzan possibly relate to me – a JCP (Jewish Canadian Princess)? As the only believer in Yeshua (Jesus) in my whole family of Orthodox Jews; and even in the entire local Jewish community, it is easy to feel like the oddball – the black sheep of the family.

Even as a very young girl, I often felt like I didn't belong, didn't quite fit in. I didn't experience acceptance from my father; always feeling an underlying sense of disapproval or suspicion (whether real or imagined); even though my mother was always very kind and loving towards me.

After I came to faith in Yeshua as my Messiah and Savior, most of my family did not understand. Had I converted to Christianity and left Judaism, the 'true faith'? *"Now that you follow 'that man', you are no longer Jewish"*, they said. *"You are not a true Jew anymore; you are not 'one of us'.*

It has always been this way – 'us' (the Jewish people) and 'them' (the goyim - the Gentile world)'. There is no in-between. My family could not see that following Yeshua as the Jewish Messiah and coming to obey the Word of God only made me more Jewish than I was before - when I lived like the world, alienated from God and ignorant of His Word.

Some in my family openly hated me now, they wouldn't speak to me; and totally ignored my very presence – as if I didn't exist any longer. They would even walk out of a room if I walked in. I was told that a mock funeral was held for me in my absence. I suffered deeply from this rejection. Sometimes I wished I had never been born.

"I have become a stranger to my brothers, and an alien to my mother's children;

because zeal for Your house has eaten me up, and the reproaches of those who reproach You have fallen on me." (Psalm 69:8-9)

But the word of God says that even if our very own mother and father forsake us, He – God Himself – will take care of us. (Psalm 27:10) What a faithful and precious Father we have in Him.

In time, I moved to Israel and met other Jewish Believers, even native born Israelis – born-again, filled with the Ruach (Spirit) of God, preaching the gospel of salvation in Hebrew. This brought some measure of comfort, some semblance of belonging. So I'm not the only one who is like this – there are others just like me. Wow!

I had found my 'real family'. **"My mother and my brothers are those who hear the word of God and do it."** (Luke 8:21)

Yeshua had no problem with insecurity. He never suffered from an identity crisis. Although born to an earthly mother, Miriam, a Jewish maiden, He knew who his real Father is. He knew where he came from and knew to where he was returning, saying, **"I am going to the Father."** (John 14:28)

Identity Crises

I see some in the Body of Messiah suffering from identity crises. Christians move into Messianic Judaism but rather than remain there, they move over into Rabbinic Judaism, which is as far from Biblical faith in its traditions as is modern Christianity in its paganism.

If only we could become so secure in our identity as sons and daughters of the King that we would not crave the acceptance and approval of people so much. If only we would be willing to follow Yeshua outside the camp, bearing his reproach (Hebrews 13:13); seeking the approval of our Father in Heaven rather than the praise of men.

It may have been easier, simpler, perhaps less painful to just remain there in Israel, in my nice, comfortable community of Believers, enjoying my inheritance in the Promised Land. But once I fully realized the spiritual danger that my people are in, I knew that, like Tarzan, I must return to the family that raised me and do what I can to help save them from the enemy.

Hasatan, the adversary hates the Jewish people and continually seeks for their destruction. He wants to keep them in the darkness of ignorance, to prevent the true Light from reaching them. But God...

"Brethren, my heart's desire and prayer to God for Israel is that they may be saved." (Romans 10:1)

There is a story of another Hannah, one of the early Zionist Pioneers, who has become an Israeli folk hero. As a young woman, Hannah Senesh left home, family, and all that was familiar in Hungary in order to make aliyah to the Land of Israel. Arriving before the outbreak of World War II, Hannah worked together with

other young and zealous Zionists to establish a kibbutz (communal settlement).

When the war broke out, however, and Hitler's evil intentions became apparent, Hannah risked everything to be parachuted back into her native country of Hungary in a daring attempt to rescue her mother and members of her family still trapped in Hungary with death quickly approaching. The Nazis captured and eventually killed this courageous young woman but at least she died trying.

What do our lives mean to us anyways? Is it just about accumulating possessions and buying a nice house and driving a decent car and paying our bills and taking our kids back and forth between school and lessons? Is it not about walking in our blood-bought destiny?

 Paul said, "**What do you mean by weeping and breaking my heart? For I am ready not only to be bound, but also to die at Jerusalem for the name of the Lord Jesus.**" (Acts 21:13)

Our calling is to say to God, "*Wherever....whenever...whatever....*" We must count the cost and then say, *"I am Yours, God, Hineinu (here am I), send me."*

We may or may not be successful in our rescue attempts, and we may or may not finally win the approval and acceptance of our earthly father. But in the end, if we have done the will of our Heavenly Father, we will one day stand before Him and know His approval when He looks us in the eye, smiles, and says, **"Well done, My good and faithful servant."**

Prayer: Thank you Father, that although we have, at times, felt different than others, rejected, and outcast, You always take care of us. We know that we have come from You and are one day returning to You. Because You are our Father we know ourselves to be fearfully and wonderfully made. Through our faith in Your son, Yeshua, we are fully accepted and beloved by You. Lead and guide each of us into our individual and communal destinies. Help us to rescue those who are being drawn towards death and stumbling to the slaughter. Save Your people, Israel, and all those oppressed by the evil one. In Yeshua's name. Amen.

Written by Hannah Nesher 2006

CHAPTER TWENTY-FOUR

Nina the Great

A Devotional on Shalom

It seems that I have inherited another dog in the Land of Israel – Nina, a shepherd/Canaanite cross. She has become quite attached to us over the last couple of years; even more so, apparently, than her real owners, our former landlords. And so, when we moved to a new house in the same moshav (village), Nina just naturally moved right along with us. She deposited herself on our front porch and refused to budge!

As our 'self-appointed' guardian, she watched over us day and night. Such fierce loyalty and devotion I have not ever witnessed before in my life. If my little grandson was scampering over the play equipment in the park, Nina was right up there with him, ever on duty.

I called them 'Mutt and Jeff' as my little Shihtzu, Pepper, and big Nina ran around the village together on our daily outings. Each morning that I walked Avi to the bus stop, Nina and Pepper would wait there with him until he left on the school bus to make sure he boarded safely.

Avi, Pepper and Nina at the bus stop

There was one problem area, however, in our route; and that was this one particular dog which always flew into a frenzy behind her fenced gate whenever Nina walked by. Why? I have no idea.

Nina may be female, but she has never been one to back away from a fight. In fact, I have seen her take on five wild dogs at a time – and win! So whenever we passed this gate, the two dogs would get into a noisy, thrashing, all-out rumble. Not that they could do much damage to one another, however, since the dog was contained, but it was still loud and disturbing – probably to the whole neighborhood.

One day, though, I noticed that Nina made a different choice. We walked by as usual, the dog kicked up a frenzy also as usual, but this time Nina just walked on by. She did not enter into this dog's fury, nor did she allow herself to be provoked. She just graciously ignored the nasty fellow; and she has done so ever since.

Not an expert on dog psychology (as is Caesar Milan, the Dog Whisperer), I can't tell you exactly what went on in her doggie mind, but I can tell you it made a difference. She came to a place of deciding that it just wasn't worth her energy to engage with this 'enemy'.

I learned a couple of valuable lessons from my friend, Nina. First of all, we don't need to 'get into it' with everyone who tries to provoke us. Usually, it does no good whatsoever to get into a quarrel with someone who seems to be just itching to pick a fight. This is just a total waste of time and emotional energy.

"It is honorable for a man to stop striving; since any fool can start a quarrel." (Proverbs 20:3)

"And the Lord's servant must not be quarrelsome but must be kind to everyone..." (2 Timothy 2:24)

We can choose to just ignore the ruckus, let it go and walk on by in perfect peace, not letting all that loud barking and snarling even faze us whatsoever, like: *"Lah, lah, lah..... I don't even hear you....."*

The other lesson I learned from this is that our enemies may make a lot of noise and can be very Intimidating but they are behind a fenced gate which is the restraining power of the Ruach Hakodesh (Holy Spirit). Even the devil himself, hasatan, was only allowed to go as far as God permitted him in the testing of Job.

"And the Lord said to Satan, **"Behold, he is in your hand, but spare his life."** (Job 2:6)

One of the names of God is *El Elyon*, meaning *'God above all'*. He has power and dominion and authority over all the powers of darkness that threaten us. Satan may make a lot of noise, like a roaring lion who seek to devour us; but if we will make El Elyon our refuge, then no evil shall befall us.

"He who dwells in the **secret place of Elyon** shall abide under the shadow of Shaddai. I will say of Adonai, "He is my refuge and my fortress; Elohai, in Him I will trust...Because you have made, יהוה who is my refuge, even Elyon, your dwelling place, no evil shall befall you." (Psalm 91:1-2,9-10)

Hebrew plaque on family home reads, "Yoshev b'seter Elyon, b'tzel Shaddai yitlonen." (Psalm 91:1 in Hebrew)

In these perilous times - of enemy attacks and missiles being fired upon this sacred Land - we place our hope and trust in these precious promises found in God's word.

The village where our extended family lives is called **Ramat Raziel**. '*Rama*' means '*high or lifted up*'; and '*razi*' means '*my secret*'. '*El*' is a name for God. Therefore the meaning of Ramat Raziel is *'my high and secret place of God'*. God has provided for us a 'secret place of Elyon' to be a refuge for us in these troubled times.

In the summer of 2015, an enemy missile struck our village on my daughter's very street. The force of the blast shattered their windows and blew up their laptop, but praise Adonai, there were no casualties. How could this be? Apparently, according to the report, the missile flew straight through all the homes, landing without incident in someone's back yard. Someone from the emergency crew that came out afterwards to survey the damage explained that the missile missing all these homes could be likened to threading the eye of a needle. She said, "Before I witnessed this, I wasn't sure of the existence of God – but now I know that God is real!" Only God could have directed this missile through a safe path as if guiding a thread through a needle.

And yet, as the missiles continued to be fired into Israel, shelters were opened and cleaned out to be ready for use in every city, town and village. Always in the back of our minds lurked the question, *"If the azaka (siren) sounds, where will we run for shelter?"*

Sometimes there is no choice but to drop to the ground, cover our heads & pray!

But we know that the most secure shelter is that of abiding under the shadow of El Shaddai – a place of safety that is available to us all.

Yeshua longs to gather us, as a mother hen gathers her chicks, just as He longed to gather the people of Jerusalem under His wings before the destruction of the Holy City. "**He shall cover you with His feathers, and under His wings you shall take refuge**." (Psalm 91:4)

The other day, I was told of an 88 year old woman who, when she heard the siren, did not have the strength to run to the shelter. She said, "*I'm going to sit right here in my chair*." The missile fell and destroyed everything around her; but she was left completely unharmed – without even a ringing in her ears from the blast! Such is the protective power of Almighty God!

And yet it is not a lighthearted, carefree time. Many women's husbands and children's fathers have been called back into military service, leaving them at home, glued to the news on radio and TV. They await Israel's decision of whether or not to send in ground troops into Gaza, which, many fear would be near to a suicide mission for these foot soldiers.

One day, at the park, we ran into a young (and very pregnant) woman, getting out of her car. She was about due to give birth, and had another little one at home besides; but her husband, Udi, had been called back along with the other reservists, not knowing when (or if) he would return. I can't imagine being in such a situation! Such is daily life in Israel.

It is one thing to just hear of this happening in Israel; it is quite another thing altogether when the people whose lives are being threatened are our friends and neighbors - people we live and work with - men, women and children whom we have come to know and love - or even members of our own family.

We also need to remember the innocents in Gaza who are suffering because of the stubbornness of their leadership in fighting against Israel, the apple of God's eye. Just as in ancient times, when God delivered the children of Israel from Egypt, many innocent men, women and children suffered through the Ten Plagues because of the hard-heartedness of Pharaoh.

It is a tragic fact that in war, so many innocent people get caught in the crossfire; however the civilian casualties in Gaza also demonstrate the horrendous practice of Hamas using their own people as human shields by firing their missiles from within densely populated areas or from schools and daycares.

Since this article was written in 2015, terrorism has been spreading across the world. This year (2017), the worst mass shooting in the history of the United States took place in Las Vegas, followed by the fatal shooting of twenty people in a church in Texas! Terrorism is no longer limited to Israel, but is happening all over the world now, as has been prophesied. How do we handle this threat to our personal safety and security? We stay in shalom.

"You will keep *him* in perfect peace, whose mind is stayed on You, because he trusts in You." (Isaiah 26:3)

Prayer: Spirit of the Living God, Ruach Hakodesh, fill us with Your peace (shalom) in these days of trouble. May Your overflowing peace calm the storm and still the frightened hearts in and around us.

Yeshua, You have promised us a peace that passes all understanding – a constant, undisturbed, quiet portion of shalom. Your name is 'Sar Shalom' (Prince of Peace). May Your blanket of shalom be a protective covering over us- a barrier from all harm - a safe and comforting cocoon of peace which surrounds us at all times, even in a time of war, turmoil and unrest.

May each one of us receive and rest in this precious, priceless gift of peace (shalom). Just as Israel has an 'iron dome' that intercepts many of the enemy's missiles and rockets. I also pray that each fiery dart of the evil one will be intercepted by God's heavenly 'iron dome' - our shield of faith that we keep over our hearts.

May God give His angels charge over us to keep us in all of our ways. (Psalm 91:11) In Yeshua's name. Amen.

CHAPTER TWENTY-FIVE

Rising up on Wings As an Eagle

A Devotional on Learning to Soar

"Those who hope upon the Lord shall rise up on wings as an eagle." (Isaiah 40:31)

It is Passover break in Israel and all the kids are on vacation – a long one – which means the necessity of finding things to do that would keep them amused enough to stop the incessant arguing and bickering that drives me absolutely nuts when they are all home together. Whew! It's quite the challenge, especially given the differences in ages and preferences.

Imagine trying to find something that everyone would like – an active, adventure - loving eight year old boy, a 'drama queen' eleven year old girl, an almost fully grown teenage 'too cool' guy of seventeen (plus his pretty girlfriend[1]); and me - the frazzled Mom. But to our surprise, we did manage to find an activity that fit everyone's tastes in a movie called Rio.

Now I am not trying to wear a new hat of 'movie critic', nor am I being paid by the producers of this movie to promote it; I am simply using the theme of this movie to illustrate a message. You see, the animated movie Rio, is about a bird that cannot fly.

Captured at an early age in the Amazon and then kept for fifteen years as a pet had conditioned this rare Blue Macaw to life in captivity. Life was *okay* for 'Blue'; in fact it was good – he had a girl who loved him and cared for him. In fact, the girl doted on her precious pet bird, even giving him hot chocolate with marshmallows each morning, just the way he liked it.

The fact that he couldn't fly never even surfaced as an issue – why fly when everything one needs is provided? But the day came when all that changed. A professor of ornithology[2] discovered Blue's existence and had vital need of him; for he happened to be the only male of his species remaining. One female Blue Macaw had been discovered and together, they could ensure the survival of their species; but without Blue, their kind would become extinct forever. And so begins the adventure.....it's off to Brazil to get the two birds together!

---

[1] Victoria later became Timothy's lovely wife
[2] Ornithology is a branch of zoology that concerns the study of birds.

Things don't go as smoothly as anticipated; however, not only when the female rejects the male, but also when bird smugglers steal the pair to sell at a handsome profit. Chained to one another, they eventually escape, but Blue's inability to fly proves to be a terrible handicap.

It's not that he doesn't try; it's not that he doesn't want to fly – he just can't! Finally at the end (not to ruin the story for you but...) to save the life of his beloved mate, Blue does finally rise up. Stretching out wings that have long lay useless, he soars on the wind into the high skies. He flies!

It's not often that an audience claps at the end of a movie but in Rio, we all clapped and cheered. Why? Blue's triumph over fear, failure, inability and limitation touches a chord in each one of us. We all, deep in our souls, want to fly. Life may be okay, but we are impatient with our comfortable – yet - boring lives. We're tired of being chronically tired – of dragging our weary selves through each and every dull, dreary day. We want to soar in the high skies and feel the freedom of the wind whistling through our feathers.

Like Blue, we have each been created unique, special, full of innate talents and abilities. But also like Blue's experience, many of us have been captured by the enemy early in life and placed in a cage of limitations, becoming complacent with an 'ordinary' life, willing to compromise with being 'average', when in fact we were created to be 'extra-ordinary'.

Like Blue, we have a specific purpose in life – a destiny that only we can fulfill. If we fail to overcome our fears, obstacles, and limitations then something essential in life may be forever extinguished. God used this simple children's story, Rio, to remind me of a message He had spoken to me many years ago.

The Honeymoon

We had boarded El Al Airlines in Canada and disembarked upon our beloved Israeli soil with such high hopes and expectations. Newly married, we were still on our honeymoon when my (then) husband and I heard the call, like our Father, Abraham, to leave everything behind and just go! Lech Lecha! – go back to the land God had promised us through Divine Covenant with my forefathers.

Radek & Hannah on the beach in Netanya, Israel (Dec 1998)

So, like most people in love, who feel (at least temporarily) invincible, we left behind mother, father, sisters, brothers, houses, lands, children; and all that was familiar to us – to go to a place that we knew by faith God would show us. And He did. We trusted God enough to take a leap of faith – to fly – and God met our faith with His faithfulness. He provided for us a home and everything we needed day by day.

Birth of Liat, with our Israeli landlords, Tovah & Amitai, & Timothy, in Ariel, Israel, Nov 1999.

We were even blessed with two more children – a baby girl, Liat, and a boy, Avi-ad, born when I was well beyond the age of childbearing. What a thrill to participate in the fulfillment of prophecies that promised the ingathering of the exiles; and that we would one day once again multiply and bear young on the mountains of Israel.[3]

Yes, we were flying! But then we crashed...

---

[3] Ezekiel 36:8-11

The Conference Disaster

My Polish-born husband, who came without official papers proving his Jewishness, was denied not only Israeli citizenship, but even a visa. This was against the law; but we did not have the financial or emotional resources left to fight their decision. The powers that be gave him fourteen days to leave the country. He had been evangelizing and they wanted him out! So we left – devastated. We had lost everything that we had built over our years together in the Land of Israel; all of our dreams and hopes lay shattered in millions of pieces at our feet.

'Fixing this' was obviously impossible. Disillusioned and feeling like complete failures, we landed at a Messianic Conference in Canada where they asked us to speak about Israel. To say that our message was not well received would be a supreme understatement – they actually removed me physically from the platform and destroyed the recording of my message.

What they wanted was to sing Hava Nagila,[4] dance the Hora and wave their Israel flags in jubilation. They certainly didn't want to hear about the sin and corruption that ran rampant throughout the Land; and a government that evicts Messianic believers because of our faith in Yeshua. And so we went back into our forced exile, to sit on our heaps of ashes and sulk in our respective cages of self-pity. It was here, in my captivity, that God began to speak to me about flying again.

---

[4] Hava Nagila is an Israeli folksong and the Hora is the accompanying dance full of energy and joy

The Phone Call – *"You Will Fly Again"*

Soon after returning home from the fiasco of this conference, I received a curious telephone call. The anonymous caller had a 'Word from the Lord' for me. He said, *"You have been shot down out of the skies by the enemy and are now like a bird with a broken wing. But the Lord has said, "You will fly again."*

I found that hard to believe. Fly? I could barely walk. The birth of my last child, Avi-ad, turned out to be a life-threatening crisis. My body was having a hard time recovering from complications following a severe haemorrhage and emergency caesarean section surgery. There were many times I had to crawl on my hands and knees to get up the stairs of our apartment.

I hated the long Canadian winters when depression set in along with the deep freeze. My soul longed to be 'home' in the Land of Israel. My marriage was crumbling, creditors were phoning, demanding their money, and I felt totally lost, alone and forsaken. Fly? Indeed the very notion seemed preposterous!

The Video – Spirit of an Eagle

So what do we do when we lose all motivation to participate in life? There are several escape hatches; but one of them is to watch the 'boob tube' – good old television to numb the pain. One night we sat watching a video that 'just happened' to have been left in the second hand VCR we bought at a garage sale. It was called Spirit of an Eagle.

In this movie, a majestic eagle had been shot down out of the sky by a hunter's bullet which had broken its wing. It could not fly.

The burly, handsome, frontiersman, Dan Haggerty (Gentle Ben series), found the injured bird and tenderly cared for it, binding up its broken wing and feeding it, hoping it would one day fly again. But the eagle showed no signs of recovering its former strength and health. One night, the man lay his head on the table and wept, crying out to the Lord to help the eagle fly again. The next day, the man set the eagle outside on a post and said to it,

"I have done everything I can for you. Now it is time for you to fly..."

Our hearts also took a leap of joy as we watched this majestic bird soar up into the skies on the winds again as it was created to fly.

Nesher means Eagle

As a blended family, we struggled with the issue of our names. It irked my husband that we each, and our children, had different last names. He wanted one unified family name, perhaps as an attempt to unify our already fractioned family. Because he didn't' want to use his Polish name, and since my maiden name meant 'eagle', we chose the Hebrew word for eagle, which is 'Nesher', as in the verse, **"Those who wait upon the Lord shall rise up on wings as an eagle (Nesher)."** (Isaiah 40:31)

In Hebrew, however, the word used is not really 'wait' but rather a more active 'hope'. In fact, the root word, 'kaveh', קוה , incorporates several nuances: 'kav' means line; 'kavanah' means intentional; 'kivun' means direction. Therefore we have the full, beautiful message behind this verse. We do not simply 'wait passively' upon the Lord; but rather we have an *intentional directing of the line of our focus in hope towards the Lord.*" Wow! It is this word which is at the root of Hatikvah, the national anthem of Israel.

The Hope
Israel's National Anthem

As long as the Jewish spirit
is yearning deep in the heart,
With eyes turned toward the East,
looking toward Zion,
Then our hope
the two-thousand-year-old hope
will not be lost
To be a free people in our land,
The land of Zion and Jerusalem.

Even in the choice of our name, Nesher, the Lord seemed to be asking me to *'hope against all hope'* in His mercy. Life continued, day after painful day, just trying to survive; but often feeling that I would not - and then a letter came in the mail. Someone had sent me a poem by an unknown author called:

'The Bird with the Broken Wing'

It lay by the dusty roadside; the people just came and went.

Not one looked down on the panting bird and its' life was almost spent.

Yes, one woman did, but she hurried on with a look of hopeless pain.

And said, *"Poor bird, you've broken your wing, you will never fly again"*.

So it fluttered all day in anguish until the sun was set, And the night came in silence, o'er the hill of Olivet.

But the Master who lay on the sod that night 'neath the trees and the open sky

Could not sleep for the sound that pierced His ear – 'twas the dying birdling's cry.

As the glory of the morning was touching the eastern hills

He came to where the weary bird lay, all faint and cold and still.

He bent His head in compassion over the shattered wing,

It was bruised, it was broken and dying, it could not soar or sing.

He drew it from the tangled grass with His
hand of healing power,
And said, "You shall soar and sing for Me as
bird never sang before".
Then He lifted it high on His blessed palm
and it spread its' wings to fly;
And then a flood of melody filled the blue
Judean sky.

It echoed over hill and plain with such a
triumphant strain
that men stood still to drink their fill, then
paused to drink again.
On wings that were strong and tireless as an
eagle on its' way
It mounted up to the throne of God past the
gates of eternal day.

It sang its' song of liberty as angels stood back
in amaze.
Then took up the song as it swept along and
all Heaven was filled with praise.
The song of the bird with the broken wing is
the song my soul is singing!
The power of His matchless love within my
life is ringing.

Out of the tangle of sin and woe His love has
lifted my soul.
For the matchless touch of the Son of God has
freed me and made me whole.

I wept as I read this poem. I kept it as a token, a
remembrance, a faint whisper of hope, and yet the
doubts remained,

"Would I, could I ever be set free and made whole? Would I ever fly again?"

In the natural it seemed impossible, but I heard that still small voice speak to my heart,

"Yes, my love, trust Me, you will fly again. And you will sing for Me again, filling the blue Judean skies with melodies of worship."

Hosea – You Will Sing Again

I well remember when I began to sing for the Lord. As a *'nice Jewish girl gone bad'*, I had left my faith and family as a rebellious teenager, choosing to follow a self-destructive path. In my earlier days, as a model student in a private Hebrew school, I had led the 'Junior Congregation' in the singing of prayers and blessings on Saturday (Shabbat) mornings. But as I entered into public school and the larger 'Gentile' community, I allowed myself to be led away captive to the world and to sin – and I reaped a harvest of sorrow.

There finally came a day when I, like Gomer, the unfaithful wife of Hosea, chased after my lovers but could not find them. I had decked myself out in jewellery and fine clothing and gone to many parties, but had forgotten my God and Creator. So He caused all my mirth and partying to cease. He hedged my way with thorns so that I could not escape. [5] I found myself pregnant and alone – abandoned and betrayed.

---

[5] Hosea 2:7-20

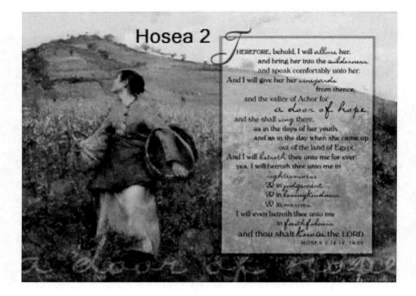

Hosea 2

THEREFORE, behold, I will allure her,
and bring her into the wilderness,
and speak comfortably unto her.
And I will give her her vineyards
from thence,
and the valley of Achor for
a door of hope:
and she shall sing there,
as in the days of her youth,
and as in the day when she came up
out of the land of Egypt.
And I will betroth thee unto me for ever;
yea, I will betroth thee unto me in
righteousness,
and in judgment,
and in lovingkindness,
and in mercies.
I will even betroth thee unto me
in faithfulness:
and thou shalt know the LORD.
HOSEA 2:14-16, 19-20

And then God wooed me back to Himself and spoke tenderly to me in the wilderness. I became betrothed to Him forever in righteousness through finding Yeshua as my Messiah.

And I read of myself in the book of Hosea and I read the promise, **"You will sing for me again as in the days of your youth..."**[6] The first thing I asked of the Lord after I received salvation through Yeshua Hamashiach (the Messiah) was a voice to sing for Him. I began to sing in the choir and loved to sing for the Lord.

But that was many years ago. Now as I sat, broken-hearted and in exile, I wondered if I would ever sing again? **How can I sing the Lord's songs in a foreign land?**

---

[6] Hosea 2:15

I could well identify with the Israelites who lamented their Babylonian exile centuries ago and wrote,

"By the rivers of Babylon, there we sat down,
 yea, we wept when we remembered Zion.
We hung our harps upon the willows in the midst of it.
For there, those who carried us away captive asked of us
a song...

How shall we sing the Lord's song in a foreign land?
If forget you, O Jerusalem,
Let *my right hand* forget it skill!
 If I do not remember you, let my tongue cling to the roof
of my mouth –   If I do not exalt Jerusalem above my
chief joy."(Psalm 137:1-8)

Yeshua is seated at the right hand of God; therefore to forget Jerusalem is like forgetting the Messiah! **"But from now on, the Son of Man will be seated at the right hand of the mighty God."** (Luke 22:69)

Take your Harp off the Willows

One of my fondest memories from our first years in Israel was our weekly ladies prayer meeting in the settlement of Ariel. It was a chance to fellowship with my sisters in the Lord, to catch up on their news, and of course to pray for one another. When I became pregnant, after having suffered several miscarriages prior, these ladies laid hands on my womb and sent up a storm of prayers to the Heavenly Throne room on behalf of my unborn child, that she would live and not die – and she did! PTL! Liat is now[7] a 17 year old lovely young lady, highly gifted in the arts, worship and dance. She also enjoys writing - like her Mom. ☺

When we engaged in the initial battle for our citizenship in the Land, these ladies even fasted and prayed one day each week to see us receive our rightful inheritance in the Land – and we did. Halleluyah! One precious woman came from America on assignment from the Lord to come to the mountains of Israel to pray. She joined our little group of prayer warriors and brought something special with her – an autoharp. This greatly enriched our meetings with the melodic sounds of her unique musical instrument. And although I had never played the harp, God placed within me the

---

[7] Nov 2016

desire to worship the Lord on an autoharp, so this became my persistent prayer request.

Years passed and I resigned myself to my apparent fate to live in exile, trying to *'make lemonade out of lemons'*. I began teaching some Hebrew lessons and spoke about Israel wherever the Lord opened a door. One day, however, my husband came home with a surprise announcement – he wanted to make an attempt to move back to Israel! Shocked, I asked how this came about. Apparently, he happened to watch my own DVD on Ruth and was touched by her pledge to never leave Naomi (a prophetic picture of the Church and the Jewish people)[8]. He repented for taking us out of the Land and asked if I would be willing to go back.

"Are you insane?" was my first reaction. We had finally begun to settle in, had just begun to get back on our feet, re-connected with friends and family, started to heal and find some sort of stability – and now he wanted to uproot us again? Leave everything and everyone behind again? Start all over again from scratch with nothing? How could I possibly do it all over again? Ridiculous anyways, I thought, since we had no money to even fly back.

And yet he looked at me and asked a question, *"If somehow, by some miracle, we had the means to fly back to Israel would you consider it?"* Thinking that this could never possibly happen, I answered flippantly, *"Sure"*, not realizing that sitting even at that very moment in my inbox was an e-mail from a business man who wrote,

---

[8] See DVD Ruth, A Righteous Gentile, www.voiceforisrael.net/shop

"Shalom Hannah. I have more air mile points than I even know what to do with. In fact I have enough air mile points to fly an entire family to Israel, and I'm wondering if you would like to use them to fly your family back to Israel."

Stunned, I had to admit that this could be the Lord's answer to the longing of my heart; and so we began the difficult process of moving across continents – again. Before we left, however, we spoke in a church about the whole issue of aliyah and our journey to Jerusalem and back. After speaking and showing our power point, a man approached me, asking if there was anything I needed to take with me back to Israel. What a question! Like what?

Well, this man further told me that he 'just happened' to walk into our meeting and stayed to listen, since his brother is a pastor and the subject of Israel interested him. Then he told me that he is the owner of a music store. *"You don't happen to have a harp do you – an autoharp to be exact?"* I asked.

Yes, he did have an autoharp and he would be pleased to give it to me as a gift to take back to Israel to worship the Lord with it. Wow!

Hannah playing autoharp

God of Second Chances – 2nd aliyah

Our second attempt at aliyah – at Ben Gurion airport (2004)

This time around, we returned to the Northern region of Israel around the area of the Galilee where we had connected with some other Messianic Believers. It was beautiful, green, quiet and peaceful – but it was still hard. The Israeli authorities still refused to give my husband a visa, which made it impossible for him to work, even though we had two children born in the Land. They demanded that he leave. He refused. He became more and more bitter; and our marriage became more and more strained (an understatement).

Far from feeling free, whole and 'flying', I still felt wounded and grounded. One evening, a group of women came from several Western countries such as the United States, Canada, and the U.K. They came with only one purpose – to encourage the Believers in the Land. The musicians led us in beautiful worship and a lovely woman began to move gracefully to the music – it was the <u>dance of the Eagle</u>. "As I wait, I'll rise up as an eagle...."

Watching her, tears began to stream down my face as the presence of the Lord began to minister to my hardened heart. I had been so burdened by the trials of life that I hadn't even felt the strength to worship the Lord with my autoharp for a long, long time.

Women began to move through the crowd, ministering in prayer to the Believers. One such woman, who did not know me from Eve, began to pray and prophecy over me. She said,

"It is time to take your harp off the willows and to sing songs of the Lord in Zion."

Later I read an article about Screaming Eagles. [9] Apparently, at some point in their lives, eagles go through a molting process. These majestic birds lose their feathers and are unable to fly. They lose their ability to see, as their vision weakens during this time. They pick up a rank odor, and stink. Calcium builds up on their beaks and they can't hold their heads up, to be the proud majestic birds that they truly are. They lose their desire to eat because they only eat fresh kill.

---

[9] Molting Eagles Need Screaming Eagles to Survive 11/5/98 by *Ken Gerry*

When the molten eagle gets in this last state, often times they will begin to peck on each other, occasionally killing another molten eagle, as they gather together in one place.

It is a most pathetic sight to see. Four or five eagles molting in the valley, where they once would only soar over to look for fresh kill. If they don't renew, they will die. They grow weaker and weaker.

Suddenly, there is a sound from the sky over the valley of molting eagles. Screaming, loudly, another group of eagles fly over head and drop fresh kill over the dying birds. The screaming is encouragement, *"Eat, Eat, Live, You'll Fly again!"* Some eat and recover, others roll over and die.

There are lessons to learn from the molten eagle. It may seem like our feathers have been plucked, people might think we smell bad, some of us maybe have lost our vision, and we feel so bad we can hardly lift up our heads. We must not lose our desire to eat of the Word of God, and we need to stop picking on one another.

"Listen, hear the sound of the screaming eagles bringing in the fresh kill. Don't die! renew! Don't retire, refire! We are still the majestic birds we've always been. If you're molting, renew!"

"Have you not known? Have you not heard, that the everlasting God, יהוה , the Creator of the ends of the earth, faints not, neither is weary? There is no searching of his understanding. He gives power to the faint; and to them that have no might He increases strength.

"Even the youths shall faint and become weary, and the young men shall utterly fall: But they that hope in Adonai shall renew their strength; they shall mount up with wings as eagles; they shall run, and not be weary; and they shall walk, and not faint." (Isaiah 40:28-31)

I knew that these women had come as screaming eagles just in time; I became determined to live and not die and declare the righteous works of the Lord.

GPS Route Recalculations

The path from there to here has not been linear; there have been many twists and turns along the way, including another return of several years into exile and the dissolution of my marriage. But, like the awesome GPS in my car, when we take a wrong turn, it doesn't berate us,

"You idiot! I can't believe you turned right when I said left! How can you be so stupid? How many times are you going to go the wrong way? Can't you even follow simple directions? I just don't know if I can do this with you anymore...." ☺

No, these may be some of the more negative, critical voices I hear in my head when I mess up; but I don't believe this is the heart of God. Instead, I hear the consistently patient, calm voice of the GPS say, *"Route recalculation. Turn back in 800 metres."*

I can imagine God in heaven saying to the angels, *"O.K. guys, we've got a route recalculation on Hannah's path to her destiny. Let's find a way to get her back on track."*

It may cost us some wasted time, and even some inconvenience, but I choose to believe that God does not condemn us when we mess up; but that He wants to help us get back on track on the path to our destiny if we will just turn back to Him and seek His guidance.

God did make a way where there truly was no way to return us home to Israel where we lived for several years on a peaceful, beautiful moshav (village) near Jerusalem with my children and children's children.

Here, overlooking the Judean Hills, I often played the autoharp and sang praises to God at our neighbors, Shirli & Yossi's place. They believed that God created this place just for me – so that these melodies would fill the blue Judean skies, just like in that 'Bird with the Broken Wing' poem I received.

Shirlee & Yossi's place overlooking Judean hills

And yet, after several years in the Land, I couldn't shake the feeling that God had something more for me than enjoying my quiet life in the village. What it was exactly, I could not quite discern. I couldn't even put into words the longing I continued to experience in my soul – but I felt it all the same. Perhaps, it is that no matter how high we fly – we always seek to fly higher. God always wants us to be growing in Him. Or perhaps it is that eternal longing we all experience to fly away to Heaven - and there - to live with our Heavenly Father forever.

When I watched that little bird, Blue, in the movie Rio, I could identify with this character's fears, insecurities and frustrations with his inability to fly. Life is good, life is comfortable; I am well cared for, and yet I knew in my heart at this Israeli movie theatre that the still, small voice of the Holy Spirit was once again speaking to me, *"Hannah, I want you to fly again."*

In November of 2015, the Ruach Hakodesh (Holy Spirit) called us to take the Word of Adonai from Zion to the nations. This is our mission, from the words of the Prophet, **"For out of Zion shall go forth the Torah, and the word of Adonai from Jerusalem." (Isaiah 2:3)**

כִּי מִצִּיּוֹן תֵּצֵא תוֹרָה, וּדְבַר-יְהוָה מִירוּשָׁלָם

It was a crazy thing to do – fly off to L.A. (cheapest ticket from Tel Aviv to anywhere) with two kids – not really knowing what we would do or how it would all work out - but God went before us and prepared a way. It is such a blessing to use our God-given gifts and talents to share the Word of Adonai in the nations. Yeshua said, **"Go into all the world and proclaim the gospel to the whole creation."** (Mark 16:15)

We have brought the Word of Torah to Poland, Japan, United States and Canada (where we are temporarily 'perching'); but we eagerly look forward to further 'flying escapades' with the Lord.

God doesn't want us to become complacent with where we are; He doesn't want us to accept an 'average' or 'ordinary' life. We are missing out on a great life when we choose comfort and security over passion. God's desire for those who know Him are to do great and mighty exploits.

There are seasons and there are seasons; but I don't believe that we are meant to pray for the ability to endure misery and mediocrity. We are called to thrive, not just survive; created to bear much fruit for Abba's glory – to enjoy a life of adventure being led by His Spirit.

I would like to share a quote from Dr. Myles Munroe's outstanding book, 'Maximizing Your Potential":

"An eagle that doesn't fly cannot fulfill its purpose. Likewise your life will lack purpose and focus until you discover your wings. This discovery will require both wisdom and courage because the thrill of flying always begins with the fear of falling. Yet you are not left alone to find your wings because God, through the prophet Moses promises to undertake for you."

"Like an eagle that stirs up its nest and hovers over its young, that spreads its wings to catch them and carries them on its pinions, the Lord alone leads you."
(Deuteronomy 32:11-12a)

Setting the Captives Free

In the movie, it took a real crisis to provoke 'Blue' into using his God-given flying skills; but I think that it's even better if we can really 'get this' before crisis hits. We need to live life with faith and courage in order to fulfill our destiny.

Most of us have been wounded at some point in life – shot down out of the sky by the enemy of our soul with his poisonous arrows. The temptation is to give up and accept a life of brokenness, mediocrity, and compromise; but this is not the passionate life of adventure that God has for us – taking more and more territory for the Kingdom of Light.

We are called to be fresh and flourishing – even bearing fruit in our 'golden years'. **"They shall still bring forth fruit in old age; they shall be vigorous and flourishing."** (Psalm 92:14)

Trouble comes into every life – or as my other used to say, *"Everyone has their tsuris.[10]"* Yeshua promised that in this life we would have trouble; but we are to be of good cheer – for He has overcome the world.[11]

If we continually '*parrot*' negative things and '*squawk*' about all the negative things in life; then we literally imprison ourselves like a bird in a cage. Every time we murmur, grumble, whine and complain, we add another bar to the cage and lock

---

[10] Tsuris – Yiddish for troubles. Hebrew 'tsurot'
[11] John 16:33

ourselves away from all the blessings that are ours to receive.

But when we refuse to give in to the darkness; and instead focus on our blessings, then we can become as free as the birds that soar in the sky. To break free of the bars of the cages that imprison us, we need to meditate continually on God's amazing love and allow His light to shine through us to others. And the truth in love will set us free.

"Then you will know the truth and the truth will set you free." (John 8:32)

In these words that Yeshua (Jesus) of Natzeret spoke, it seems to me, that we have all the wisdom we need to live the abundant life that He came to give us.

Enjoy your flight!

Love Hannah

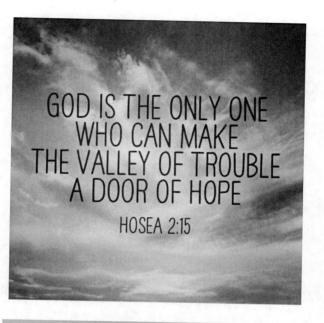

GOD IS THE ONLY ONE
WHO CAN MAKE
THE VALLEY OF TROUBLE
A DOOR OF HOPE

HOSEA 2:15

*T*hose who hope in the **LORD** will renew their strength. They will **SOAR** on wings like eagles they will run and not grow weary they will walk and not be faint.

Isaiah 40:31

וְקוֹיֵ יְהוָה יַחֲלִיפוּ כֹחַ יַעֲלוּ אֵבֶר כַּנְּשָׁרִים יָרוּצוּ וְלֹא יִיגָעוּ יֵלְכוּ וְלֹא יִיעָפוּ:

ישעיה מא:31

CHAPTER TWENTY-SIX

Running out of Fuel

A Devotional on Finding Balance in Life

"One hand full of rest is better than two fists full of labor and striving after wind." (Ecclesiastes 4:6 NASB)

Shalom from Israel!

I may just be rambling, but I have some things I've been pondering in my heart lately that I would like to put down on paper and share with you, in hopes that, perhaps these ramblings may help someone else as well.

Today [1], the village where I live on the top of a mountain in Israel was shrouded in a thick, deep fog. You couldn't really see a thing! As I was waiting with Avi at the bus stop, we couldn't even see the school bus approaching – all we could see were its headlights.

Sometimes it feels like we're walking around in a fog. I think they even have a term for it now – *"brain fog."* But really, in today's complex and speed-driven world, the sheer mass of information overload and endless choices and demands of daily life can leave us feeling like we are trapped in a thick fog of confusion.

We peer intently through the heavy mist, but cannot quite discern the next step to take, even if it's right there in front of our face.   Have you ever felt like this? I know I have... maybe even today!

It seems to me that our only hope to get through the fog is to keep watching and waiting for the headlights – that which will be a lamp at our feet and a light to our path. [2]

Yeshua said **"I am the light of the world. Whoever follows me will not walk in darkness but in the light of life."** (John 8:12)

[1] Written March 4th 2012
[2] **Psalms 119: 105**

A foggy winter day in Israel

Some of us are not necessarily walking in pitch black darkness but more of a grayish misty fog. For my life and for yours, may the true Light guide our paths into truth, clarity, wisdom and righteousness.

In my last e-mail, I wrote about running out of fuel to heat the house and how it got me thinking about the parable of the ten virgins, which I had just written about in Parashah Tetzaveh [3] with regards to the anointing oil. I asked the Lord how I may be

<hr />

[3] Torah portions (parashot) www.voiceforisrael.net

walking in foolishness? We have to be careful what we ask the Lord, because He is so faithful to give us an answer to our questions ☺.

And just in case I hadn't quite got the point about running out of fuel, when I lit the burner on my gas stove, guess what happened? That's right – nothing. No more gas left in the propane tank to light the stove. I wasn't worried, though, because we have two gas tanks outside the house – one to use and one for reserve. We just switch to the reserve tank when the first one is used up. But for some reason, even the reserve tank was also empty. Oye vey!

So we sat. No fuel for heat. No fuel to cook. Outside was a storm complete with hail and snow! I could see my breath *inside* the house and it is the first time I have actually heard a dog's teeth chatter! ☺ Poor Pepper.   I finally had to admit that these things happened because I didn't make sure I had enough fuel on hand.

Running on Adrenaline

I wonder if we keep driving ourselves beyond our limits; running on adrenaline – our reserve energy – that 'second wind'. This may be acceptable occasionally, but what about when we use caffeine, stimulants, and sheer will power to push ourselves even when we know that we desperately need to slow down and be renewed.

The Good Shepherd promises He will *make us* lie down in green pastures; lead us beside quiet waters, and refresh our soul.[4] He will bring refreshing and restoration, but sometimes He has to '*make us*' lie down first.

When I woke up one Shabbat morning, I simply couldn't move. It was like nothing in my body wanted to function. I have become accustomed to living with chronic pain and fatigue, but this was beyond anything I had experienced. It was a total shut down – a body gone on strike.

The day prior had been very stressful, emotionally and physically; but then not really so different from many other days. I wrote in my journal, "*It feels like my fuel has just completely run out.*" I prayed, "*God I need a miracle!*"

As part of my devotional time that morning, I read a chapter out of a Christian author, Dr. James B. Richards' book, The Anatomy of a Miracle. In this chapter, he wrote about living according to the laws of harmony and the consequences of breaking those natural laws upon which God created the universe.

I was particularly touched by what Dr. Richards wrote about in this chapter about living in harmony. In the Old Testament, even the land needed a rest and the people were forbidden to plant or harvest on the land every seven years. As human beings, we are

---

[4] Psalm 23:2-3

also commanded by our Creator to take one full day of rest out of every seven and to observe the Sabbath.

I will quote some of Dr. Richard's writing, since he says it a lot better than how I'm trying to explain it.

"Since we don't get energy from our much needed restful nourishment, we have chronic fatigue, heart disease and a host of other diseases that come from pushing our bodies into extreme acidic inflammation...."

"If we refuse to harmonize, we exhaust our energy. When we can't push ourselves any further, we collapse into the total inability to function...It is not a judgment from an angry God...It is what happens when our force runs out..."

What I like about Dr. Richards' writing, is that he not only explains the problem so accurately, he also gives us the "*God prescription*" for healing.

"An innumerable host of modern diseases simply would disappear if we only took more vacations, relaxed more often and learned how to play."

How does this relate to Yeshua's parable of the five wise and five foolish virgins? I had always interpreted this parable in a spiritual sense – that I must stay filled with enough 'anointing'. This still holds true, but perhaps there is another level of interpretation. Through these recent experiences I have had with running out of fuel, I am seeing this parable in a new way.

I feel the Lord is warning me about the way I have been living: pushing my body beyond its limits on a continual basis, allowing myself to get stressed and upset over little things, refusing to relax or have fun or play because of all the work and pressing demands of my life. This is just plain foolishness! And I realize now that if I continue to run off reserve fumes, this too will one day run out, just like the gas tanks for my stove.

If we refuse to heed the Lord's counsel and make some changes to our stressful lifestyle, then just as it happened for the five foolish virgins, one day we may find ourselves out of fuel, out in the cold, and unfortunately by this time it may be too late for anyone to do anything about it.

We cannot keep repeating our same mistakes, which create the same problems, which requires seeking a supernatural deliverance through miracles. Dr. Richards writes, *"That is the way of the foolish! We must harmonize our lifestyles with the laws of the miraculous and live an entirely different quality of life."*

As I think about this, I think about my Dad. Surely he is not perfect, but when I look at his life, I see that he lived according to laws of harmony and wisdom. He usually took a 'power nap' every day, often listening to his favorite classical music on headphones while reclining in his easy chair. He kept regular hours as a dentist, worked outside in his garden, and enjoyed a happy, peaceful marriage with the same wonderful woman (my Mom) for over sixty years. He attends synagogue regularly, belongs to a community of faith, sings in the choir, and plays piano every day.

Today, he is 82 years old [5], Baruch Hashem (praise the Name) and still drives his car, does the shopping, travels, cuts his own lawn in the summer, and stays active in a number of good service works.

My Mom served as his faithful helpmeet for over 60 years; and was the most amazing mother to all four of us children. Unfortunately, she never took the time to develop any interests outside her home and family. She never took cat naps; never indulged in hobbies or listened to music. She was so chronically tired that if they ever took a night off to go to a movie or concert, she immediately fell asleep and missed the whole thing.

She was the model of how to live a completely self-sacrificial life. Today, however; she has dementia to such an extent that she is unable to even communicate; and must reside in a nursing home where strangers have to care for her most basic needs.

---

[5] Written in 2012. This year in 2017, my Dad is turning 87 years old & is still going strong! PTL!

Could it be possible that a tiny bit of 'selfishness' might actually be good for our health? Could it be that the universe will actually continue to exist if we take some time out for our own enjoyment of life?

I also have this childhood memory of my Dad sitting back in his recliner every Shabbat afternoon, after coming home from the synagogue and having enjoyed a nice, home cooked meal. He would put on his favorite music (usually opera or classical which we intensely disliked) but nevertheless, he would close his eyes, listen to his music and just relax. In fact, almost every day, he would purposefully take time to consciously relax in his 'easy chair'.

My parents made consistent right choices that have guided them in paths of peace and prosperity. My Dad worked hard in school and chose a profession that would allow him to come home each day at 5:00 P.M. for supper and to be home with his wife and family every weekend. They chose their marriage partner wisely as a godly person from a reputable family who would be faithful and loving and honest.

Together, they cooperated and considered one another, endeavoring to keep the peace in our home. They each worked hard, but they rested every Shabbat. They took vacations as a couple and also together as a family – often just relaxing in the summer months at the local pool.

My parents gave generously to the poor, to charitable causes and to the synagogue where they faithfully attended and participated. They taught us the value of generosity, kindness, and hospitality. Although generous givers, they also saved and invested wisely for the future.

They were stable, living in the same house that they built and where they raised their family for the next sixty years. They often met with family to celebrate life and enjoyed a solid social network. They kept their priorities straight. They lived according to wisdom, with balance, goodness, honesty and integrity. And well into their eighties, they were reaping the benefits of peace, health, and prosperity. My Dad, however, took time to renew his mind, body and soul; whereas my Mom did not.

Mom and Dad at their 60th wedding anniversary

The Torah says this:

"Blessed are those who find wisdom, those who gain understanding, for she is more profitable than silver and yields better returns than gold. She is more precious than rubies; nothing you desire can compare with her. Long life is in her right hand; in her left hand are riches and honor. Her ways are pleasant ways, and all her paths are peace. She is a tree of life to those who take hold of her; those who hold her fast will be blessed." (Proverbs 3:13-17)

We may have made some foolish choices in our lives (who hasn't?). By not following the path of wisdom we may therefore find ourselves suffering the consequences. But today is a new day. There is yet hope for us. Just as a doctor is not for the healthy, but the sick; Yeshua did not come for the righteous but for sinners. There is yet time to make changes. We can choose to heed the Word of our 'Wonderful Counselor' (Peleh Yo'etz), to slow down and take time to 'smell the roses', to see more sunsets, and to take more walks in the park.

We can spend time just hanging out with the people we love to strengthen those relationships, and take time to engage in the things we enjoy doing, even if completely non-productive. We can take that vacation we've been putting off for a more 'favorable time'. And we can sit back in our comfy chair, put the earphones on, listen to our favorite music, and just relax.

The inbox will wait and so will the housework. I promise.

Yeshua said, "The thief comes only to steal and kill and destroy but **I have come that you may have life and life more abundantly.**" (John 10:10)

L'CHAIM (TO LIFE)!

CHAPTER TWENTY-SEVEN
SCAREDY-CAT

The fear of man bringeth a snare: but whoso putteth his trust in the LORD shall be safe.

Prov. 29:25

משלי כט:כה

חֶרְדַּת אָדָם יִתֵּן מוֹקֵשׁ וּבוֹטֵחַ בַּיהוָה יְשֻׂגָּב:

A Devotional on Overcoming Fear of Persecution, Bad Hair Days, & Other Calamities

"Be merciful to me, O God, be merciful to me: for my soul trusts in you: yes, in the shadow of your wings will I make my refuge, until these calamities have passed by." (Psalm 57:1)

There is a tendency in Jerusalem, especially, to keep silent about our faith. Perhaps it is because of the zealousness of the anti-missionaries here. Or perhaps our flesh just succumbs to a fear of man. We were shocked, when we first arrived in the Land of Israel[1], to find so many believers in Yeshua who seemed to keep quiet about Him, for fear of offending the Jewish people. "*Shh*!!!" they would hush us if we happened to mention the name of Yeshua too loudly in a public place.

Or in their home they might whisper, "*What if my neighbors hear you*!?" Of course not all are like this. There are some who publicly proclaim the gospel and suffer persecution; but most realize that they must live here in the community and they, as well as their children who usually attend the local schools, would likely suffer greatly if the fact that they are Messianic Believers (followers of Yeshua) became public knowledge.

Friends of ours had the dubious honor of seeing that the anti-missionaries had printed their photo on a poster which they put up all over their neighborhood warning people to stay away from these so-called '*dangerous Christian missionaries*'. It actually backfired because most of their neighbors know and love these people; and rallied around them with demonstrations of support and respect.

A scripture leaped out at me the other day promising that God has His people in the city.

---

[1] Dec. 1998

"Do not be afraid, but speak, and do not keep silent, for I am with you, and no one will attack you to hurt you; for I have many people in this city."(Acts 18:9-10)

I was reminded of two incidents that occurred which confirmed the fact that God has many of His people strategically placed throughout this city of Jerusalem.

When the cold weather came upon us recently, I took my children shopping for warmer clothing. The store where locals usually shop for bargains is generally a madhouse. Clerks often scream, argue and shout at one another openly across the clothing racks. Often they will vent their tempers upon a customer who dares ask for help. I've learned to just muddle through and do my best.

But one clerk, perhaps an Ethiopian, appeared noticeably different. There was a peace - a serenity about her that caused her smiling face to shine. She actually approached us and sought to be of courteous assistance. Unbelievable for Israeli customer service! It felt like a shower of refreshment in a dry desert. She watched my children play hide and seek under the racks and commented on how clever they seemed to be. "*Of course!*" this Jewish mother proudly agreed.

When it came time to leave, I couldn't find the little ones so I called out in a strong voice, "*Shmuel[2]!! Liat!!*" and out they scurried from their hiding place into my arms. My son said, "*Mommy, I couldn't see you but when I heard your voice, I knew right away it was you and I knew where to find you.*"

Seeing this as an opportunity to teach my children 'as we walk alongside', I replied, "*Yeshua said the same thing. He said that His sheep hear His voice and they follow Him.*" (John 10:27)

"And when he brings out his own sheep, he goes before them, and the sheep follow him, for they know his voice. Yet they will by no means follow a stranger, but will flee from him, for they do not know the voice of strangers."(John 10:4-5)

The clerk who had been helping us suddenly looked at me with surprise and ran over. "*You know the One you speak of?*" she asked.

"*Yes...?*" I said.

"*I know Him.*" she proudly stated, her face beaming.

We quietly looked into one another's eyes, smiling, knowing we had found a '*member of the family.*' As the children and I walked home, we talked about how Yeshua in this woman's heart has made her different than all the other clerks - she stood out as a

---

[2] Shmuel was Timothy's Hebrew name in Israel

light in that dark place. And this is how it should be here in the Land, as in all the nations.

It felt good to break though cultural taboos to speak the name of Yeshua publicly, and to find a kindred spirit.

In another incident, I took my children to the neighborhood park to play, and I noticed a woman sitting by the carousel (merry-go-round) whom I had met previously. I knew only that she was an Israeli married to an American, with two rambunctious boys. We struck up a conversation and in my mind I was praying, *"Lord, please help me to share Yeshua with this precious Israeli woman."*

Liat with a basket of kitties in the park in Jerusalem 2001

After a few minutes of conversation, this woman asked me which synagogue I attend. This was my open door. *"I go to a Messianic Congregation off Ben Yehudah street,"*[3] I replied. Her mouth visibly dropped open and there was a moment of silence until she exclaimed the first names of our ro'eh kehilla (congregational leader) and his wife.[4] She knew them well and even used to attend their congregation. Her husband is actually a pastor from America! She couldn't believe that here was another Messianic Believer in the same neighborhood. We were very glad to exchange phone numbers and looked forward to fellowship together.

Being Counted Worthy to Suffer

Not all believers are so quiet about their faith in Israel, however. Some boldly proclaim their faith in Messiah Yeshua and often pay a heavy price. When our congregational leader called for a testimony one Shabbat, a dark-haired Israeli man came forward to share about his desire for the boldness to be a faithful witness for the Lord Yeshua.

Hitchhiking (called '*tramping*' in Hebrew) into Tiberius one morning, he caught a ride with a da'ati man (da'ati is the Hebrew word for 'religious', from the root da'at, which means knowledge). Fear rose up within him, but he prayed to God for the courage to speak of his faith.

---

[3] At that time we attended Kingdom Ministries Jerusalem congregation which has since disbanded

[4] This couple became my daughter's in-laws when she married their son in Jerusalem.

As he began to share, this religious Jewish man became very angry and agitated, ordering him to get out of his car! My (then) husband, David, smiled at this point, remembering occasions when he had also witnessed to the religious (da'ati), but being the driver, they couldn't really kick him out of his own car. As a captive audience, they had to sit there and listen until they came to their destination.

After making it home, this man went out to share Yeshua with people in his village. Shortly thereafter, a burly man knocked loudly on his door. This man was very angry, but like a good Sephardic Jew, [5] he kept a calm exterior and no emotion could be read openly on his face. Still, his words spewed forth like venom. He forbid this believer from speaking of Yeshua and threatened to burn his house down and organize a group to physically harm him if he persisted in speaking about '*Yeshu*'[6].

This Israeli went on to testify that his courage faltered and his heart was troubled by these threats so much that he couldn't sleep at night. In the morning, he still had no peace; but when He prayed, the Lord returned his peace and courage. He was able to rejoice that he had been **"counted worthy to suffer shame for His name."**(Acts 5:41)

---

[5] The Sephardic Jews are those originating from Spain, Morocco, and Arabic countries rather than the Ashkenzi which come from Russia, Poland, and Eastern Europe

[6] Many Orthodox Jews call Yeshua by the name 'Yeshu' which is a derogatory reference – an acronym meaning "May his name be blotted out forever and ever."

Like the early apostles, he determined to obey God rather than man: **"not to cease teaching and preaching Yeshua as the Messiah."** (Acts 5:42)

Overcoming Fear of Man

There is something liberating in overcoming that fear of man; and being willing to suffer shame and persecution, even from our own brethren, for His name's sake – as did the first apostles in the book of Acts. Yeshua is returning to His people Israel and there is much opposition.

I sometimes feel like we are re-living the book of Acts in Jerusalem. The Jewish people whose mission it is to oppose the gospel in Israel can be very intimidating. They have stormed congregations and ripped infants out of their mother's arms; burned New Testaments, surrounded Messianic fellowships chanting curses; videotaped believers entering places of worship[7], slashed tires, firebombed apartments, smeared dog excrement on doorways, and painted swastikas and other forms of offensive graffiti on dwellings or ministries of followers of Yeshua. They actively lobby to evict Messianic Jews from the Land; and to convert them back to rabbinic Judaism.

Even if these overt acts of violence are not experienced, most still face their painful accusations

---

[7] They use these video tapes to try and evict Messianic believers from the Land & revoke citizenship

that we are not really Jews anymore because of our faith; or that we have betrayed and blasphemed our God by worshipping a false God (Jesus). And so it is not surprising that many of us usually act more like Peter before the resurrection – subtly denying or covering up the fact that we know Him and have been with Him.

Believers in Israel deal with persecution for their faith in Yeshua on a daily basis, as do many Christians in other nations. But this is an issue that each one of us who believe in Him will one day be required to face in the End Times.

In theory, it sounds so lofty, so noble, so heroic to suffer persecution for His sake; but when it comes down to it; our flesh goes through great gymnastic contortions to avoid pain and discomfort. Our flesh is totally pleasure and comfort orientated. So how do we overcome the fear of persecution?

The answer, of course, is not to stop fearing, but to replace the wrong kind of fear with a godly fear. We need to fear God rather than man. How is it possible to do this? Only through living our lives with an eternal perspective – we must add eternity to our thinking.

Fearing God not Man

I recall attending a prayer meeting for a certain ministry in Jerusalem; and was saddened to discover that they did not mention the name of Yeshua in any of their literature, nor would they even use any New Testament Scriptures. They justified this glaring ommission by explaining that they focus on their specific humanitarian mission and do not want to jeopardize this by becoming perceived as 'Christian missionaries'.

We were even rebuked for speaking of Yeshua in a normal tone of voice on the stairs leading up to their office and on the street, in case anyone overheard us. They were afraid that their landlord would kick them out of their rented space if word got out that they followed 'that man'.

This shocked and upset me deeply. I thought of how in the book of Acts, it was the religious Jewish leaders who forbid the Jewish Believers from speaking the name of Yeshua on the streets of Israel. **"And the Cohen Hagadol (high priest) asked them, saying, "Did we not strictly command you not to teach in this name?"** (Acts 5:28)

But now, ironically, fellow believers were forbidding other believers from publicly speaking His name! And yet, **"we ought to obey God rather than men."** (Acts 5:29)

At other times, we noticed this '*Hush! Hush!*' attitude among Messianic Believers in the Land, who hid their faith in Yeshua in order to make aliyah (immigrate to Israel). They did not want to jeopardize their citizenship (or safety) by openly sharing their faith.

Why? Fear of man. Fear of persecution. It is now in our times as it was then with the first disciples. Many

Jewish people believed in Yeshua , even among the rulers, but they would not openly confess Him because of the Pharisees (the religious Jews of their day) **"lest they should be put out of the synagogue; for they loved the praise of men more than the praise of God."** (John 12:42-43)

It seemed a similar situation with this Christian ministry that would not openly confess the Lord Yeshua because of the fear of being thrown out of their office space by the landlord. I will admit that the persecution here in Israel can be intense. The leader of this ministry was sharing that he has had religious men, thinking that he was evangelizing while handing out their pamphlets and literature on the streets, try to put a cigarette butt out in his face.

Another threatened to slit his throat if he ever came back again. And this is without even mentioning the name of Yeshua or even the New Testament! This can happen when they even remotely suspect that someone may be evangelizing. We have seen actual video clips of religious Jews spitting on someone preaching Yeshua on the streets of Jerusalem.

Persecution can come against Believers in many forms; even home groups can be a target. Several years ago, our son, Shmuel, who was at that time eleven years old, attended a small home fellowship meeting with his young friends. A group of Orthodox Jews surrounded the house, calling out threats, making it necessary to call for police escort to get our son and the other children out to safety.

In order to understand the religious Jewish Israelis' abhorrence of Christianity and especially its shlichim (*sent ones or missionaries), we must study the history of anti-Semitism between the Jewish people and the Christian Church. Unfortunately, a long and bloody period of history in which the so-called Church persecuted the Jewish people has resulted in an intense distrust of anything Christian.

Ask my son, Shmuel! He tells me that in school, the teachers often mention Notzrim (Hebrew for Christians), but usually in the context of Christians being one of the 'enemies' of the Jewish people. So intense is their avoidance of Christianity that even in the subject of mathematics, Israeli students do not use the symbol of a cross as a plus sign, but only a 'half cross'.

Orthodox Christians in Israel during Easter

Most Jewish people despise Christianity because of the horrors that have been perpetrated against the Jews in the name of 'Jesus Christ'. The Crusaders, the Spanish inquisition, the Russian pogroms, and even the Holocaust were all associated with

Christian anti-Semitism. In fact, some of the early Church fathers were the worst anti-Semites of all! [8] And so, some followers of Yeshua prefer to keep their faith a private affair.

Enemies of the Gospel but Beloved for the Fathers' sake

We must always remember, though, that even if those who persecute us are enemies of the gospel, they are still beloved for the sake of the Fathers.[9] But the intensity of their hatred and zealousness to oppose the gospel and any of Yeshua's emissaries can be intimidating if not downright frightening.

A congregation in Be'er Sheva was surrounded and attacked when the Orthodox religious Jews of the

---

[8] See books describing the history of Christian anti-Semitism such as 'Our Hands are Stained with Blood' written by Michael Brown.
[9] Romans 11:28

city heard that baptisms were taking place inside. Nursing babes were snatched out of their mothers' arms. Many of the children suffered from nightmares afterwards. Some of the young Jewish zealots said they were only waiting for their rebbe's (Rabbis) consent to kill them (the Messianic believers).

The Word of God does warn us that there will come a time when they think that in killing us, they are doing God a favor.

"They will put you out of the synagogues; yes, the time is coming that whoever kills you will think that he offers God service." (John 16:2)

Indeed, even now they believe that in persecuting Jewish Believers in Yeshua (Jesus), they are doing the will of God, since they consider Yeshua a 'false God' that Christians worship. The Torah speaks strongly against tolerating any kind of false worship or idolatry.[10]

While on a speaking tour in America[11], an Orthodox Jewish man who previously lived in Israel and still had children here, came to the home of the couple hosting us in order to challenge our faith. He looked directly at me and threatened,

"If you ever share Jesus with my children in Jerusalem, I'll break your legs!"

---

[10] Deuteronomy 13:6-10
[11] 2002

It is ironic that many Christians give to Orthodox Jewish causes and ministries - the same ones that have this attitude towards Jewish Believers – brothers and sisters in the Lord. Would you give money to someone who threatened to break your sister's legs or tried to put your brother in prison?

But many Christians do just that, rather than supporting the Messianic Jewish community in the Land. Sadly, this man's daughter was later murdered in a terrorist attack and we never had the opportunity to share the gospel with her.

At a conference in Jerusalem, members of the militant Yad L'achim (a fanatical anti-missionary organization, dedicated to opposing Yeshua and the gospel) infiltrated the meeting, dressed as more moderately religious Jews, and attacked the Believers inside.

This same organization forced a believing couple out of their home by threatening to burn it down. These are just a few recent examples of persecution that I, personally, am aware of. I'm sure there are many, many more.

And so, although we Jewish Believers are not yet imprisoned and tortured for our faith, as some are in Muslim nations and other parts of the world, still - the persecution in Israel is not theoretical; it is very real.

And the fear of this persecution can cause us to become as quiet as field mice about the Lord if we're not careful.

True Confessions

I remember a mighty woman of God who helped us make aliyah[12]. She heard my testimony at a conference on our first day in the Land and offered us her own apartment in Netanya as temporary accommodation until we could get settled. This was a tremendous answer to prayer! Roni's mission was to help Believers make aliyah and to be a blessing to the Body of Messiah in the Land through prayer and intercession as well as practically and materially.

Going out with her one day, however, we noticed something strange. Whenever we tried to mention the name of Yeshua, she hushed us and looked around furtively. She had moved into an apartment in the old city of Jerusalem, the Jewish quarter, which is populated by many of the religious community. Here, it was even worse – we were not allowed to mention anything about Yeshua even in her own home, lest any of her neighbors overheard and discovered in Whom she believed.

We thought, as the '*new kids on the* block', that we just didn't understand yet how things work in Israel. But shortly thereafter, this precious woman declared that Yeshua was no longer relevant in her life and she dissociated herself from anyone professing faith in Him. Silence can be deadly. It can cost us our eternal salvation.

I am not sitting here on my lofty seat of righteousness, pointing my finger at those who fear

---

[12] Aliyah – to immigrate to Israel

to openly confess their faith. I am examining the plank in my own eye first. This has required for me a time of soul searching; of wrestling with God through this issue of fear of man.

There exists but one way of avoiding persecution and that is, "*Keep our mouth shut!*" If we never confess our faith in Yeshua with our mouths, but only keep it in our hearts, then no one will ever know, and consequently no one will ever care to persecute us (at least not for our faith). Obviously this is not an option for anyone truly committed to the Lord.

The Word of God states that if we confess with our mouth the Lord Yeshua and believe in our heart that God has raised Him from the dead, we will be saved... **"For with the mouth confession is made unto salvation."** (Romans 10:9-10)

Yeshua also said this about people who refuse to confess Him before men: **"Therefore whoever confesses Me before men, him I will also confess before My Father who is in heaven. But whoever denies Me before men, him I will also deny before My Father who is in heaven."** (Matthew 10:32-33)

 If we are seeking approval, acceptance and praise of men, even the religious community (with whom we may identify and of whom we may even have great love for), then we have become man pleasers and not God pleasers. By this we have essentially ceased in serving as a faithful bondservant of the Lord.

The apostle Paul said, **"For if I still pleased men, I would not be a bondservant of Messiah."** (Galatians 1:10)

If anyone could boast of suffering from persecution, it was Paul (Shaul in Hebrew). He was one who knew the story from both sides – first persecutor and then persecuted. Paul had been chief among those religious zealots who persecuted the Jewish Believers, (those who followed 'The Way'), to death, binding and delivering men and women into prisons. But suddenly the Light penetrated the darkness. He fell to the ground and heard a voice saying, **"Shaul, Shaul, why are you persecuting Me?"** (Acts 22:7-8)

Yeshua revealed the truth that those who persecute His children are in actuality persecuting the Lord, Yeshua of Nazteret (Nazareth). This life changing event transformed Shaul, the persecutor, into Paul the persecuted. He could have remained silent with his testimony and avoided all the suffering he endured, but he chose to serve the Lord, to please and obey Him rather than man.

When commissioned by the Holy Spirit to testify in Jerusalem, his brethren pleaded with him not to go, knowing the suffering he would face there, but Paul said, **"What do you mean by weeping and breaking my heart? For I am ready not only to be bound, but also to die at Jerusalem for the name of the Lord Yeshua."** (Acts 21:13)

How did Shaul overcome his fears of persecution? He had seen the Light. He had heard the Voice. He had gained the perspective of eternity.

Persecution not only comes against Jewish Believers from our fellow Jews; we must keep in mind that Christians are suffering all over the world for their faith in Yeshua. Many are being tortured, imprisoned, and even martyred by their non-believing countrymen. Yeshua promised us this, **"And you will be hated by all for My name's sake. But he who endures to the end will be saved."** (Matthew 10:22)

As they hated Him, so must we expect to be hated. For the servant is not above the master [13]. As He suffered, so must we expect to most likely suffer, if we follow His example and walk in His footsteps. This promise is just as sure as the one that He came to bring us life and life more abundantly[14]. Some preach only abundance, blessing and prosperity, but we must keep a balanced perspective – Yeshua also warned us that in this life we would suffer trials and tribulations as well. (John 16:33)

Overcomers Inherit the Kingdom

Why do I keep harping on and on about persecution? Is it to inspire fear? No, it is to cause us to face our fears, since persecution is something that all of us, in these End Times, will be required to face. It is a test we must pass in order to be called 'overcomers' and inherit the Kingdom of God.

"He who overcomes shall inherit all things, and I will be his God and he shall be My son." (Revelation 21:7)

The next line goes on to say that the 'cowardly' (as well as the unbelievers, abominable, murderers, sexually immoral, sorcerers, idolaters, and liars) will

---

[13] **(see John 15: 20)**
[14] **(see John 10: 10)**

not inherit the kingdom but rather will have their part in the lake of fire. Obviously, fear is an issue we need to deal with head on.

Shmuley Boteach, rabbi and author of <u>Face Your Fear</u>, said this, "*Don't be pushed by fear. Be pulled by promise.*"

We are all running the race set out before us. But do we run for the prize, straining towards the promised reward? Or are we being driven by fears? Fear of insignificance, fear of financial lack, and fear of loneliness....many fears can drive us to run; but these are hard taskmasters, like Pharaoh of Egypt. If we are under his whip, then we are not free; but if we are being led by the Holy Spirit, then we are running with joy for the prize set before us.[15]

Running for the Promise with JOY!

God gave me this picture that illustrates the difference. When I come home after being out, my little dog runs down the hallway to greet me. You can just see his joy in the way he bounces and leaps to greet me. It is so much fun to watch him run his little heart out just to be close to me and to be with me again, even after just a short absence.

But when we went for a walk in the woods, he seemed to be afraid of every little noise and rustle in the bushes. Now what if a bear appeared and began

---

[15] (see Hebrews 12: 1 - 2)

to chase him? He would surely run just as fast, but this time, his running is fear-based, not joy-based.

Why are we running our race? I think this is a good question to ask ourselves as we search our hearts for an honest answer. How do we truly feel about running our race? Do we have joy and delight? Or are we running scared?

When she was a little girl, my daughter, Liat, had been laboring at a certain computer game for quite some time. Apparently, the goal was to successfully complete various tasks in order to receive more and more 'keys'. Once all the keys are collected, the child 'wins' the prize. Liat did not know what the prize actually consisted of, but she was determined to win it. She would not give up until she had collected the keys.

Each time she worked on the game, her excitement mounted as she drew closer and closer to obtaining the prize. Finally, that moment came! And what happened? Not much... The horse and its little mouse rider approached a locked gate, used the keys to open it, and rode off into the sunset. The end.

"*That's it?!*" Liat cried in righteous indignation. She couldn't believe that after all her labor, this boring scene was the 'prize' that she had won at the end. She felt betrayed, cheated & tricked.

Perhaps some of us worry about it ending up this way when we pass through those pearly gates into heaven. After all the persecution we will endure - after faithfully standing through each trial and persevering through every form of tribulation - will we end up disappointed? Will we look around us and cry, "*I've been shafted, cheated, hoodwinked!*"? I think not.

Yeshua possesses the key of David and with it, we have the right to enter through the gates into the city and have the right to the tree of life! (Revelation 22:14) **"Open to me the gates of righteousness; I will go through them, and I will praise the Lord. This is the gate of the Lord, through which the righteous shall enter."** (Psalm 118:19-20).

Yeshua is the gate for the sheep. Whoever enters by him will be saved and find pasture. (John 10:7, 9) When we go through that gate, I highly doubt if we're going to have a look and say, like Liat, "*Ho Hum, how boring.*" The Word promises that God has more for us than we could ever possibly imagine, even in our wildest dreams.[16]

"Eye has not seen, nor ear heard, nor have entered into the heart of man the things which God has prepared for those who love him." (1 Corinthians 2:9)

If we do not believe this by faith, we may never possess the courage and strength we will need to stand up under persecution that is here now and will increase in these End Times. Yes, it will all be worth it! We must hold onto our confidence.

Men and women performed many great and mighty exploits by faith as described in Hebrews chapter 11: **"Women received their dead raised to life again."** (Heb. 11:35).

I would like to be one of these mighty women of faith with access to this resurrection power who see the dead raised to life. But we must consider the whole picture:

"Others (women?) were tortured, not accepting deliverance, that they might obtain a better resurrection." (Hebrews 11:35)

Hannah & Her Sons

In the book of the Macabbees, we read about a woman named Hannah who had seven sons. Rather than accept deliverance, they all chose martyrdom, that they might obtain a better resurrection.

---

[16] Ephesians 3:20

As she watched in anguish, each of Hannah's sons were tortured and killed. When it came to the youngest, the king urged the mother to convince the little boy to submit in order to save his life and receive riches and honor as a reward. Instead, this Jewish mother laughed scornfully at the king and spoke thus to her only remaining son:

"My son, I beg you to remember that God created the heaven and the earth and everything in it. We have no existence without Him. Fear not this butcher, but proving thyself worthy of thy brothers, accept death so that by God's mercy I will receive all of you back again."

Hannah and her youngest son were then executed together. They did not fear man, who could only kill their bodies, more than God who has the power to cast their souls into Sheol (hell).[17]

We also may be persecuted and suffer, but we need not fear, for the Lord has said to us, **"Be faithful, even unto death, and I will give you the crown of life."** (Rev. 2:10)

The Crown of Life

Blessed is the man who perseveres under trial, because when he has stood the test, he will receive the crown of life that God has promised to those who love him.

James 1:12

---

[17] **(see Matthew 10: 28)**

I once heard it said that any Believer who fears death does not really know where he is going after he dies. Do we have this assurance? Yeshua promised us that whoever believes in him, though we may die, yet we shall live! Do we truly believe this? (John 11:25-26).

What will be our response to persecution because of our faith? Will we allow God to examine us, to search us for any hidden fears, so that we might be prepared to face the End Times when this persecution does come into full force?

"Search me, O God, and know my heart; Try me, and know my anxieties; (fears) and see if there is any wicked way in me, and lead me in the way everlasting." (Psalms 139:23-24)

Bad Hair Days & Other Calamities

Fear is not limited to persecution; and not all our fears are life threatening. One morning my then eleven year old son, Timothy (Shmuel in Hebrew), came under attack by fear. Fear of what? His hair. The night before, I had tried out my new, handy dandy hair clipping kit, bought for the outstanding price of sixty shekels at the shook (market). I was so proud of my increasing ability to bargain with the Middle Eastern merchants. I paid only ten more shekels than what the guy originally told me was the price of fifty shekels. (don't ask... ☺)

Anyways, I thought of all the money I would save by cutting the family's hair myself rather than use the barber. I finally convinced Timothy that Mom is really a professional hair dresser in disguise and would make him look fantastic. And he trusted me.

But those _____ clippers wouldn't work and I botched the job and, well, needless to say, Timothy of necessity wore a hat to school that morning.

As he got ready for school, he kept saying over and over again, *"I'm scared. I'm scared. I'm scared."*
"What are you scared of?" I asked.
"The kids." he replied.

He was scared that the kids at school would tease him when he got a look at his 'home made' hairstyle. I challenged him to stop chanting fear and to start speaking the Word, **"God has not given us a spirit of fear, but of power and of love and of a sound mind."** (2 Timothy 1:7)

Whether our fears are as seemingly trivial as Timothy's fear of a bad hair day; or as serious as fear of martyrdom, we need to deal with our fears lest they stop us from doing the will of our Father in Heaven.

How do we deal with our fears? We may either:
1) run
2) hide or
3) stand and fight.

Scattercats

I have noticed that the cats in our village manifesting these three distinct reactions to the threat of attack. When Sheba, my cat-chasing dog indulged in her favorite pastime, I watched the neighborhood cats resort to one of these three options.

1. The first is most common – they run like the dickens as soon as they see her coming! Scrambling madly up a tree, barreling into a thorn bush, or diving into a garbage can – anything becomes a potential place of refuge – as long as it takes them out of Sheba's reach. There's a time to run!

2. The second feline reaction is quite pitiful to behold. The cat curls up with a dour expression on its miserable face, and hopes the dog will simply go away. Perhaps it is living in denial, pretending the dog doesn't really exist, or perhaps the fat old cat is just too stubborn to move.

Nevertheless, this is a dangerous position to assume, since this cat is at Sheba's mercy, which could potentially attack at any time. The cat is also going nowhere as long as Sheba is around.

Fear can cause us to become stuck as well. My then five year old daughter, Liat, got a new bike which she loved to ride around the village. There were times, however, when she would ride into a rut and although she was still peddling like mad, the back tire simply spun in mid air and she 'ain't going nowhere fast'. So, too, when we are held in bondage to fear, we may be working like crazy, busy all the time, and yet we seem to make no progress.

There may be a time for hiding, for covering and for keeping quiet. Esther was commanded by her cousin Mordechai who raised her, not to reveal her identity as a Jewess to anyone when she came into the King's house. (Esther 2:10)

But Esther did not hide her identity out of fear; but rather, in obedience to Mordechai (symbolizing the Holy Spirit who tells us when to speak and when to remain silent). Esther's silence was only temporarily in order to fulfill a very specific purpose. She would courageously unveil her identity in God's perfect timing, again in obedience Mordechai (Holy Spirit) in order to bring salvation to her people.[18]

If we are hiding our identity as Believers we must ask ourselves, *"Am I remaining quiet about this out of fear of persecution and rejection, out of cowardice, or out of a heart of obedience to the Holy Spirit – until such a time as this?"* (Esther 4:13-14) Perhaps only the Holy Spirit can reveal the true motives of our hearts.

3. The third and most amazing feline response is the cat who, although small in comparison to her much larger opponent, hunches up her

---

[18] See book by author, <u>Messiah Revealed in Purim</u> or DVD <u>Esther's Last Call to the Church</u> www.voiceforisrael.net

back, sticks out her hair in every direction and gives a loud, clearly defined 'HISS!!!!!!!!!" sound, followed by snarls, yowls and growls. I've yet to see Sheba pursue a cat who takes this bold stance.

On another morning, I saw a cat with the chutzpah (Yiddish expression for 'the nerve') to stand up to Sheba in just this manner. When Sheba's muzzle came close enough for the kitten to feel her hot breath, she shifted in an instant back to plan A and took off like a shot up the nearest tree.

Sheba could easily have caught her and devoured the kitten in a single gulp but didn't – proving she's in it for the chase only, not for the kill. This may prove to be the one essential difference between this kitten's adversary, Sheba, and our own – the devil is not playing games; he goes for the kill: **"Be sober, be vigilant; because your adversary the devil walks about like a roaring lion, seeking whom he may devour."**(1 Peter 5:8)

This scripture was given in relation to the sufferings of the Body of Messiah in the world. Yeshua said that the thief comes only to steal, to kill and to destroy. (John 10:10) Therefore, we cannot be careless in dealing with this issue.

If the thought of standing up under persecution fills us with dread, I believe we need to confront this spirit of fear, which is not of the Spirit of God. We need to stop being so defensive all the time and get on the offence! The righteous are bold as a lion[19], not timid little mice.

I believe we must also take this bold stance against the spirit of fear – whether that be fear of man, fear of persecution, fear of rejection, or some other fear that holds us in bondage. If we run, we will be running all our lives and at the mercy of this tormenting spirit. We will never simply stand and obediently do what God has commanded us.

If we pretend the fear doesn't exist, we will always be held at bay, never being able to progress, in case we are found out. But if we stand firm, hunch our back, mess up our hair and snarl, "BACK OFF, JACK!!!" to that spirit of fear, we may very well find to our surprise that as we have resisted the devil, he has left us.[20]

Fear will never be cured through appeasement or compromise. We can't give in to fear by giving it what it demands.

---

[19] Proverbs 28:1

[20] James 4: 7(b)

There is a time for running. Yeshua said that when they persecute them in one city they should flee to another. (Matt. 10:23) He also foretold of a time when His followers in Judea would need to flee to the mountains when they see the abomination of desolation in the holy place. (Matt. 24:16) Yes, there is a time to run; but there is also a time to refrain from running – a time to boldly take our stand.

HAIRY MACLARY

Our youngest son, Avi-ad, had a favorite book that he loved for us to read together called <u>Hairy Maclary Scattercat</u>. [21] Hairy Maclary, a frisky, cat-chasing dog, chased Greywacke Jones high up into a sycamore tree, chased Butterball Brown under a door, chased Pimpernel Pugh over a wall, chased Slinky Malinky into a drum full of weeds, and chased Mushroom Magee through a hole in the hedge – until the day he met his match...

That day finally came when Scarface Claw, looking like he's been around the block a time or two (and is not about to stand for any monkey business), chased Hairy Maclary - all the way home! That was Avi's favourite part. ☺ Perhaps now has come the time to say,

"I'm not going to be Greywacke Jones any longer, nor Butterball Brown, Pimpernel Hugh, or Slinky Malinki for that matter. No Mushroom Magee for me either; 'cause here I come – SCARFACE CLAW – and fear, you are going to stop chasing me; I'm going to chase you – all the way home!"

---

[21] Hairy Maclary Scattercat by Lynley Dodd

<u>Closing prayer:</u> Dear God, thank you that You have not given us a spirit of fear; but of power, love and a sound mind. But Father, You know that there are times when we are tempted to give in to fear. You know the fears that torment us and rob us of our peace – even preventing us from having a good night's sleep. We may have all sorts of fears and anxieties about so many, many things, Lord; and yet You have promised us a peace that passes all understanding.

You have commanded us, just as You commanded Joshua, to be strong and of good courage. Your Word says that as we wait upon You, trust in You and continue to believe, You will strengthen our heart and give us the courage to overcome. Please give us wisdom to know when to run and hide, when to ignore; and when to stand and fight. Help us to forgive and pray for those who persecute us.

Thank you that we are always safe and secure in You —resting in Your shadow and finding shelter under the refuge of Your wings.

I will both lay me down in peace, and sleep: for thou, LORD, only makest me dwell in safety.

Psalms 4:8

and don't forget your prayers!
Good night!

Meow from Israel!

John 16:33
I have said this to you,
so that in me you may have peace. In the
world you face persecution. But take
courage; I have conquered the world!"

יוחנן טז
33אָמַרְתִּי לָכֶם אֶת הַדְּבָרִים הָאֵלֶּהכְּדֵי שֶׁבִּי יִהְיֶה לָכֶם שָׁלוֹם.
בָּעוֹלָם – צָרָה לָכֶם, אַךְ הִתְעוֹדְדוּ:
אֲנִי נִצַּחְתִּי אֶת הָעוֹלָם.יי

תהלים לד:ה
דָּרַשְׁתִּי אֶת־יְהוָה וְעָנָנִי וּמִכָּל־מְגוּרוֹתַי הִצִּילָנִי

"I sought the LORD,
and he heard me, and delivered me
from all my fears."

Psalms 34:4

CHAPTER TWENTY-EIGHT

SHEKET! BE STILL!

A Devotional on 'When Rebuking the Storm Doesn't Work'

Jesus stilling the tempest, painting by James Tissot, Brooklyn Museum

"And He got up and rebuked the wind and said to the sea, "*Sheket (quiet) be still.*" And the wind died down and it became perfectly calm." (Mark 4:39)

I love the story about Yeshua rebuking the wind and the waves in the midst of a violent storm at sea. There arose a 'fierce gale of wind', the water was filling the boat; and the disciples of Yeshua thought they were goners for sure! Yeshua, completely unperturbed, remained asleep (on a cushion yet) in the boat until his disciples woke Him up, saying, *"Master, don't you care that we are about to perish?"*

I would say this describes most of my adult life – going back and forth from one side of the shore to the other, most often facing fierce, gale-force winds and boat-capsizing sized waves in the middle. The thought comes to me that *'this time I'm not going to make it for sure'*; and when, in my desperation, I look for Yeshua for help - it seems He is blissfully snoring away the crisis.

We love it when we can say, *"I rebuke this storm in the name of Yeshua Hamashiach[1]!"* and we experience a wonderful 'sheket' (quiet) as the wind and waves become perfectly calm once more. But what about when it just doesn't work? If we are honest, there are times (more often than we may care to admit) when all our rebuking seems to have no effect whatsoever on the storms raging in our life. How do we deal with this seeming 'failure' in our prayers of authority over the wind and waves?

---

[1] Yeshua Hamashiach – Jesus the Messiah

I am reminded of the day my eldest daughter, Courtney, was about to be wed to her beloved Emanuel. It was going to be the most beautiful wedding that Jerusalem had ever seen or experienced in her entire  history! Well, at least that's the way we perceived it. First of all, because Courtney was the most beautiful bride ever; and Emanuel surely the most handsome bridegroom. Truly! ☺

Emanuel, as an amazingly gifted music composer and talented videographer, had choreographed the entire event. His originally composed music matched perfectly with each step we would take down the stairs as we would walk towards the chuppah (wedding canopy). The outdoor setting near the promenade in Jerusalem, overlooking the valley, was as beautiful as it was perfect.

Emanuel's mother, Batya, being especially talented in all things bright and beautiful had finished with all the lovely decorations. Courtney's gorgeous, classic, wedding dress had been picked out, the guests had been invited, and we were all set – or so we thought – until the storm blew in.

I received a phone call from a tearful Courtney early on the morning of her intended wedding day. Through her sobbing, I managed to catch the gist of what she was saying: *"The wedding is off!"* *"Why??"* I asked. *"The storm has ruined everything!"* Courtney replied.

We all ran down to the scene of the carnage and witnessed firsthand how the fierce winds had torn down all Batya's beautiful decorations and the pouring rains had drenched everything in sight. Not to be defeated by a simple storm; and mighty, prayer warriors that we thought were, we began to rebuke the storm.

Shimon, Emanuel's stepfather, just happened to be the Pastor of one of the largest, most vibrant, Spirit-filled Messianic congregations in Jerusalem at the time. So he led the way: *"We rebuke you – in the name of Yeshua Hamashiach! We command this wind and rain to stop NOW!"*

We all chimed in – shouting and rebuking until our rebukers were plain worn out! The more we called for sheket (quiet) the worse the storm seemed to become. Eventually we simply gave up and went home, dejected, wondering whatever had happened to our *'authority in Christ'*?

Meanwhile, a great miracle happened in the Holy City that day. Somehow, Batya was able to find an indoor venue for the wedding at the very last moment and against all odds, they were able to move the entire event into Binyunei Ha'uma – a large auditorium in central Jerusalem that was secured by several Israeli armed guards. The wedding was still on – halleluyah!

With a great sense of relief, Courtney, Batya and I went downtown to get our hair and makeup done professionally at a salon. While in the process of becoming 'beautified' for the occasion, we heard a loud 'boom!', followed by the radio blaring its report that a suicide bomber had just blown himself up at a location very near to us in downtown Jerusalem.

The hairstylist immediately hollered for someone to turn off the radio. *"There is a bride in here, people! She doesn't want to hear about suicide bombings on her wedding day!"* So that was the last we heard about the incident – until after the wedding....

It was a lovely affair and everything went off with the usual minor glitches: the flower girl, sweet little Victoria, ran out of petals before the end of the runway so, after stopping and looking perplexed for a few moments, she just 'faked it', tossing out imaginary blossoms until she reached her end position. The ring bearer, my middle son, Timothy, couldn't find the ring for a few tense moments. Yes, this is the same Victoria that Timothy later fell in love with and chose for his own beautiful bride (but that's another story....)

Timothy and Victoria (Vicki) wedding photo, Israel, 2014

Once Emanuel had 'kissed the bride' and they had danced their beautifully choreographed dance together, we all sat down to enjoy the delicious meal. This is when we found out from one of the guests who had connections with the Mossad[2] (Israeli Secret Service); that they had been tracking this suicide bomber (who blew himself up in downtown Jerusalem near the hair salon) for quite some time.

The day of the wedding, they had followed him to the very site of Courtney & Emanuel's outdoor wedding. Apparently, when this terrorist saw that the site had been devastated by the storm and that obviously no guests were arriving (for him to murder), he changed

---

[2] Mossad is responsible for <u>intelligence collection</u>, <u>covert operations</u>, and <u>counterterrorism</u>, as well as bringing <u>Jews</u> to Israel from countries where official <u>Aliyah</u> agencies are forbidden, and protecting Jewish communities.

his mind and carried out his terrible deed in a different location.

We were shocked – but also incredibly thankful that God had refused to answer our prayers! Had it gone our way - had the storm stopped and the wedding resumed at its originally intended location – we might not be here today to tell the story. Had Yeshua rebuked the wind and rain and caused sheket to come that wedding day – it may very well have been a disaster beyond comprehension.

Because God turned a deaf ear to our pleas for the storm to cease, Courtney and Emanuel have been married for fifteen years; and now have four beautiful children (my grandchildren). A whole new generation of Messianic Jewish believers are growing up strong and healthy in the Land of our forefathers because God, in His mercy, allowed a storm to ruin the way that we had planned, in order to save us!

 We can thank God, not only for the prayers He answers; but also those that, in His infinite wisdom, He chooses not to answer according to 'our way'.

I think of this now, as I walk through my current 'storm' of sickness, disability and discouragement over unanswered prayer. When every fiber of my being just wants Yeshua to shout, "SHEKET!!" to the wind and waves in my life and make everything perfectly calm, I remember this story; and I say,

"Thank you God that Your ways are so much higher than my imperfect ways and your grand thoughts infinitely higher than my own petty thoughts." [3]

God sees things that with our limited vision, we can't possibly see. He knows the end from the beginning. He has our very best and highest good in mind; and He is still on the Throne. Only He can cause all things to work together for our good.

We may not always understand why God allows the storms of life to rage on without an end in sight; and yet - in this as in all things – we can trust Him, declaring, **"*Though you slay me yet will I trust You*."** (Job 13:15)

Prayer: Yeshua, sometimes I get frustrated and upset when faced with a fierce storm while you seem to be asleep in my flimsy boat. There are times when I also cry out with faulty faith, *"Master, don't you care that I am perishing?!"* But the truth is that You always care about us; and You are both willing and able to help us in our times of need. Thank you for Your Word that reminds us of Your power and authority to calm the same seas that You walked upon. Help us learn to simply be still and to draw our strength from quietness; trusting in God's faithfulness and mercy – even in the middle of the storms of life. Amen v'Amen.

---

[3] Isaiah 55:9

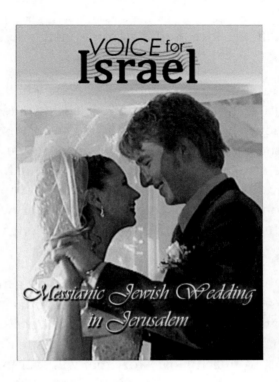

Messianic Jewish Wedding in Jerusalem

Emanuel Nahum is one of the most unusual young men you will ever meet. Born in Austria, raised in Tel Aviv and Jerusalem, he began composing classical music as a small child, and even as a young teen was performing before the highest government officials in the Israeli Knesset. He helped lead powerful, anointed praise and worship at KMJ, his parents' Messianic congregation in the heart of Jerusalem as well as composing music for Hollywood.

When Courtney, Hannah's eldest daughter, first walked into the congregation and heard Emanuel sing, she thought she was listening to the worship of angels. It was love at first sight! A match made in heaven!

When Emanuel met Courtney Rebecca, who had immigrated to Israel from Canada as a teenager, he knew her to be the love of his life. They both had taken the 'true love waits' vow at an early age and now determined to wait until their wedding for even their first kiss! Their wedding is a triumph and a testimony to young people and singles everywhere of the virtues of sexual purity. Here's what one young woman said,

Emanuel choreographed the entire wedding and composed much of the music himself for his bride. In the ancient city of Jerusalem, city of our God, this wedding brings the viewer into an exquisite drama of the most wonderful love story that will ever take place -that of the Messiah, the Bridegroom, coming upon the call of the shofar to re-unite with His beloved and beautiful *Bride.*

The most wonderful part of the story is a real life miracle - God actually created a terrible tempest to force the re-location of the wedding ceremony at the last minute in order to avert a likely terrorist attack. Come be enraptured by the pure love expressed in this Messianic Jewish wedding in Jerusalem.

"Yet again there shall be heard... in the cities of Judah, and in the streets of Jerusalem.   The voice of joy and the voice of gladness, the voice of the bridegroom and the voice of the bride." (Jeremiah 33:10-11)

Od Yishama
b'harei Yehudah
Uv'chutzot Yerushalayim

Kol sason v'kol simcha
Kol chatan v'kol kalah

עוֹד יִשָּׁמַע
בְּעָרֵי יְהוּדָה
וּבְחֻצוֹת יְרוּשָׁלַיִם

קוֹל שָׂשׂוֹן וְקוֹל שִׂמְחָה
קוֹל חָתָן וְקוֹל כַּלָּה

Rabbi officiating at Jewish wedding www.goisrael.com

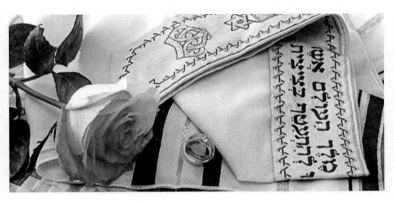

CHAPTER TWENTY-NINE
A SHELTER OF GARBAGE
A Devotional on God's Protection

"For in the day of trouble he will keep me safe in his dwelling; he will hide me in the shelter of his sacred tent (sukkah) and set me high upon a rock." (Psalms 27:5)

A curious mystery emerged in our household this past week – the mystery of the moveable garbage. I was sure I had set out several bags of garbage by the door in the evening; but by the next morning, I found it all piled up in a heap in the middle of the living room. How could it have moved? My first assumption was that my husband, who has asked me more times than I'd like to admit to NOT put the garbage behind the door (as if I have anywhere else to put it...), had thrown all the bags of garbage into the living room in a fit of frustration. But surprisingly, it was not my husband who moved the garbage.

Then it must have been my teenage son, I thought, "*You know teenagers and their hormone- induced moods and strange behaviors.*" But no, Timothy hadn't done it either. So we went on down the line, asking everyone how the garbage could have moved from the door, down the hall and into the middle of the living room. Finally, it was our youngest son, Avi-ad, who confessed to the dastardly deed.

"*Why did you do it?*" we asked him. Looking a little sheepish, he admitted that he had heard some strange noises in the early morning before anyone else was awake - noises that sounded to him like ghosts, and so he became frightened.

"*But what does this have to do with the garbage?*" I asked.

"*It was my shelter*", he explained.

In his sweet and silly way, Avi had constructed a shelter for himself out of whatever was nearest at hand – which just happened to be the bags of garbage – to protect himself from the scariness of life – ghosts and all. We tried not to laugh, because even though his 'shelter of garbage' was absurdly inadequate as a fortress against powers of darkness, we didn't want to hurt his feelings.

Later, I began to see how I, at times, do something equally silly – I attempt to construct my own flimsy shelter to protect me from the things that frighten me instead of relying on the shelter that God has provided for us.

"The Lord יהוה is my rock and my fortress and my deliverer; My God my strength, in whom I will trust; my shield and the horn of my salvation, my stronghold. I will call upon the Lord who is worthy to be praised; so shall I be saved from my enemies." (Psalms 18:2)

But instead of relying on the Lord to protect, defend and save us, we may try to put together our own pathetic little fortresses – shelters of garbage. We cover ourselves with shame, guilt and condemnation to hide from the things that frighten us - from the pain of rejection and failure, from our inability to deal with the sin in our lives.

We hide under a frail shelter of passivity, refusing to confront the manipulation and control which the Lord instructs us to stand against in liberty and freedom. We put walls up around our heart – impenetrable walls of bitterness, hatred, resentment and unforgiveness - wrongly thinking that these things will protect us from further hurt and pain in relationships. We hide in our isolation.

The Word of God says that His name, יהוה, is a strong tower; the righteous run into it and are safe.

(Proverbs 18:10) He is the One who will hide us in the shelter of His wings if we are willing to run to Him instead of hiding from Him when we are in trouble.

Yeshua wept over Jerusalem, *"Yirushalayim, Yirushalayim, the one who kills the prophets and stones those who are sent to her! How often I wanted to gather your children together, as a hen gathers her chicks under her wings, but you were not willing!"* (Matthew 23:37)

How sad to read of Yeshua's longing to protect Jerusalem's children; and their unwillingness to come under the shelter He wanted to provide. Yeshua forewarned that their house would lie desolate until they would say, *"Baruch Habah B'shem Adonai"* (Blessed is He who comes in the name of the Lord יהוה).

This Hebrew phrase, 'baruch habah', is another way of saying *'welcome'*. Until we welcome Him and run under the shelter of His wings, we will remain desolate. Once we take courage, throw off the bags of garbage and face the scary things in our lives, we will find comfort and peace.

We must stop grabbing what is nearest at hand – a smoke, a drink, a drug, an immoral relationship, the gossip line on the phone, or even the tub of ice cream and bag of chips (comfort food) – and instead run into our heavenly Abba (Daddy's) arms, singing:

"You are my hiding place; You always fill my heart with songs of deliverance. Whenever I am afraid I will trust in You. I will trust in You. Let the weak say I am strong in the strength of the Lord." [1]

While living in Israel, we lived with the constant threat of enemy attacks, bomb threats and the danger of terrorism. No one (it seemed) was safe, since any bus, any café, any gathering of Jewish people was a potential mark for suicide bombers. Anyone could be a potential terrorist – even someone we had lived beside and worked with for years. One day he could decide to run over a group of pedestrians waiting at a bus stop; or stab a husband out buying groceries for his pregnant wife.

But we lived there without fear, knowing that our lives are in the hands of the Almighty – El Elyon and all of our days appointed for us are in His book of Life. One day I picked up a religious Jewish woman who was hitchhiking. Her parents had made aliyah (immigrated to Israel) and now she was raising her own children in the Land. I asked her, *"Are you not afraid to hitchhike?"* She answered, I do not fear – not the Arabs and not hitchhiking and not living in Israel - because I know my God is with me.

More and more today, it seems like fear attempts to rule our daily lives – if it's not the threat of terrorism, it's the bird flu or some other kind of plague that everyone is worried about. And if it's not

---

[1] <u>You are my Hiding Place,</u> **Michael Ledner** **(Psalm 32;6-8)**

terrorism or plagues, then it is the predicted financial collapse. I cannot even shop for my groceries now without hearing over the speaker system about all the diseases that they say we are likely to contract if we're not careful – diabetes, breast cancer, skin cancer, heart disease – you name it, they'll warn you about it.

Fear can become a part of our consciousness without even realizing it. The news certainly doesn't help matters with all its reports of kids killing kids in schools, political unrest, and all manner of murder and violence in our cities and countries. Recently, terrorists (mostly in the name of ISIS) have carried out terrible attacks in Western countries as well: a vehicle ramming in New York city, a bomb exploding on a London subway, van ramming in Barcelona and London, attack outside an Ariana Grande concert in Manchester, England; and on and on...

It feels like the days of Noah again with all this evil and violence surrounding us. And as if this wasn't enough; fires, floods, hurricanes and other natural disasters have been destroying property and lives around the world. So how can we find protection from all these threats and dangers?

Psalm 91 promises that those who dwell in the secret place of Elyon shall abide under the shadow of Shadai and nothing shall come near us – not plague, nor pestilence; not terrorism nor warfare. It shall not come near us.

"He shall cover you with His feathers and under His wings you shall take refuge." (Psalm 91:4)

God does not promise us a trouble-free life; but He has given us the power of His name as a strong citadel of protection. One week everyone was getting the stomach flu. Both my kids had it, then my husband got it and after that, even the dog had the characteristic vomiting and diarrhea. I always boasted that mothers don't get sick, but one night I felt my stomach start to cramp. I lay there moaning and groaning, scared that I too was succumbing to the flu. But through the night, the Lord brought this scripture to mind,

"Because you have made the Lord, who is my refuge, even the Most High (Elyon), your dwelling place, no evil shall befall you, nor shall any plague come near your dwelling; (Psalm 91:9-10)

Something rose up in me and I began to speak out loud these word, *"I dwell in the secret place of the Most High God, El Elyon and abide under the shadow of El Shaddai. The Lord is my refuge, therefore no evil shall befall me and no plague, no sickness and no flu shall come anywhere near me! In the name of Yeshua Hamashiach!"* [2]

I was truly amazed when all the stomach pains disappeared immediately and never came back to bother me again. Halleluyah!

---

[2] Jesus the Messiah

I wish I could say I do this all the time but I don't. Too often I use Avi's kind of childish shelters instead of walking in 'child-like' dependence on the refuge of God. But what freedom and light we would experience if we could tear down our weak and flimsy man-made shelters and instead trust in Adonai, saying,

"For You have been a shelter for me, A strong tower from the enemy, I will abide in Your tabernacle forever, I will trust in the shelter of Your wings." (Psalm 61:3-4)

For You have been
a shelter for me,
A strong tower
from the enemy.
I will abide
in Your tabernacle forever;
I will trust
in the shelter of Your wings.
(Psalm 61:3-4)

4כִּי־הָיִיתָ מַחְסֶה לִי מִגְדַּל־עֹז מִפְּנֵי אוֹיֵב:
5 אָגוּרָה בְאָהָלְךָ עוֹלָמִים אֶחֱסֶה בְסֵתֶר כְּנָפֶיךָ סֶּלָה:

תהלים סא

Prayer: Thank you Adonai that you are my shelter, my refuge and my fortress - my defense, my strong tower against the enemy - and against all the things that scare, trouble, and worry me. I now tear down and throw off all strongholds that have been constructed around me through fear.

Thank you that even when the storms rage and I can't see through the darkness, You are still with me, watching over my life, keeping me safely under the shelter of Your wings.

I know I am Your child and You are my Father ('Avi' אבי) and so I willingly and gratefully come running to you, trusting that You will help and protect me because of Your goodness and faithfulness that never fails.

Your love is forever and mercy is everlasting.

Hodu L'Adonai Ki tov; ki l'olam Chasdo. Amen.

CHAPTER THIRTY

SPRING IN A SNOWSTORM

A Devotional on Faith

"For behold, the winter is past, the rain is over and gone. The flowers appear on the earth; the time of the singing has come." (Song of Solomon 2:11-12)

On April 27th, 2009, it hailed. Yes, hailed. Selah. (Pause and think about that). For all of us Edmontonian Canuks, longing for freedom from our eight-month long winter housebound state, this spring storm came as a bitter blow.

Bad enough when the sun began to hide behind the clouds, casting us back again into that non-descript grayness; bad enough when the first snowflakes began to fall again – but hail?

I could literally feel myself sliding down that slippery slope into my gloomy pit. Notice I had begun to call it *'my pit'*. It had almost become a familiar (if not quite comfortable) abode - the miry clay of depression, despair and hopelessness.

My dog and I sat together, shivering in the cold. You see, I had foolishly thought that spring had finally arrived when I scheduled Pepper's spring haircut for April 20th. But no.......it seemed he still needed his winter coat in this God-forsaken, frozen tundra. Too late. His winter fur was gone. What was I thinking?!

It seems that many of us are experiencing winter storms these days, as our little boats head closer and closer into the end of days as we know it. Everything that can be shaken is shaking. But we have this assurance – Yeshua is in the boat. Just as Yeshua spoke peace (shalom) to the wind and the waves that threatened the lives of His disciples, so can He speak shalom to the storms in our lives as well, bringing a calm that we so desperately need.

"He arose and rebuked the wind, and said unto the sea, "Peace, be still." And the wind ceased and there was a great calm." (Mark 4:37-39)

I don't know about you, but going through the dissolution of my marriage, single parenting at fifty years old, and homeschooling to boot (I know, foolish woman...), I could sure use some of that calm right about now. We fear the storms - those things that force change in our lives. Even if we despise our lives as they are, we still fear the unknown. We panic when the storm comes to destroy that which is familiar to us; and we see it all being swept out into the raging sea.

We wonder what we have done to deserve this trouble? And where is God in all the mess? We cry out, **"Master, don't you care that we are perishing**?" (Mark 4:38)

I love what Kirk Franklin speaks as an introduction to his beautiful CD, <u>Songs for the Storm Volume I</u>:

"The myth is that storms have to do with punishment; that they are God's response to sin, or His disappointment in us as His children. May I suggest that it is actually the opposite - It is the confirmation that we are flowers of the Father, He has planted and He desires for us to grow. No matter how painful or inconvenient, it is necessary – for the flowers' beauty."

His message to us through these songs is, *"Don't be afraid to grow."*

This is the message that I am receiving as well, that I would like to pass on to you, just in case you may be struggling to hold on through a storm raging in your own life. These storms are not to harm us, but to help us grow – in Him. We are not alone in the storms; we have a Savior who hears us when we cry out to Him. We have a God who is faithful to His people.

When our hearts are shattered by the storms of life that have torn it apart; and we wonder when the healing will even begin – He is there. Yehovah Shamah – God is simply *'there'*. God will never take His love away. When we fall, He is there to catch us – underneath are His everlasting arms. Weeping will last for a night but joy will come in the morning. (Psalms 30:5)

The storm comes only to help us grow. God's purpose in the storm is redemptive – to bless us, to do us good, and to bring about restoration.

In her book, <u>Broken Open, How Difficult Times Can Help Us Grow</u>, Elizabeth Lesser writes of her own personal journey through the storms of life. Walking through the Old City of Jerusalem one morning, she came across a beautiful picture of a flower in bloom in a tiny shop in the market.   Under the photo was written this quote:

"And the time came when the risk to remain tight in a bud was more painful that the risk it took to blossom." (Anais Nin)

Perhaps this time has come in my life; maybe it has come in yours - when living half a life is not enough anymore. Time when our soul is crying out to experience the abundant life that is our birthright - when remaining in our tight, safe little bud of merely going through the motions becomes more painful that the risk of breaking open and embracing whatever it will take to blossom. We are meant to live with joy and passion. It's called growth.

May God grant us the grace, strength and hope to weather the storms and come out on the other side a new creature, truly restored to His original design. It means moving beyond other people's expectations and all their demands of us, in order to find out who God created us to be and what He has called us to do in this lifetime and for eternity.

Let us praise Him in the storms, knowing that we know that we know, that somehow (and we may not see how) but somehow... He is going to work this thing out and cause all things to work together for good. He makes all things beautiful – in His time. (Ecclesiastes 3:11)

It seems to me that last year we experienced a spring snowstorm as well. You would think I would be used to them by now. Just before our scheduled Passover Seder, in April of 2008, our city was hit by the worst snowstorm in twenty years! It really took faith for my children to get up and sing, *'Simcha Rabah, Simcha rabah, Aviv higiyah, Pesach bah!'* (Great joy, great joy, spring has arrived, Passover has come.)

Several years ago, just after being exiled from Israel because of our faith in Yeshua, we experienced a whopper of a Canadian Prairie spring snowstorm. It was a real shock, but it inspired me to write this devotional on faith.

SPRING HAS SPRUNG

Suddenly, spring has sprung. Grass is sprouting where previously it lay buried by snow; the shining sun has left puddles everywhere which meant a trip to the store to buy rubber boots. The weather has warmed to the point where we kidded ourselves into believing that we could run outside without a coat on (until the still pre-season chilliness of the air sent us scurrying back to the house for a jacket or sweater). The birds' singing their sweet songs announced that spring had arrived.

I even checked my calendar and noted that yes, the official first day of spring had come and gone and we were officially and legally in the blessed season of spring after a long, hard, dreary, miserably cold winter. [1]

When it seemed as if I could not bear to suit up one more child one more time in all their winter gear just to poke their noses outside for a few minutes before it threatened to freeze right off their faces; and when it seemed that I couldn't stand one more Donut Man video played for the thousandth time because it was just too darn cold to go out (no offense, Donut Man – they're great videos, but ....); just when it seemed

---

[1] This article was written originally in April 2003; later updated in May 2008

almost too good to be true, too much to hope for.... finally, finally, spring brought blessed relief from the cabin fever claustrophobia and depression of winter.

And how very welcome this season seems; especially this year, after our first winter back in Canada. Even though I grew up in this prairie climate and my hardy grandparents pioneered in the Peace River Country in Northern Alberta, living in a little log cabin they had built with their own two hands, I had grown accustomed to the mild winter seasons in Israel which rarely saw snow. In fact, a snowfall in Jerusalem becomes an occasion for celebration and hilarity. People fashion various snowmen on the backs of their cars and drive around with them until they have melted. The whole nation shuts down and everyone enjoys a 'snow day' off school and work.

Liat & Avi build a snowman in Israel

How grateful I now felt for the first signs of spring in Canada – the tiny buds on the trees, the first blades of grass poking their heads through the snow; the bird singing and bunnies hopping. I felt especially thankful for the light of the sun and the ability to walk and play outside. I could feel, with every cell of my being, the delicious sense of new beginnings and the faint stirrings of renewed hope.

Only a few days after this breakthrough in the warmer spring-like weather; however, a snowstorm dumped its heavy load back upon us. Gone was the warmth, the sunshine, the singing birds and carefree spring to my step. It was back to snowsuits and boots and hats and mitts and gloves and scarves and... *"Arrhhh!! Where is that other mitt anyways?"*

And *"Avi, stop that screaming when I put on your snowsuit before I lose my mind!"*

And *"Liat, keep that hat on your head! It's freezing outside."*

Snowplow clearing roads after a snowstorm in Canada

I felt myself sinking back into the grey, winter gloom. But through this experience, God gave me a beautiful word picture and strengthened my faith.

I felt God place a question in my heart, *"Hannah, is it still spring?"*

I had to stop and think for a moment. *"Well, yes, technically it is still spring,"* I answered.

How did I know it was spring? I knew it was a fact that we had crossed the line from winter into spring because technically, spring begins on a certain date (March 20th); and since we were still past that date, then by logical deduction, it was still spring.

The Holy Spirit then asked me, *"Is it as much spring now that you are in the midst of a snowstorm as a few days ago when the sun was shining?"*

I had to admit that yes, officially and legally and by the calendar, it was still spring. None of what my five senses could discern would tell me it was spring. Nothing I could see with my natural eyes or hear with my ears or feel with my body or my emotions told me it was spring; but the truth I knew deep inside was that it was truly spring.

This then, is our experience of faith. When our world is crashing in around us; when we feel that no one loves us; when we have lost everything or simply lost our way in a maze of confusion, we may still stand upon the truth of God's Word. When we feel defeated, we may know that we are still more than conquerors through Him who loves us.[2]

When we fail, we may trust and believe that He will always lead us in triumph through the Messiah Yeshua. When we are sick and in pain, we can stand on the legal truth that by His stripes we are healed.[3] When we don't have enough to pay our bills and the rent is due and creditors are waking us up in the morning with their harassing phone calls, we not only can but we must stand on the truth of God's word that He will meet all of our need according to His riches by the Messiah Yeshua. [4]

When we are weak, we say we are strong in Him and His grace is sufficient for us each day. When we feel upset, nervous and frantic, we say we are seated in heavenly places with the Messiah and have entered into His rest. When everything is going wrong, it seems, we can be assured that all things work together for good for those who love God, to those who are called according to His purposes.[5]

When everyone seems against us, we can say that if God is for us, who can be against us? (Romans 8:31) When we have fallen so low that we think even God could not love us now, we proclaim that nothing can separate us from the love of God which is in Messiah Yeshua Adoneinu (our Lord). [6]

---

[2] Romans 8:37
[3] Isaiah 53:5
[4] Phil. 4:19
[5] Romans 8:28
[6] Romans 8:38-39

We cannot trust our eyes, our ears, our sense of smell, and especially not our emotions. For the just shall live by faith.[7] It is what is unseen that is more real than the seen. What we experience here on this earth is only temporary; there is an eternal reality.

"Therefore we do not lose heart...while we do not look at the things which are seen, but at the things which are not seen. For the things which are seen are temporary, but the things which are not seen are eternal." (2 Cor. 4:16 -18)

Faith is the substance of things hoped for which we now do not yet see. If we could already see it, we wouldn't call it hope.

"...but hope that is seen is not hope; for why does one still hope for what he sees? But if we hope for what we do not see, we eagerly wait for it with perseverance." (Romans 8:24-25)

What do we hope for that we do not yet see? Restoration of our health and strength? The return of a prodigal son or daughter? Guidance and direction to know God's will? Family reconciliation? Freedom from debt? A loving, faithful husband or wife?

We may not see these things yet with our natural eyes; but through the eyes of faith we hope and wait with perseverance.

So may we not lose heart when we thought it was finally spring, and then suddenly a winter storm dumps its icy load on us again – when we thought we

---

[7] Habakkuk 2:4

had the breakthrough only to find that we have just made one more trip around that same mountain.

We need to remember that despite what we see, hear and feel, it is still spring. No matter the trials and storms we face in life, the promises of God are still yes and Amen.

When we go through a difficult 'season' of our lives, we may given in to the temptation to lose heart and become discouraged; but the changing of the seasons in nature gives us reason to hope continually in the mercies of God.

Everything else in our lives is subject to change; but God is the Rock, the unchangeable, stable, solid, eternal, everlasting and forever God.

Are you suffering? Let us stand on the promise that after we have suffered 'a little while', the God of all grace will *'perfect, establish, strengthen, and settle you.'* (1 Peter 5:10)

Recently, I came across this beautiful poem (of unknown authorship) giving us a life lesson from the changing of seasons. It showed the exact same scene in nature at the four different seasons of the year.

How different it looked in spring, summer, fall and winter! How different our life can appear in the different seasons we go through as well.

Lessons of Life

There was a man who had four sons. He wanted his sons to learn not to judge things too quickly. So he sent them each on a quest, in turn, to go and look at a pear tree that was a great distance away.

The first son went in the winter, the second in the spring, the third in summer, and the youngest son in the fall. When they had all gone and come back, he called them together to describe what they had seen.

The first son said that the tree was ugly, bent, and twisted.

The second son said, no it was covered with green buds and full of promise.

The third son disagreed; he said it was laden with blossoms that smelled so sweet and looked so beautiful, it was the most graceful thing he had ever seen.

The last son disagreed with all of them; he said it was ripe and drooping with fruit, full of life and fulfillment.

The man then explained to his sons that they were all right, because they had each seen but only one season in the tree's life.

He told them that you cannot judge a tree, or a person, by only one season; and that the essence of who they are - the pleasure, joy, and love that come from that life - can only be measured at the end, when all the seasons are finished.

If we give up when it's winter, we will miss the promise of our spring, the beauty of our summer, fulfillment of our fall.

Moral:
Don't let the pain of one season destroy the joy of all the rest.

Don't judge life by one difficult season.

Persevere through the difficult patches and better times *are sure to come sometime sooner or later.*

Just Trust in Yeshua, He is our only answer.

Prayer: Dear Lord, sometimes what I experience does not line up with the truth of Your Word; but I choose by faith to believe that Your Word is true. You are not a man who can lie. I hold to the reality of what Your Word promises; rather than trusting in the information that my five senses and my emotions are telling me.

Thank you for the hope that I have in You and for the truth of Your Word. Help me to persevere through the winter storms, the bitter cold, and the barrenness with hope that, as I wait upon Your timing, this season will surely change. It may feel like winter, but I trust that Aviv (spring) will arrive, the colorful flowers will again appear in my life; and the season of singing will come.

Thank you Adonai that it is already completed in Yeshua the Messiah. May the faith we have in You always fill us to overflow with peace, joy and hope.

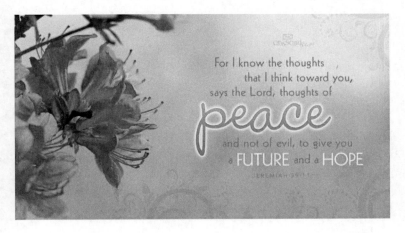

For I know the thoughts that I think toward you, says the Lord, thoughts of *peace* and not of evil, to give you a FUTURE and a HOPE
JEREMIAH 29:11

Liat & Avi & Hannah shoveling 'spring snow'

Written in May 2003; updated May 2008 & April 2009

CHAPTER THIRTY-ONE

THE ACCUSER OF THE BRETHREN

A Devotional on Freedom from Condemnation

"Therefore, there is now no condemnation for those who are in Messiah Yeshua." (Romans 8:1)

When we first moved to this pretty, peaceful little village in the Galilee, it was to connect with a particular family that we had 'met' over the internet. We intended to serve the Lord together, thinking that surely two families are better than one. Not long after we arrived, however, cracks in this picture-perfect scenario began to appear. Actually, not just cracks, but huge crevasses into which we seemed doomed to fall headlong.

First of all, our children could not seem to get along with theirs; and major issues materialized that prevented the children from even playing together. They accused my son Timothy of striking their daughter (a crime to which he vehemently denied). There were obvious disappointments in the relationship between us parents as well – issues surfaced that had not been apparent in our on-line communications previous to the move.

Things were not completely 'kosher' and everyone knew it. But I was devastated to receive a letter full of wicked accusations against us; and their twisted reasons for their decision to reject us from even fellowshipping together with them. Some of the accusations were blatant lies – specifically the accusation that we were physically abusive to our children.

Unfortunately, Timothy had stepped on a rake in the yard and the stick had slipped up and thwacked him - hard – right in the face! Funny in cartoons like Bugs Bunny but not so funny in real life. Oye! It left him with a serious black eye – a real shiner! Yes, ok, it did look like someone had punched him in the face; but honestly it was the rake. You have to believe me!

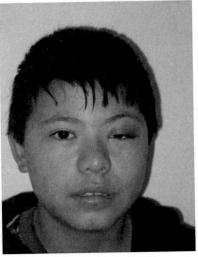

That same week, my youngest son, Avi (then a soother- sucking 2 year old), took a flying leap off the bed and struck his forehead on the open door on his way down. This left him with a nasty, big bruise and huge goose egg right in the middle of his forehead. Oye Vey! Two kids in one week — no wonder they thought we were using our children as punching bags — but it just wasn't true. These were both accidents — occurrences that seemed all too common in our family in Israel.

Our family in the Galilee (2005). Timothy with a black eye and Avi with a goose-egg on his forehead

I remember that when our daughter, Liat, was a little girl in the Negev (desert), she hurt herself so often that we even considered putting her in a helmet and full body armor! Seriously — she would walk down the aisle in a grocery store and a can would fall off the shelf and hit her in the head. Then the whole grocery cart she was sitting in would fall over! Oye!

Years later, I, myself, was bitten on the toe by a tarantula in our village while walking the dog atop some dried palm branches where they had been discarded after sukkot. Well, this was the way Pepper wanted to go that day! Ya live and learn eh?

Later, that very same day, Avi came home from the basketball court crying and holding his arm. By the way it was dangling at an odd angle; it was all too obvious that it had been seriously fractured – probably in more than one place. Hey – we were able to deal with both calamities in the same trip to the hospital. ☺ Now that's taking the practice of looking on the bright side a bit too far, I'd say....

Avi playing 'Nerf' on his 11th birthday with a cast on his arm

These incidents happened not long after I sustained serious injuries in a car accident along the road to Beit Shemesh in which I was sandwiched between two vehicles and my car was completely totaled.

'Stuff' happens. Sometimes more 'stuff' than others. We live in a fallen world that still suffers under many curses, misfortunes and tragedies, which in Israel, seem all too commonplace. Anyone who has followed the Lord for any time has soon discovered that being a disciple of Yeshua does not give us immunity from suffering.

Tarantula bites hurt and so do broken arms; but false accusations seem to be one of the most emotionally painful. Betrayal can be excruciatingly difficult to deal with in a righteous way.

Yeshua understood the pain of betrayal when one of His close disciples, Judas, with whom He shared the matzah on his last Passover, betrayed him with a kiss. In a Messianic prophecy, it is written,

"Even my close friend, someone I trusted, one who shared my bread, has turned against me." (Psalm 41:9)

Granted, some of the accusations leveled against us contained a measure of truth. No, we did not use our kids as human bowling balls; but we did have faults and weaknesses which the Holy Spirit had already shown us; and that we were working on by the grace of God.

Yes, we did sometimes argue as husband and wife; and yes, I did occasionally (hard to believe I know but true) raise my voice in anger. Who was to know that Israeli homes are not built to be sound-proof and that anyone standing outside can hear everything being said inside? ☺

This couple's accusatory letter, however, caused me to feel utterly ashamed, rejected, worthless, hopeless, defeated and discouraged. Even so, I decided to walk to our weekly home fellowship meeting, thinking that perhaps being with other Believers and worshipping the Lord in spite of it all was the right thing to do. Although the Lord is our glory and the lifter of our heads, I walked in shame with my head hung low.

I was not even sure if I would be accepted into this home fellowship group any longer if they had heard all these terrible accusations against us. But of course, these warm and wonderful people made a special point of making it known that we are always welcome in their home and in their fellowship.

The leader of the group, Ben (also principal of the Messianic Believers' school in Tiberius), shared an excellent teaching on discerning the difference between the discipline of the Lord and the attacks of the enemy.

Discipline or Attack?

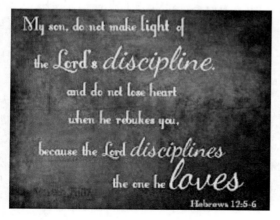

My son, do not make light of the Lord's *discipline*. and do not lose heart when he rebukes you, because the Lord *disciplines* the one he *loves*

Hebrews 12:5-6

One thing Ben said that really ministered to me is that even though God's discipline is not pleasant at the time, His correction is evidence of His love for us.

God's discipline is meant to turn us in the right direction towards righteousness and obedience (as in the story of Jonah). Its purpose is not to destroy us, or to make us feel worthless, useless, hopeless and forever condemned. The thief, however, comes only to steal, kill and destroy. [1] Condemnation is one of his favorite evil tactics intended to bring us down.

The Accuser of the Brethren

We call our spiritual enemy Satan, but this is not his name. Rather, it is a title, coming from the word, '*l'satan*', which means to oppose or stand in opposition to. Even the donkey in the story of Balaam was called a 'Satan' (one who stands in opposition).[2]

Another name for this evil one is the '*accuser of the brethren*': **For the accuser of the brethren, who accuses them before our God day and night, has been cast down."** (Revelation 12:10)

I had not previously shared with anyone from the home group what had been going on between us and the couple who had accused us (who did not fellowship with this group or any other.) But the Holy Spirit's ministry is awesome. He knows what to speak into our lives at the perfect time.

---

[1] John 10:10

[2] Numbers 22

And let us run with perseverance the race marked out for us

The purpose of the accuser is to hurl accusations against us until we feel like a terrible person and perhaps become so discouraged that we give up even trying to serve the Lord; but God is faithful to lift us up and encourage us to keep running our race with perseverance (Hebrews 12:1).

Ben went on to give a powerful illustration that makes me even more thankful for what Yeshua did for us. Yehoshua (Joshua), the Cohen Hagadol (the High Priest), stood before the Lord with hasatan at his right hand to oppose (l'satan) him. The Lord rebuked hasatan, took away Yehoshua's filthy garments and exchanged them for clean, rich robes.

To Joshua, He said, **"See, I have removed your iniquity from you and I will clothe you with rich robes."** (Zechariah 3:4)

God did not even address the validity of the enemy's accusations against Joshua. He merely made the exchange. This is such a powerful picture of what Yeshua has done for us. Because of Yeshua's death on the cross, God covers us with robes of righteousness.

Many of us have received salvation but we have not received the revelation of our righteousness that comes from God through Yeshua. We are clothed with salvation but covered with righteousness. Wh en we actually 'get it', this should cause us such great joy and rejoicing:

"I will greatly rejoice in the Lord, my soul shall be joyful in my God;' for He has clothed me with the garments of salvation, He has covered me with the robe of righteousness." (Isaiah 61:10)

This verse is not just for Israel. Through the New Covenant, all who are in the Messiah can walk in this righteousness and glory that is from Him. Many of us, though saved and bound for Heaven, walk in shame, guilt and rejection because of woundings and hurts from our past. Yeshua took all of this upon Himself on the cross so that we could be set free; but we must be willing to receive it!

"Yeshua... for the joy that was set before Him endured the cross, despising the shame, and has sat down at the right hand of the throne of God." (Hebrews 12:2)

Yeshua understands rejection. He experienced the most horrible rejection of all — far worse than the rejection of father or mother or friend or spouse — the very rejection of Father God Himself! While dying on the cross, He cried out with a loud voice, **"Eli, Eli (My God, My God), lama sabachtani? (why have you forsaken /abandoned /rejected me?)"** (Matthew 27:46)

He took upon Himself this rejection so that we may be accepted! Yes, we are accepted in the Beloved. **"He chose us in Him before the foundation of the world, that we should be holy and without blame before Him in love ... by which He made us <u>accepted in the Beloved</u>."** (Ephesians 1:4-6)

As God's children, we are not just tolerated; we are welcomed! Some of us have been treated as little nuisances as children by our parents. We just got in the way and took them away from what they really wanted to be doing. (Or have we, perhaps at times, treated our own children like this?) But we are not annoying little nuisances to God, taking Him away from His 'important' work.

We may, at any time, not just once a year on the Day of Atonement (Yom Kippur), come boldly into the Holy of Holies (Kadosh hakdoshim) to an intimate place with God; and this privilege is no longer reserved for the Cohen Hagadol (high priest) but for each one of us — we are all cohanim (priests) through the blood of Yeshua (Jesus), by a new and living way. (Hebrews 10:19-20)

God welcomes us into His presence at any time. There have been times when I have felt terribly neglected, ignored, and not cared for. Especially at times like these, the enemy of our souls, the liar, tells us that God doesn't have time for us either – that He is not really listening, not really caring for us as He should. But this is not the truth and we need to resist this lie, speaking the truth that God loves and cares for us; He is always willing to receive us.

Yeshua's disciples thought that the children were bothering such an 'important' man – the very Son of God, the Messiah, son of David – the KING! But Yeshua rebuked them, saying, **"Let the little children come unto Me."** (Mathew 19:14)

The disciples did not yet understand the heart of the Father. We are all inside still like little children, needing love, needing acceptance, needing affirmation, especially that which we did not receive while growing up from the people closest to us.

For what parent is perfect? What friend? What spouse? And yet the Father loves us with a perfect love. This perfect love casts out fear[3] – fear that we are not good enough; fear that we don't belong; fear that we will be rejected.

Children sometimes chant the well known refrain, *"Sticks and stones can break my bones but names*

---

[3] 1 John 4:18

will never hurt me." But we all know that this is a lie. Name-calling can cause deep hurt.

Years ago, a little girl came over to play with my daughter, Liat. We were trying to clean up the playroom and Liat, (then age 5), was doing her utmost to participate. But it wasn't good enough for her older and more 'efficient' friend. So she called Liat a '*baby*' and said she was not really working but only playing.

Liat later came to me and, with tears welling up in her eyes, said, *"Mommy, I really was trying hard to clean up, but when she said this to me, it made me feel like I'm not a good child."* This girl's unkind remarks not only caused Liat to feel that what she had *done* wasn't good enough; but that she herself as a person did not measure up – that she is not a good child! Even as adults, it's hard to separate our 'who' from our 'do', isn't it?

For a long time afterward, Liat did not refer to this girl by name but as '*the one who called me a baby*'. Labels can stick. Most of us were called names as children (or even as adults!). I know I've been guilty of labeling other people in moments of anger, and calling them unkind names. Some of us have accepted these labels, these accusatory names, as our very identity: stupid, lazy, bad, selfish, slow, fat, ugly, unloved and unlovable.... The list is endless.....

But the Word of God says that one day He will give us a new name. **"To him who overcomes...I will give him a white stone, and on the stone a new name written which no one knows except him who receives it."** (Revelation 2:17)

God Himself, the Lover of our souls, will call us by new names: Beloved, Accepted, Friend, Beautiful Jewel, My delight is in her, Chosen and Faithful.

"You shall no longer be called Forsaken, (Azuvah) nor shall your land any more be termed Desolate; but you shall be called Hephzi-bah (My Delight is in her) and your land Beulah (Married)." (Isaiah 62:4)

In the future, the Lord of Lords and King of Kings will defeat the beast and the whole anti-Messiah system; and those who are with Him will be called, **"chosen, (Nivharim) and faithful (ne'umanim)."** (Revelation 17:14)

Where we lived in the Galilee, everything is green by February. The rains come and water the ground, causing it to flourish with new growth. When I would get up in the morning and open the door for my son as he left for school, I would stand still and quiet for awhile just to drink in the visual feast set before my eyes. Lush green plants, beautiful flowers of every color, shape and size, and all manner of fruit trees stood as a silent but powerful witness for the Lord.

This land that was called Desolate by all who saw it, because of the sins of the nation of Israel, is now fruitful and flourishing. Why? Because of the mercies of God who brings forth life from the dead. He has done it for this Land of Israel; and He can do it for each one of us if we will receive this new life.

Yeshua said, **"I am the resurrection and the life."** (John 11:25)

We no longer need to live in guilt, shame and rejection; we can be called '*Hephtzi-Bah*' and know that God delights in us through Yeshua! We can stand against the voice of the accuser, clothed in the garments of salvation and covered completely in righteousness that is from Him alone.

"For He made Him who knew no sin to be sin for us, that we might become the righteousness of God in Him."(2 Cor. 5:21)

As we experience His love and grace, we can grow in an ever deeper appreciation for what Yeshua has done for us; and for the amazing grace of God, so rich in mercy. Though our sins are as scarlet, yet we will be white as snow only by the blood of the Lamb. (Isa. 1:18) Halleluyah!

I hope that this application of the Word of God will help to set others free from the heavy weight of condemnation caused by the Accuser of the Brethren; so that we will have the strength to press on towards our High calling in Adonai.

Of course we have all done things that we regret and would do differently given what we now know. We are all imperfect human beings with sometimes glaring faults and weaknesses. But we need to remember that Yeshua said to the men standing ready to stone the woman caught in adultery, *"Let he who is without sin cast the first stone." (John 8:7)* All the men put down their stones and left. And to the woman, Yeshua said, *"Neither do I condemn you. Go and sin no more."*

Neither do I Condemn You

Yeshua did not come to condemn the world, but to save it! [4] We are all so easily drawn into judgment over others; but if we are walking in the spirit of Yeshua, we will not delight in judgment but in mercy. We may face many 'accusers' in our lifetime as we go about trying in our own imperfect ways to do the will of our Father. But God's word says that we who trust in Him will never be condemned.

Yeshua does not condemn us – He stands at the right hand of the Father interceding for us. There is no man or woman on earth without sin who can cast stones against us. We are God's elect and no one can legally bring an accusation against us.

"Who shall bring any charge against God's elect when it is God who justifies? Who shall come forward and accuse those whom God has chosen? Will God, who acquits us? Who is there to condemn us? Will Messiah Yeshua, who died, or rather who was raised from the dead, who is at the right hand of God actually pleading as He intercedes for us? Who shall ever separate us from Messiah's love?" (Romans 8:33-35)

Sometimes we feel utterly unloved and unlovable. People can be so mean and cruel; as has been said, *"Hurting people hurt people"*. But we can stand on the Word of God that nothing – absolutely nothing – can separate us from the love of God that is in Messiah Yeshua!

---

[4] John 3:17

There are those who will curse, but God will bless! [5] The prophet/sorcerer Balaam tried to curse the people of Israel as he was hired to do for King Balak. But at the end of the day, Balaam declared that he could not curse those whom God has blessed. (Numbers 22-24)

This is not *'greasy grace'* which gives us license to continue in our sin. Yeshua said, "Go and sin no more." We are not to engage in willful sin, thinking flippantly that, *"Oh well, God will forgive me - the blood of Jesus covers all my sins..."* The word that we are not under law but under grace is given in the context of having been set free from the power of sin.

 God's grace gives us a supernatural power to walk in holiness. The Holy Spirit will bring conviction when we step out of line, not to condemn us, but to bring us back to the narrow path that leads to life. The commandments are all for our good to give us life. But we don't need to strive; we can rest assured that He who began a good work in each of us will be faithful to complete it (Philippians 1:6).

This is a work of the Holy Spirit in our lives. It is a process that continues throughout our lifetime. We are all under construction and those who think they have arrived are deceived. We all need to heed wise counsel and receive loving correction. Whoever does not do so is a fool. But the fact that we are not yet perfect does not make us unworthy.

---

[5] Psalm 109:28

So the next time some 'well-meaning' brother or sister comes with thinly veiled judgments and unfair accusations, we can resist condemnation and defeat judgment by affirming our heritage as servants of the King of Glory (Melech Hakavod).

"No weapon formed against you shall prosper, and every tongue which rises against you in judgment You shall condemn. This is the heritage of the servants of the Lord, and their righteousness is from Me, "Says the Lord."(Isaiah 54:17)

The law and truth came through Moses, but grace and mercy through Yeshua Hamashiach. [6] In Him mercy triumphs over judgment. [7]

In the book of Hebrew it is written,

"The sprinkling of His blood speaks better things than that of Abel. " (Hebrews 12:24)

---

[6] John 1:17

[7] James 2:13

What did the blood of Abel speak of? When Cain killed his brother Abel, his blood cried out to God from the ground. [8] It called out for vengeance, judgment, and retribution. But Yeshua's blood cried out from the cross, *"Father Forgive them, for they do not know what they are doing."* (Luke 23:34)

The precious blood of our Messiah cries out to the Father these very same words on our behalf as well.

Instead of being clothed with shame we can be clothed with His righteousness, that His glory will be seen shining upon, in and through us to the world.

Let your light so shine before men, that they may see your good works, and glorify your Father which is in heaven.

Matthew 5:16

"Arise, shine; for your light has come! And the glory of the Lord is risen upon you." (Isa. 60:1)

---

[8] Genesis 4:10

Prayer: Thank you Yeshua that the accuser of the brethren has been cast down, for You made a public spectacle of him and all demonic powers when you died on the cross. Thank you for Your awesome love – that You accept me and call me Your own.

When I begin to feel guilty and condemned, help me to stand on Your word that say there is therefore now no condemnation for those who are in Messiah Yeshua.

Show me Your ways, O Lord, and teach me Your paths, that I may live in a manner worthy of my calling. I thank you and praise Your for the work of Your grace in my life by the power of Your Holy Spirit. Amen.

Written By Hannah Nesher in Neve Oved, Galil, Israel, 2005

CHAPTER THIRTY-TWO

THE GOOD SHEPHERD

A Devotional on Deliverance from Torment

"I am the good shepherd. The good shepherd lays down his life for the sheep." (John 10:11)

Upon leaving Israel[1], we left behind many precious brethren in Israel who were struggling and suffering in many ways: financially, physically, spiritually and emotionally. Israel is so much more and different than what is shown on travel tours and in glossy brochures. Here in Canada, however, I have come to realize that we all have our own struggles.

---

[1] We received 14 day notice to leave Israel in May 2003. Article written in 2007

It seems that, even though our enemies are not as obvious as violent terrorists, our unseen spiritual enemies are just as deadly and dangerous. I wanted to share something with you that I hope will bless you as much as it has me. It's about the Lord יהוה as our shepherd.

Most of us have read this verse from the 23rd Psalm. It is the standard word of comfort recited at most Jewish funerals.

> A Psalm of David. "The LORD is my shepherd; I shall not want." (Psalm 23:1)

מִזְמוֹר לְדָוִד : יְהוָה רֹעִי, לֹא אֶחְסָר
Adonai Roi Loh Echsar[2]

Yeshua called Himself a shepherd - in fact, a good shepherd (Roe ha'tov) – one who would even give His life for the sheep.[3] I think we can all relate to the

---

[2] Literally meaning 'nothing is missing'
[3] John 10:11

first several lines of the Psalm: I shall not want, He makes me lie down in green pastures, leads me beside the still waters, restores my soul, leads me in the paths of righteousness.

He even leads us through the valley of the shadow of death with his rod and staff. In all this we can visualize the shepherd leading, guiding, and caring for His flock of sheep. But what about anointing our heads with oil? What's up with that?

"You have anointed my head with oil..."
(Psalms 23:5)

What happened to the imagery of a shepherd with his sheep? How does anointing oil relate to the job of a shepherd?

This is something I had never thought of before; but in his book, <u>Travelling Light</u>, Max Lucado shares an aspect of shepherding that has revealed special meaning to this line of Scripture.

Tormented Sheep

Tormented Sheep

Apparently, sheep are at times tormented by swarms of flies in the pasture. They even fly into the sheep's nostrils and lay eggs. These hatch into larvae which wiggle about and drive the poor sheep just about crazy.

At times, the sheep will bang their heads on trees and boulders to such a degree that they may even kill themselves just in a desperate attempt to find relief from the torment.

Have you ever felt like banging your head on something really good and solid? Have you ever felt that even death would be a relief if you could just get away from the relentless aggravation, stress, and frustration of life? I know I have felt this way at times.

Lord of the Flies

One of the names that people use for the devil is 'Beelzebub'. This actually comes two Hebrew words -

Baal (Lord) and zvuv (fly) { בַּעַל זְבוּב }. So we could say that the devil is *'Lord of the flies'*. According to Catholic views, he is one of the seven princes of Hell.

His name is linked with the Canaanite god (Ba'al); and was also the name of the god of the Philistine city, Ekron. In the Bible, a reference is made to Baal – zvuv in the book of 2 Kings:

Beelzebub as depicted in <u>Collin de Plancy</u>'s *Dictionnaire Infernal* (Paris, 1863)

"Now Ahaziah had fallen through the lattice of his upper room in Samaria and injured himself. So he sent messengers, saying to them,

"Go and consult Baal-Zvuv, the god of Ekron, to see if I will recover from this injury."

But the angel of the LORD said to Elijah the Tishbite, "Go up and meet the messengers of the king of Samaria and ask them,

'Is it because there is no God in Israel that you are going off to consult Baal-Zvuv, the god of Ekron?' (2 Kings 1:2-3)

Sheep Gone Astray

The Prophet Isaiah compared us to sheep. He said we are like sheep who have gone astray.

"All we like sheep have gone astray; we have turned, every one, to his own way; and the LORD has laid on Him the iniquity of us all." (Isaiah 53:6)

Don't you sometimes just feel like a dumb, lost sheep? I know I do - in fact - more often than I care to admit. The good news is that we haven't been left on our own to try and find our own way home. We have a good shepherd who gently leads and guides us; and who tenderly holds the lambs close to His heart.

"He tends his flock like a shepherd: He gathers the lambs in his arms and carries them close to his heart; he gently leads those that have young." (Isaiah 40:11)

I especially like this verse because, as a single Mom, I so often feel woefully ill-equipped and totally unqualified to be leading our family along right paths. So many decisions need to be made on a daily basis; and some of those decisions are potentially life-changing and irreversible. How can a simple ewe, with an annoying tendency to go astray, find peace in this situation? Only through knowing our Good Shepherd is faithfully guiding us.

Sometimes, however, in the marathon of life with all of its trials, we can lose sight of this truth and feel lost. Even those who do have a wise and godly spouse may experience challenges with knowing the way in which we should go. When my (then) husband and I lived in Israel, there came a time when we needed to move from our apartment in the settlement of Ariel - the only problem being – we had no idea where to go next!

We had decided that we would go anywhere except Jerusalem which, in our view, was much too crowded, too expensive, too noisy, and entailed too much spiritual warfare. So we searched all over the country for our new home – everywhere except Jerusalem – but to no avail. We simply could not find anyone who would rent to us. It seemed ridiculous! Everyone wanted co-signers and thousands of dollars deposit on every apartment we looked at.

 I was reduced to tears in a realtor's office on Yom Hashoah (Holocaust Memorial Day) lamenting the fact that when the Jewish people came back to this Land from out of the horrors of the holocaust they surely did not need co-signers and a couple thousand dollars deposit just to find a place to lay their heads. But still, we could not find a place. We would drive by abandoned, half-demolished buildings and (in my desperation) I would think, *Maybe we could just camp out there for a little while."*

We tried asking people to co-sign for us; or to lend us the required deposit but were met with only polite refusals. Finally, after all our best efforts had failed to secure us a home, and our furniture had been thrown out on the street (literally), my husband and I began to walk around a park, literally 'baaahhing' like a couple of meshuganah (crazy) sheep.

We were saying to the Good Shepherd, *"Here we are Lord, a couple of your lost sheep. We don't know where to go or what to do. Please come and find us."*

Well, the Lord didn't suddenly appear with his staff and rod and show us the way to our new apartment; but I did finally get the message: surrender. I needed to submit my own plans and to say, *"Not my will but Thine be done – and yes - even if it means Jerusalem!"*

That very same day that we surrendered our will to the Lord's, we received a phone call from someone about an available apartment – in Jerusalem of course! ☺ We went straight there and by the end of that day had signed the lease – no co-signers or deposit required! Halleluyah!

In hindsight, we could see that the move to Jerusalem was in God's perfect will – it was there that my daughter, Courtney, met and married her beloved husband, Emanuel. Fifteen years and four children later they are still thriving and flourishing in the hills of Judea (just outside of the city of Jerusalem). My middle son, Timothy, also received a good education in Jerusalem, which is home to Makor Hatikvah - one of only two Hebrew – speaking, Messianic believers' schools in the country.

It was a good move; but we never would have done it without the guidance of our Good Shepherd. Even with knowing Yeshua, however; life can leave us feeling crushed by all the stress, pressure and turmoil in the world.

Just like these flies that drive the sheep crazy, demonic forces can bombard our lives with such torment that we also may be driven to insanity – or at the very least - despair.

What is the solution and how does this relate to Psalm 23?

Apparently, a good shepherd is one who applies oil to the head of the sheep as a kind of insect repellant. The flies smell the oil and stay away, giving the sheep badly needed relief. So when our Good Shepherd anoints our heads with oil, it repels those demonic forces buzzing around our heads and gives us a measure of peace (shalom).

One Flock, One Shepherd

Yeshua said that He came for the lost sheep of the house of Israel 4 ; but also that there are others, not of this flock, who will also come under His watchful care.

"I have other sheep that are not of this flock. I must bring them also. They too will listen to my voice, and there shall be one flock and one shepherd." (John 10:16)

May we experience the rest, comfort, provision, and protection that come from being under the care of the Good Shepherd. Let us worship Him, for He is our God and we are the people of His pasture – the flock under His care.

"Come, let us worship and bow down, Let us kneel before the LORD our Maker. for He is our God and we are the people of his pasture, the flock under his care." (Psalm 95:6-7)

---

4 Mathew 15:24

Prayer: Thank you, Lord, that You are our faithful, good shepherd. May we clearly hear Your voice and discern Your will for our lives. Help us to follow You and never be led astray by the voice of a stranger.

Amidst all the aggravations of living in this fallen world and the sorrows of living amongst an evil and perverse generation, anoint our heads with oil so that those annoying flies may not alight.

Anoint us for our calling, God, and especially as we get older, anoint us with fresh oil, so that we may still flourish and bear fruit in our latter years.

May Your Word remind us of eternity and give us comfort that one day we will live again in Gan Eden (Garden of Eden) forever through Yeshua Hamashiach (the Messiah).

"**I am the good shepherd** (Ani roeh hatov). **The good shepherd gives His life for the sheep. My sheep hear My voice and I know them, and they follow Me.**

And I give them eternal life, and they shall never perish; neither shall anyone snatch them out of My hand."

(John 10:11,27-28)

Safe in the Shephard's arms

Be still and know that I am God
Psalm 46:10

CHAPTER THIRTY-THREE

THE ROAD OF LIFE

A Devotional on Transitions

After being unceremoniously kicked out of Israel,[1] we moved back to my hometown in Canada and rented a run-down, small apartment in a large, low-income housing complex. It was depressing (for more reasons than one); and although we often wanted to move to more spacious and comfortable living quarters, we felt the Holy Spirit restraining us whenever we made an attempt.

One particular morning, as I sat in my dumpy but comfy 'devotional chair', feeling so empty, and so distraught; I pleaded with the Lord for a 'Word' that would bring clarity to my mind and peace to my soul.

I opened a devotional book, <u>From the Father's Heart,</u> a collection of letters representing God's

---

[1] In 2003. See the story in '<u>Journey to Jerusalem</u>' by the author.

thoughts towards us, written by Charles Slagle. I had not read from this book in a long time, but it fell open at a page marked by an advertisement to the International Christian Embassy Jerusalem's live musical presentation of 'The Covenant'. [2]

It was at this exact place in the book that I read these words addressed to: **"Bewildered Deliverer,**

What is this emptiness you are feeling? I will tell you. <u>You are in transition</u>. In the midst of change, there is no choice but to move. In the process of moving, settling in is out of the question. So of course you feel rootless! A tree being transplanted cannot be rooted until it is planted again in good soil.

Ponder this truth and remember it — there is no way to enjoy the comforts of a home, and move at the same time. And it is impossible to harvest fruit from a vineyard yet to be.

I know it has seemed like a long journey, but it will be shorter if you will keep this in mind: you aren't supposed to feel satisfied where you are. This isn't home. This is travel. Meantime, why not enjoy the scenery? You will never pass this way again, and one day you will cherish the memories of this trip...

Helpfully,

Dad

I wept as I read these words, a message that my heart already knew — it was time to move on and we needed to prepare to say goodbye... again.

---

[2] Musical production by Elizabeth and Robert Muren

This devotion was based on Scripture that has played a key role in my life:

"By faith Abraham obeyed when he was called to go out to the place which he would receive as an inheritance. And he went out, not knowing where he was going.

By faith, he dwelt in the land of promise as in a foreign country, dwelling in tents with Isaac and Jacob, the heirs with him of the same promise, for he waited for the city which has foundations, whose builder and maker is God." (Heb. 11:8-10)

It was not Abraham but his father who was called to leave the land of Ur and travel to the Land of Canaan. They set off for the Land but settled in 'Haran'. **"But when they came to Haran, they settled there**." (Genesis 11:31)

All too often we 'settle' somewhere; becoming comfortable where we are and choosing to stay there permanently. I felt that God was challenging us not to settle here in our *'Haran'* but to go all the way back to the Promised Land.[3]

Haran was both a place and a person. It was the name of one of Terah's sons who died in this place. Haran, therefore, represents death – not only physical death, but also spiritual death: death of dreams, death of destiny, and death of God's plan for our life. It comes through settling for the good instead of the best; for being satisfied with mediocre instead of striving for excellent.

---

[3] This was our second attempt at aliyah (moving back to Israel) in 2004 to the Galilee

Testing God

Although I received this as a 'word in due season', you know how it is – we question in the darkness the words we receive in the light. And so I decided to test it one more time. I noticed an ad for a house for rent that sounded fantastic – everything were hoping for – a yard for the kids and the dog, space for an office and even room to teach some classes – and for not much more rent than what we were paying for our apartment.

It was so tempting! But we prayed on the way to view the house and asked God for His wisdom. When we arrived at the appointed meeting time, the house was locked, dark and empty – no one was there. After waiting for some time, we returned home and I went down to the laundry room, still pondering this and staying in a prayerful stance. Something *sticky* on the floor of the laundry room caused my slippers to become *stuck*. Then I placed my laundry card in the slot to start the machine and it also became *stuck*. I couldn't pull it out no matter how hard I tried.

Hmmm....was there a message here? Was it a sign from above? Could it be that the Holy Spirit was trying to tell me, "If you rent this house, you could get *'stuck'* here"? I have seen sillier ways that the Lord has used to get a message across to me (as anyone who has read my stories from Israel can attest to).

But no, this house looked so good, we had to keep trying. So we arranged another meeting and saw the house. It was so great! Although a simple bungalow, it seemed like a mansion compared to what we were living in at the time. And my son Timothy would even have his own room in the basement – complete with his own bathroom and shower – heaven for a teenager!

"We'll take it!" we told the landlord. But later we noticed that we had both lost our peace. Strife began to rear its ugly head again in our family. What was wrong? Everything had looked so good.

That Sunday we went to a meeting to hear Roger, an aboriginal brother, preach at a First Nations Ministry meeting. It was an awesome time and everyone had a chance to share from their heart. I was hoping he wouldn't call me because I had nothing prepared and had no idea what I would say, but of course he did call me up to share.

When I opened my mouth, what came out was an encouragement that in these last days, we must listen for the voice of the Good Shepherd, and obediently follow the guidance of the Holy Spirit, not giving in to fear.

"For as many as are led by the Spirit of God, these are sons of God. For you did not receive the spirit of bondage again to fear, but you received the Spirit of adoption by whom we cry out, Abba, our Father." (Romans 8:14-15)

I don't remember much of what else was said at the meeting except for these words, *"Don't look to Egypt - to what looks good. Don't give in to temptation. For our Father has mansions prepared for us in heaven."*

These words pierced my heart – I knew what the Spirit was saying to me and I needed to receive it as truth. Here's the twist – the landlord of this house was an Egyptian! God has such a sense of humor! ☺ Egypt (mitzrayim in Hebrew) may also represent 'limitation', or 'second best'.

My (then) husband and I both felt the same way and together agreed that we would not *settle in Haran*- not settle for less than God's best for us.

We decided with finality to decline the 'mansion in Egypt' (exile), choosing instead to follow the Holy Spirit all the way to the Promised Land and look to the reward of greater treasures in heaven. We need to keep an eternal perspective.

"By faith Moses...choosing rather to suffer affliction with the people of God than to enjoy the passing pleasures of sin, esteeming the reproach of Messiah greater riches than the reassures in Egypt; for he looked to the reward." (Hebrews 11:24-26)

Many people are currently in transition – being called out from where they have been comfortable; and not yet having arrived to where they are going to end up. We have only the lamp at our feet as a light; we can only see the next step, not the whole path.

We must each face our fears over what God is calling us to and even 'do it afraid'. Perfect love casts out all fear.[4]

---

[4] 1 John 4:18

We need to get out of the '*safe zone*' and into the '*faith zone*'. [5] We sometimes get sidetracked by forgetting that we have not been called to a safe or comfortable life; but have been called to a great adventure with the Lord with Him in the driver's seat, not with us controlling the steering wheel and brake pedal.

I love the following poem that came across my path by an unknown author which expresses this sentiment beautifully.

The Road of Life

At first I saw God as my observer, my judge
Keeping track of the things I did wrong,
So as to know whether I merited heaven or hell
when I died.

He was out there sort of like a Prime Minister.
I recognized His picture when I saw it,

---

[5] See Sukkot Devotional <u>Living as a Sukkah</u> www.voiceforisrael.net

But I didn't really know Him.

But later on, when I met the Messiah,
It seemed as though life were rather like a bike
ride,
But it was a tandem bike,
And I noticed that Yeshua was in the back,
helping me pedal.

I don't know just when it was that He suggested
we change places,
But life has not been the same since.

When I had control, I knew the way.
It was rather boring, but predictable;
It was the shortest distance between two points.

But when He took the lead, He knew delightful
long cuts,
Up mountains, and through rocky valleys at
breakneck speeds;
It was all I could do to hang on!
Even though it looked like madness, He just said,
"Pedal".

I worried and was anxious and asked,
"Where are you taking me?"
He laughed and didn't answer,
And I started to learn to trust.

I forgot my boring life and entered into the
adventure,
And when I'd say, "I'm scared!"
He'd lean back and touch my hand.
And I'd know by the look in His eyes that He

knew where we were going.
He'd been there before.

He took me to people with gifts that I needed,
Gifts of healing, acceptance and joy.
They gave me gifts to take on my journey, My
Lord's and mine.
and we were off again.

He said, "Give the gifts away;
They're extra baggage, and others need them."
So I did, to the people we met,
And I found that in giving, I received,
and still our burden was light!

I did not trust the Lord at first, in control of my
life
I thought He'd wreck it; but He knows bike
secrets.
Knows how to make a bike bend to take sharp
corners,
Knows how to jump to clear high rocks,
Knows how to fly to shorten scary passages.

And I am learning to just be quiet
And pedal in the strangest places.
And I'm beginning to enjoy the view
And the cool breeze on my face
With the delightful constant companion and guide,
Yeshua the Messiah.

And when I'm sure I just can't do anymore,
He just smiles and says, "Pedal!"

And I do.

I laughed at this poem, remembering the summer I determined to buy an attachment for my bike so that my youngest boy, Avi-ad, could sit on the back and pedal with me. We tried this tandem riding but just couldn't quite get the hang of it - making it only around the parking lot once or twice before giving up. I think I have a lot to learn still about riding tandem bikes but I look forward to the adventure ahead of me with the Lord in control.

It seems as though we are often given the choice of accepting the high call, venturing out into the deep water which involves an element of risk; or settling for second best, which always involves compromise and resignation. There lies before us the *'blessing road'* or the *'glory road'*. We can choose the blessing road, and God will bless us simply because we are His children, but we will know inside that we 'settled for second best'.

Or we can face our fears and choose the glory road, even though it looks dangerous; even though we have no idea where it leads. We can only see the lamp at our feet and the light at our path. We can only see the next step at our feet, but we know that

God is taking us to a place of greater glory, even though it means sacrifice and sharing in the fellowship of His sufferings – perhaps even suffering His reproach outside the camp.

It is in the 'deep waters' that we may take in a haul. Yeshua told His disciples to go out into the deep for the big catch of fish. He has made us fishers of men now. [6] There may be a period of waiting on the Lord to strengthen us and confirm the call, but we cannot wait until conditions are perfect before making the leap.

"He who observes the wind (waiting for all conditions to be favorable) will not sow and he who regards the clouds will not reap". (Eccl. 11:4)

We will never feel completely ready. We must first jump off the cliff and find our angel wings on the way down. Trust and obey, for there's no other way to be happy in Yeshua than to trust and obey. [7]

---

[6] (Luke 5: 4 ; Matthew 4: 19)
[7] John H. Sammis, 1887

Prayer: Dear God, even now, after all our adventures together and remembering Your great faithfulness along the way; I still find myself afraid to face an unknown future. Sometimes I feel too weak, too alone, too unsure of myself to step out into the deep. It's scary to know we're in over our heads, and not know how long we're going to have to tread water.

Sometimes I feel like settling here, Lord, in my safe little boat, no matter how confining, dull and dreary; simply because I am frightened to step out and walk on water again. Help me to see Your outstretched hand and to know that no matter what, You will not let me drown.

When I pass through deep waters they will not overflow me and when I walk through fire I shall not be burned because You are with me.[8]

Be my faithful guide in this time of transition and lead me to my true place in life where I will be in position to fulfill my destiny and the assignment you have given me to complete for Your glory and pleasure.

I'm ready to jump, Lord, so catch me if I fall; and save me if I start to sink. Give me angel's wings for a safe flight. How exciting to know that we are about to embark on another exhilarating adventure together – but this time You drive, ok? Todah rabah (thank you so much) ! ☺

---

[8] Isaiah 43:2

CHAPTER THIRTY-FOUR

USED – UP BEAR

A Devotional on Aging

"Do not cast me off in the time of old age; do not forsake me when my strength fails." (Psalm 71:9)

"They shall still bring forth fruit in old age; they shall be fresh and flourishing;" (Psalm 92:14)

I can sympathize with Used-Up Bear. [1] This loveable but pathetic teddy bear in my daughter's bedtime story feels and looks so over-used, that he considers himself not much good to anyone anymore. And

---

[1] Carmichael, Clay, <u>Used-Up Bear,</u> North-South books, New York, 1998

especially not to Clara, who has loved him for a very long, long time.

Sadly, he gazes at his reflection in the mirror and notices that his once white fur is now as dingy as an old sock. Stuffing shows through the frayed place down the middle of his back. One of his eyes is loose, and his nose sometimes drops off altogether and skitters under the bed. *"I'm a worn-out, used-up bear,"* he says.

I, too, took a glance at myself in the mirror the other day (on a rare moment when I actually had time to look in the mirror), and was dismayed at the image staring back at me. My once clear complexion now showed ugly, brown age spots and discoloration.

My hair used to be my glory – long, full, wavy brown luxurious locks which were the envy of my favorite cousin, Shauna (who had to set her hair in rollers, then lie still on each side for hours, and then iron it for a finishing touch to keep it from going too fuzzy). But lately mine had become thin, stringy, and graying in all too noticeable places.

I'm not sure if it's post-partum hormones, or excessive stress that causes the hair to fall out in nasty clumps at each shampoo or brushing, but either one – it's not a pretty sight.

My daughter can no longer boast, as she did at one time to her teenage girlfriends, that *her* mother is the skinniest mother in town. The curse of *'fat after forty'* seems to have unjustly descended upon me. Five children and one life-threatening caesarian section later, my stomach muscles seem to have healed in a permanent sag that droops down to my ....well, suffice to say any sagging is less than desirable.

I decided one day, to take advantage of the health club next door. Taking courage in hand, I showed up for their beginner 'step' class. Not wanting to appear ignorant of fitness trends, I did not ask what a 'step' class was. I assumed we would 'step' on something or other and in the process, lose weight and get fit which were my two primary goals.

My (then) ten year old son, bless his innocent heart, decided to accompany me. I was relieved to know that this 'beginners class' was for those of any age and ability. Besides my son and me, one other woman showed up. Surely at least a decade older than I, she was obviously beyond the 'beginners' level, and had to keep modifying the program with double time steps and such to accommodate her obviously superior fitness level. Clad in the latest, hot, skin-tight outfit, the instructress – herself a teenage bundle of fitness energy – led us through our 'step' paces.

A few minutes into the class and I knew I was in trouble. I could barely step up and down on the lowest step level and I was fading fast. My son looked over at me, concern showing in his eyes. Giving some lame excuse, I bowed out early and limped home, tail between my legs, wanting only to hide and lick my wounds.

My friend Betty showed up shortly thereafter, just to 'chat'. She has been like a second mother to me, always ready to lend a listening ear or a shoulder to cry on. Herself a veteran of life's battles, she knew that we need to be there for each other. She took one look at me and asked, *"What's wrong?"*

"I'm old, I'm ugly, and I'm fat; that's what's wrong," I managed to reply before bursting into tears. Betty couldn't, however, suppress a giggle when I explained about my failed fitness class attempt. People like Betty never go to fitness classes.

Helping me to put things into perspective, she reminded me that at least Yeshua has saved my soul even if my body is deteriorating. And yet, I remained troubled. Used-up Bear was troubled too. He had seen what happened to worn-out, used-up things people didn't want anymore. They became dust rags. They were tossed in the cellar where it was dark and spidery. They were dropped in the thrift box and sold for ten cents.

"*Soon Clara won't want me anymore. No one will,*" Bear said, and wiped a tear from his one good eye.

"*I know exactly how you feel, Bear,*" I thought. My kids seem to only want me when their tummies are rumbling or diapers need changing or they're bored and want me to amuse them. If I become any more incapacitated than I am now, surely they will find a replacement. My husband doesn't seem to want to be around much anymore. Oh, I know he says he has to actually work for a living, but surely this is simply an excuse!

Bear decided to adopt a strategy designed to help him last longer. He tried to be very still and quiet so that he wouldn't wear out any faster. When Clara asked him, "*Where should we go now and what should we play?*" he said, "*I think I'll stay inside and rest today.*"

Rather than sleep with Clara in her bed, he slipped off to sleep on the sofa so he wouldn't get used up any sooner. I tried that strategy myself. I thought, "*If I put my kids in daycare and have more rest and peace, than I too won't get so worn out so fast.*" Rather than sleeping in bed with my husband, I crept off to the sofa or some other place where I

could sleep alone. I tried staying home, being very still and quiet, but like the little Bear, I ended up feeling lonely and cold.

To make matters worse, the other animals made fun of Bear. They taunted him with songs like, "*Worn-out bear, used-up bear, pretty soon you'll have no hair.*" And as they sang they showed off their newness and their fur coats, thick and soft and shining. They were really jealous of Bear's relationship with Clara, because he was really her favorite.

So they lied to him and scared him with their threats. "*She'll shut you in the attic,*" Panda told him, "*and the moths will eat you alive.*"

"*She'll take you to the dump,*" said the monkey, "*and the seagulls will peck out your eyes.*"

"*She'll make one of us her new best friend,*" said the lion. "*Who'd want to be seen with a rag like you?*" And then they laughed, while Bear crept to the far end of the sofa, afraid every scary thing they had said would soon be so.

I also heard the taunts and laughter of the voices that predicted my doom and destruction. "*You're a failure!*" they jeered. "*Look at you. Who would ever want to be friends with someone like you? You're worn out. You're used up. You're a has-been. You've really messed up bad this time. It's too late. You have no future. There is no hope for your life.*" Haven't we all heard these nasty voices at one point or another?

Yeshua (Jesus) said that we have an enemy who is a liar- actually the Father of lies. He seeks only to kill, steal and destroy, but Yeshua said He came to bring us life, even abundant life. Somewhere in my heart, I must know that the words the liar speaks to my soul in my darkest moments are not the truth, but sometimes it sure feels like he's hit the mark.

Like the Bear, we may want to creep to the far end of the sofa and dwell on our fears, to isolate ourselves and nurse our depression. Perhaps the severity of the enemy's attacks stand as evidence that, (like the lion and other animals in the story), he is jealous of our relationship with God. We are special to God — this I know — for the Bible tells me so.

"Also today the Lord has proclaimed you to be His special people, just as He promised you...He will set you high above all nations which He has made, in praise, in name, and in honor..." (Deuteronomy 26:18)

God first chose the nation of Israel to be His special treasure, like a precious jewel. "...**the Lord your God has chosen you to be a people for Himself, a special treasure above all the peoples on the face of the earth...because the Lord loves you...**" (Deuteronomy 7:6-8)

When I look at my reflection in the mirror, I don't feel like a special treasure and I certainly don't look like a precious jewel. But God has a wonderful promise for us when we are going through the midst of the storms of life.

"O you afflicted one, tossed with tempest, and not comforted, Behold, I will lay your stones with colorful gems, and lay your foundations with sapphires. I will make your pinnacles of rubies, your gates of crystal, and all your walls of precious stones." (Isaiah 54:11-12)

Wow! I may not look like a gem today, but one day I will be glorious!

Even more wonderful is the fact that becoming a special treasure and precious jewel to God is not the exclusive privilege of the people belonging to the nation of Israel. No one has to endure the complex and difficult process of converting to modern-day Rabbinic Judaism, to become part of God's family.

No, we don't have to wear a kippah or learn to bake challah. [2] God decreed that anyone of any tongue, tribe, or race of people may join His family and enjoy every blessing and benefit of the seed of Abraham. There is only one condition – faith in the Jewish Messiah, Yeshua (Jesus).

"Therefore remember that you, once Gentiles in the flesh...at that time you were without Messiah, being aliens from the commonwealth of Israel and strangers from the covenants of promise, having no hope and without God in the world. But now in Messiah Yeshua you who once were far off have been brought near by the blood of Messiah...For through Him we both have access by one Spirit to the Father. Now, therefore, you are no longer strangers and foreigners, but fellow

---

[2] kippah – headcovering; tzitzit – fringes worn on garments ; challah – traditional braided load of sabbath bread

citizens with the saints and members of the household of God." (Ephesians 2:11-19)

So shalom! (greetings, peace) fellow citizen, saint (tzadik), and member of the family. You are now part of the 'chosen people'. The writer of the book of Peter says we may be rejected by men, but we are chosen by God – and precious. He says we are a chosen generation, a royal priesthood, a holy nation, His own special people.

So the next time those mean voices taunt us with their evil threats and fearful forebodings, we can tell them all to go jump in the lake of fire, because we are chosen by God and precious – His special treasure. Our hearts cry out, "Abba! (Daddy)"

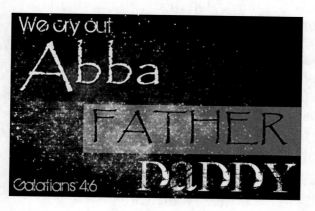

We cry out
Abba
FATHER
Daddy
Galatians 4:6

It seems that this issue carries more weight (excuse the pun) with women than with men (although I can only speak from a woman's perspective). The reason is because of a gender difference. Generally speaking, men choose; women are 'chosen'. Now before you get all uptight and defensive on this, just think of it. At that all important school dance in junior high school who does what? Girls line the walls of the gymnasium waiting for the nervous, sweaty boys to choose someone to dance with. The girls wait to be chosen; the boys choose.

With regards to dating, the only advice I received from my mother was this – *"Don't phone boys!"* Actually, I'm not being quite fair – she did give me one more essential piece of dating advice: *"Don't choose spaghetti off the menu on a dinner date – too messy."* ☺

Ok, I know times have changed and now the girl may be the one to take the initiative rather than the guy but I need this illustration to prove my point, so please have grace for someone born before the invention of cell phones, lap tops, and internet banking; and just 'bear' with me.... ☺

Although the tables have turned somewhat in the younger generation and often, girls are now as aggressive (if not more so) than the guys in initiating contact, traditionally, we women have been the ones to wait for that phone call; we wait for the object of our affection to choose us.

What about marriage? Not too many women, even in this 'enlightened age', say the words, *"Will you marry me?"* Okay, Ruth did it with Boaz, but remember I said, 'generally speaking'. In most cases, women wait for their beloved to pop the question. Women wait to be chosen as a marriage partner; men choose a marriage partner. Except for those delightful 'Sadie Hawkins' days at summer camp when the roles are reversed and the girls chase the boys to share their picnic lunch, it is traditionally boys who choose and girls who are chosen.

Perhaps for these reasons, body image may become a significant issue for women as we get older. When we become less physically attractive through the ravages of time or illness or just 'life', we wonder if we are still desirable – are we still worthy of being chosen?

During my last two pregnancies (after the age of forty), I developed pain in my hips and started walking with a limp. This only became worse over the years, especially after a car accident in Israel – to the point where I could only barely gimp around slowly using a cane.

One day, sitting around a campfire with my Israeli hippie neighbors, Shirlee and Yossi, the subject of dating came up (they are also in their fifties and have also been through three marriages each). They asked if I would ever consider dating again. At this point, I hadn't been on a date in over a decade!

I pointed to my cane and said, "*Who would want to go out with me with this thing?*" Yossi, being the 'sensitive male soul' that he is, admitted, "*Ken, yorid*" (meaning, yes, it lowers your worth). Sigh....

Because of this emphasis on feminine youth, beauty and physical attributes, it is vital that we know that we know that we know that our God has chosen us. He loves, accepts and values us today, no matter how badly this 'outer shell' of a body is deteriorating.

"For we know that if the earthly tent we live in is destroyed, we have a building from God, an eternal house in heaven, not built by human hands." (2 Corinthians 5:1)

Of Zion – a land that had become barren, dry and forsaken – the Lord said, "**You shall no longer be termed Forsaken, nor shall you land any more be termed Desolate, but you shall be called Cheftzi-bah** (which means 'my delight is in her') **and your land B'ulah** (married). (Isaiah 63:4)

Although it may seem for a time, that by all appearances' sake, we are desolate, God's delight is in us and we are married (betrothed) to Him eternally: "**I will betroth you to Me forever**;" (Hosea 2:19)

Yes, we are chosen. Our Redeemer has chosen us. We are called The Holy People, the Redeemed of the

Lord...Sought Out, not Forsaken. (Isaiah 62:12). We can use these words to combat the lies of self doubt and feelings of rejection or worthlessness. Truth can overcome lies; light can banish the darkness.

Poor Bear, however, didn't as yet see this great revelation. In the depth of his despair and hopelessness, he slipped out the back door, sat on top of the garbage can, and simply waited to be hauled away. Isn't that sometimes the way we act?

"Well, my life is over. I think I'll just sit here and wait for the garbage truck to haul me away with the rest of the trash. Don't even bother putting me in with the recycling, because surely I cannot possibly be of any use to anyone ever again."

But no matter how low we may feel, or how scared, or lonely – God always has a plan – and it's always a good one. **"For I know the plans that I have for you,' declares the LORD, 'plans for welfare and not for calamity to give you a future and a hope."** (Jeremiah 29:11)

At the end of the story, Bear woke up snug as a bug in Clara's bed. Someone had sponged him clean and white, mended his frayed place, and fastened his eyes and nose on tight. Bear sat upright and found on the bed a small package from Clara.

The card said: *"For my best friend Bear to wear at night, so I can always hug him tight."*

Inside was a red flannel bear suit, as soft and warm as fur, with two pockets for his ears, in exactly his size. He admired himself all morning in the mirror.

One day, of which the date and hour only our Father in heaven knows, we will wake up with Him and will no longer inhabit these worn out, dilapidated bodies.

We will awake in the likeness of God, no longer looking worn out and used up; and we will be truly satisfied.

"As for me, I will see Your face in righteousness; I shall be satisfied when I awake in Your likeness." (Psalms 17:15)

In a moment, in the twinkling of an eye, we will be changed. **"Behold, I tell you a mystery: We shall not all sleep, but we shall all be changed – in a moment, in the twinkling of an eye, at the last shofar.[3] For the shofar will sound, and the dead will be raised incorruptible, and we shall be changed."** (1Corinthians 15:51-52)

Bear turned to all the sofa animals who had made fun of him and told them, *"Maybe someday, you'll*

be loved enough to have a red suit made for you."

We are loved enough to have a white robe of righteousness[4] made just for us (in exactly our size). Someone has loved us enough to send His own son to die for our sins, so that we may live forever.

---

[3] A ram's horn, used to give a loud 'alarm' call; commonly translated as trumpet.
[4] Revelation 3:5

"For God so loved the world that He gave His only begotten son; that whosoever believes in Him should not perish but have everlasting life." (John 3:16)

And on that blessed day, when we inhabit our resurrected bodies - instead of wincing at our reflection in the mirror, we will probably admire ourselves all morning as re-created in the perfect, beautiful, image and likeness of our God. ☺

What a blessed honor to be thoroughly 'used up' in serving our beloved Kin Yeshua.

Prayer: Dear God, it is so easy to become dismayed and discouraged as we get older and our bodies begin to fail us. We may feel less worthy in the eyes of the world; but I thank you God that in Your eyes, we are ageless.

I do pray, YHVH Rophe, for Your blessed healing over our bodies, so that we may be strong, vibrant and full of vigor until the very end – like Moses; and like Calev – that old, faith-filled Hebrew warrior - who said, *"Give me a mountain to conquer"* at the advanced age of eighty-five years old. [5]

I know that You can heal us, Lord, but even if You don't we will still love and trust You. *"Heal us O Lord and we shall be healed; save us and we shall be saved; for You are the One we praise...."* (Jer. 17:4)

Continue to use us, God, in whatever way You choose (even if we are broken-down, used-up vessels). We want to serve You with joy and gladness all of our days.

In Yeshua's name. Amen v'amen.

---

[5] Joshua 14:10-12

CHAPTER THIRTY-FIVE

VALLEY OF ACHOR

A Devotional on Turning Trouble into Hope

"The son of Carmi was Achar, the troubler of Israel, who transgressed in the accursed thing."
(1 Chronicles 2:7)

Life sometimes feels like walking through an endless valley of trouble. In Hebrew, this valley is called *'Achor'*. How does this word relate to the transgression of Achar, whose very name means *'trouble'*? If we explore this in Scripture, we may discover a way out of the dark valley.

According to Hebraic tradition, we need to search the Scriptures for the first time the word or concept is used. For this, we turn to the seventh chapter of the book of Joshua for the account of Achar and the transgression of the *'accursed thing'*.

Here we find Joshua on his face before God, asking why Israel has been defeated by their enemies. *"Why have You brought us over the Jordan only to be delivered into the hand of the Amorites to destroy us?"* (Joshua 7:7)

This defeat followed right on the tail of their stunning victory in Jericho. Just after the mighty walls of Jericho came crashing down with just the blast of their shofarot[1], Israel ends up being chased, tails between their legs, by the insignificant army of Ai. *"Therefore the hearts of the people melted and became like water."* (Joshua 7:5)

Don't we sometimes feel discouraged like this when walking through our valley of troubles? We ask, *"Why God? Why have you saved us just to let us be defeated by these troubles, destroyed by even the weakest of enemies? If I can't even get victory over this insignificant issue, how can I expect to deal with the really serious trouble in my life?"*

What is God's answer to Joshua? *"Get up! Israel has sinned. They have taken some of the accursed things and put it amongst their own stuff."* (Joshua 7:11)

God revealed the reason behind Israel's defeat. He was no longer giving Israel victory because of the accursed things. In Hebrew, the word used is Herem {חרם }. Until these accursed things were removed from their midst and destroyed, Israel would not be able to stand before their enemies. They were

---

[1] Plural for shofar, ram's horn, used in spiritual and physical battle

doomed to destruction! God's presence would not be with them anymore. (Joshua 7:12)

God had warned Israel not to take anything from the spoils of Jericho lest they bring a curse and trouble upon themselves. (Joshua 6:18)

Here the Hebrew word used is from the same root for trouble – achar. Who could have brought this trouble upon Israel? A man whose name actually means trouble – Achar. It also means '*gloominess*'. Enough trouble in our life can make us gloomy, pessimistic, always expecting something to go wrong. Interestingly enough, here the man's name is not Achar but Achan , a slight variation to the one used in the book of Chronicles, but one with the same lineage – son of Carmi (Ben Carmi).

In his greed, Achan had taken a beautiful Babylonian garment, as well as some gold and silver, hidden it under his tent, (thinking no one would ever discover it which automatically reveals his unbelief in God who sees all things). This brought defeat upon Israel.

What was God's remedy for defeat? Destruction of the 'herem'! When the accursed things were found under Achan's tent (evidence of his sin of covetousness and disobedience) they carried all that belonged to him - his sons, daughters, donkeys, sheep, oxen, the accursed things, and even his tent – to the Valley of Achor. There, they were all stoned to death and then everything was burned with fire.[2]

---

[2] Joshua 7: 20 - 26

Joshua said, *"Why have you troubled us? The Lord will trouble you this day."* (Joshua 7:25).

This contains a lesson for each of us. There is no remedy for sin but its complete removal. How is this possible? How can we eradicate sin from our midst since we are sons and daughters of Adam, infected with sin from the beginning in Gan Eden? As the Word of God tells us, "All have sinned and fallen short of the glory of God." (Romans 3:23)

For answers to these questions, we must follow the trail of the Valley of Achor to the book of Hosea. Here is a woman I can well identify with as the woman I was in the past – having a spirit of harlotry – she decked herself in flashy earrings and jewelry and chased after her lovers without a thought to the One who is her true Beloved.

But God has His ways. In His incredible kindness and mercy, He absorbed all the rejection and wooed her back unto Himself. Hedging her way with thorns, and walling her in so that she could no longer catch her lovers, causing all her 'mirth' and immoral partying to cease, He then allured her, brought her into the desert (midbar) and spoke comfort to her there.

The midbar (wilderness or desert) is a place where God speaks. Midbar מדבר comes from the root 'daber' דבר which means 'speak' or 'word'. It was here that God spoke to Moses in the burning bush. It was in the desert that God spoke to the adulterous woman, Gomer. It is in the dry and parched places of our lives where God often speaks a Word to our hearts as well.

Now God speaks an amazing word: **"I will give her vineyards from there, and the Valley of Achor as a door of hope; She shall sing there as in the days of her youth..."** (Hosea 2:15)

"I will ... transform her Valley of Troubles into a Door of Hope." Hosea 2:15 LB

God actually promises to turn the Valley of Achor (trouble) into a door of hope! How can the valley of our troubles be turned into a place of hope? How is the curse of Achor turned into a blessing? What (or should I say who) is the door? The Hebrew word for door is *'delet'*, but the word used here is *'petach'*, which means 'an opening'.

In the New Testament, Yeshua (Jesus) uses a metaphor well known to the people of Israel – a shepherd with his sheep. He says, "I am the door (sha'ar = gate) of the sheep." (John 10:7). He repeats, *"I am the sha'ar. If anyone enters by Me, he will be saved, and will go in and out and find pasture."* (John 10:9)

Yeshua is the opening through which we may enter into life. He is the good shepherd (Ro'eh Hatov) who leads His sheep to lie down in green pastures. The enemy comes to steal, kill and destroy, but Yeshua said He has come to give us life and life more abundantly.[3] He laid down His life for us. No one took it from Him but He lay it down of Himself as He was commanded by His Father. [4]

Yeshua is the One who has turned the curse of Achor into the blessing of hope (tikvah). The Messiah redeemed us from the curse: *"Messiah has redeemed us from the curse of the torah, having become a curse for us."* (Galatians 3:13)

Because of the curse of sin, we were doomed to destruction, just as were the Israelites under the curse of Achor. But Yeshua took the sin upon Himself so that we may have hope and walk in righteousness. *"He who knew no sin became sin for us that we might become the righteousness of God in Him."* (2 Corinthians 5:21)

The blood of bulls and goats in the Old Testament sacrificial system could never truly remove or destroy our sins. The sacrifice had to be repeated over and over again, and even then the sin was only temporarily covered, not destroyed. But Yeshua entered the Holiest place with His own blood, thereby completely eradicating our sin. [5] It has been destroyed as surely as was Achan and all that belonged to him in ancient Israel.

Because of the accursed things we hold unto our bosom, our 'herem', those things devoted to destruction that we refuse to relinquish, we are

---

[3] John 10:10
[4] John 10:18
[5] Hebrews 9:12

doomed to sure defeat (even from the most insignificant opposition such as the feeble army of Ai); but in Messiah, we may walk in victory. Thanks be to God, who gives us the victory through our Lord, Adoneinu, Yeshua Hamashiach. [6]

We are more than conquerors through Him who loved us.[7] Our 'herem', our accursed sin, dooms us to eternal separation from God. But through Yeshua we may be forgiven and have eternal life in God's presence. He is Immanu-El (God with us). [8] Death is swallowed up in victory. [9] Halleluyah!

In the book of Hosea, the Lord promised a wayward, weak, sinful woman that He would give her an opening of hope (Petach Tikvah) instead of the misery of a perpetual walk of condemnation through the Valley of Achor. He granted her an eternal covenantal relationship and promised that she would sing again in His presence as she had in the days of her youth.

As a young Jewish girl, I used to lead the singing of prayers and worship in our children's congregational Sabbath services. But as I grew older, I forgot my God and rejected my faith; choosing instead to walk in the ways of the world, looking for love in all the wrong places. When God hedged my way in with thorns, causing my lovers to abandon me, and my mirth to cease, I thought I would never sing again. It felt like my life was over; my hope had been cut off forever.

---

[6] Our Lord, Yeshua the Messiah, 1 Corinthians 15:57
[7] Romans 8:37
[8] Isaiah 7:14
[9] Isaiah 25:8, 1 Cor. 15:54

But then God performed a miracle in my life - He revealed Himself to me as a God of covenant, betrothing me to Himself forever in righteousness, lovingkindness, mercy and faithfulness through the Jewish Messiah, Yeshua. He said, *"I will never leave you nor forsake you."* My first request was to sing for Him again; and He gave me that desire of my heart. The Valley of Achor has been turned into a door of hope and I sing to Him again as in the days of my youth.

Why are so many who have, by faith, walked through the sha'ar, the gate – this Petah Tikvah – opening of hope – still walking in hopelessness, despair and defeat? It is because of our stubborn refusal to take hold of everything that Yeshua died to give us. He came to give us life and life more abundantly.

He came to give us an inheritance of peace, love, joy and righteousness in the Holy Spirit. But we can be like prisoners, sitting in the gloom of our cells, depressed and discouraged; while the doors stand wide open - the brightness and warmth of sunshine along with the musical sounds of birds singing beckoning us to freedom.

We are accepting a heavy covering of guilt and condemnation instead of the garments of praise and righteousness. "Therefore there is <u>now no condemnation</u> for those who are in Messiah Yeshua, who live and walk not after the dictates of the flesh, but after the dictates of the Spirit." (Romans 8:1)

If we already know Yeshua as our Messiah and yet feel as if we are always walking in the Valley of Achor

- in defeat, despair (hopelessness) and destruction, perhaps we need to also examine our lives for evidence of herem – accursed things. Could there exist things in our possession, even unknowingly, that should be devoted to destruction?

I have visited very few homes of Believers where I did not see evidence of some kind of witchcraft, idolatry, or occult. It may take some spiritually discerning 'snooping' to cleanse our homes from this herem, asking God to reveal anything in our possession that may be causing us to walk in defeat. It may be a statue, a piece of jewelry, or even a children's toy.

A friend of mine, a young mother, recently related an incident when one day, her baby would not stop crying. The mother became more and more irritated with her child to the point where she felt enraged. Thankfully, she was spiritually discerning enough to realize that the enemy was at work and she noticed a small toy that a homeless person had given to her child. Looking closely at this toy figure, she could see the rage and demonic expression on its face. She immediately took it outside, her husband smashing it under his heavy work boots; and shortly, the crying and the rage completely disappeared.

How many of us are living with the presence of the enemy in our homes because of herem – items devoted to destruction? Are we allowing our children to watch television, movies or play video games that are an abomination to God in our homes? Is there pornographic material being viewed or read behind closed doors? We must be willing to give up and even destroy anything the Holy Spirit shows us that is not pleasing to Him. A return of God's favor and presence is well worth the sacrifice of whatever material possession that may be.

"Nor shall you bring an abomination into your house, lest you be doomed to destruction like it. You shall utterly detest it and utterly abhor it, for it is an accursed thing (herem)." (Deuteronomy 7:26)

What is our personal Valley of Achor? Surely some measure of trouble is part and parcel of real life in this fallen world amongst imperfect people. Job wrote, with a somewhat negative outlook that some would simply call realistic, *"Yet man is born to trouble, as the sparks fly upward....Man who is born of woman is of few days and full of trouble."* (Job 5:7, 14:1)

Another reality is that we do have an adversary – an enemy of our souls who seeks to kill, steal and destroy and can definitely 'trouble' us. However, sometimes our 'herem', which continually brings trouble into our life is spiritual, emotional or mental rather than physical. We may have wrong attitudes, wrong thought patterns that need to be destroyed.

Perhaps the fiery coal of an angel needs to touch our unclean lips and change the way we speak.[10] The Word warns us that a root of bitterness will not only cause trouble in our own lives, but will also defile the lives of many people we come into contact with. [11]

---

[10] Isaiah 6: 6-7
[11] Hebrews 12:15

Sobering thought, but well worth considering if we continually struggle with trouble.

Even a close relationship with one who is covetous and disobedient may cause our destruction. We are warned not to keep company with an idolatrous, covetous person, even if he or she claims to be a 'Believer' – not to even eat with such a person! [12]

Bad company surely does corrupt good character. All of Achan's family were destroyed along with him. We must pray fervently that those in authority over us walk in the Spirit and not in the flesh.

Let's pray together:

God of Abraham, Isaac, and Jacob (Israel), thank you for revealing to us the sin of Achan and providing the remedy for the Valley of Achor through the Door of Hope (Petach Tikvah). Thank you, Yeshua, that You are the gate by which we may enter into eternal life by faith. Please reveal to us any 'herem' in our lives – physical possessions, wrong relationships, sinful attitudes, thought or speech patterns - that may be causing us to keep wandering in the Valley of Achor - in perpetual trouble.

Show us what we are holding onto or hiding that should rather be devoted to destruction. Burn it all away - for You, O God are a consuming fire. Forgive us and cleanse us. Help us to walk in the freedom that You died to give us. Teach us to walk in the peace, joy and righteousness that is our inheritance

---

[12] 1 Corinthians 5:11

in You. Bring us through to victory, Lord, for Your namesake and to You be all the glory. Amen.

"For I know the thoughts that I think toward you, says the Lord, thoughts of peace (shalom) and not of evil, to give you a future and a hope (tikvah)." (Jeremiah 29:11)

CHAPTER THIRTY-SIX
We are Sorry, But...
A Devotional on Purity

HE WHO **OVERCOMES** SHALL BE **CLOTHED** IN **WHITE GARMENTS**

REVELATION 3:5

"I will greatly rejoice in the Lord, My soul shall be joyful in my God; For He has clothed me with the garments of salvation, He has covered me with the robe of righteousness ..." (Isaiah 61:10)

When I went to pick up my coat the other day from the drycleaners, the lady handed it over to me with an apology, pointing to the little note pinned to the plastic protective cover. You know those little notes – the ones that read, "We are *sorry, but... we've tried and tried but we are unable to remove the stain on this garment without possible injury to the color or fabric.*"

It's an off white winter coat, totally impractical I realize, with three children at home and a busy lifestyle (not to mention a dirty car), but I love this coat - which is why I spend the money to dry clean it when it becomes too embarrassing to wear in public. I still wear the coat, even with a stain. After all, you can barely see it – and yet I know it's there. I am fully aware of its subtle presence, marking my beautiful, off-white parka with the fur-lined hood as somewhat imperfect, flawed, perhaps even of inferior quality.

This got me thinking about another garment I have been promised – a clean, white, heavenly robe of righteousness. Have my sins, like the mud and oil that had soiled my winter parka, made my robe so filthy that when my time comes to pick it up, will I hear an apology and see one of little notes pinned to it as well? "We're *sorry, but... we angels tried our best, but just couldn't get that nasty stain out completely.*"

Paul said that the Messiah came to present us to God as a chaste virgin - a pure bride, glorious, holy, without spot (stain) or blemish (imperfection or flaw).[1] I think that, if we study the Word, we know this intellectually, but how many of us feel, deep in our hearts, that we have committed some sin so

---

[1] Ephesians 5:27

terrible, so grievous, so irreversible that it can never be washed away?

Perhaps it is some kind of sexual sin – promiscuity, perversion, pornography, adultery; it could be abortion, the sin of shedding innocent blood, or homosexuality - the list is endless – but the effect of sin the same. They mark our soul, causing us to feel shame and guilt, believing that we are somehow 'defective', flawed - a lesser quality of person within the ranks of humanity.

How may we overcome these feelings of inferiority and shame in order to walk in the sense of purity and holiness that the Messiah died to give us? Paul said that He (Yeshua) would sanctify and cleanse her (His bride) with the washing of water by the word. (Eph. 5:26). Maybe this was the problem with my coat – I 'dry' cleaned it!

Later, we checked the label and sure enough, it could be washed in the machine on a gentle cycle and hung to dry. Great - saves me some money. But better yet, it shows me that to be really clean we need the washing of water by the Word. We need the water and the Word, Spirit and truth – the Word to show us the truth and the Spirit of God to convince us of its truth for us personally.

The key is to look at Yeshua's righteousness and not our own. I think if there was anyone who could have claimed to be righteous before God by crossing all his T's and dotting all his i's, it would have to be Paul: 'circumcised on the eighth day, of the stock of Israel, of the tribe of Benjamin, a Hebrew of the Hebrew, a Pharisee ...concerning righteousness which is of the torah, blameless – even he put no confidence in his own righteousness but in the Messiah's.

"Not having my own righteousness, which is from the torah; but that which is through faith in Messiah, the righteousness which is from God by faith..." (Philippians 3:5-9)

It is a sad fact that we must come to accept – that our own righteousness is like filthy rags before the Lord. [2] One commentator has said it even more graphically, 'like used menstrual cloths'. If our own righteousness is this gross and disgusting before the Lord, then how may we become clean, pure and holy?

"He made Him who knew no sin to be sin for us, that we might become the righteousness of God in Him." (2 Cor. 5:21)

Yeshua was a perfect picture of the Passover lamb without blemish. We do not have to keep striving for perfection or wallowing in shame and condemnation

---

[2] Isaiah 64: 6

over our sins because Yeshua Hamashiach (the Messiah) has taken them all upon Himself as the scapegoat (in Hebrew - the Azazel of Yom Kippur) to make atonement for us so that we too may be presented to God as pure, holy and without any stain or spot. There is such release and freedom in accepting this wondrous truth!

I have a stain remover I sometimes use on my laundry called 'Shout'. But we don't have to 'shout out' the stains in our soul; all that is needed is sincere repentance: **"If we confess our sins, He is faithful and just to forgive us our sins and to cleanse us from all unrighteousness."** (1 John 1:9)

It has been said, *"One cannot beat the darkness away with a stick; the only solution is to turn on a light."* Yeshua is the light of the world. Whoever follows Him will never walk in darkness but have the light of life. [3]

The Hebrew prophet, Jeremiah (Yirmiyah), prophesied a day when a branch of righteousness would arise out of the line of David, a king who would reign over all the earth with justice and righteousness. Judah will be saved and Israel will dwell safely. His name will be called,

---

[3] John 8: 12

"The Lord our Righteousness (YHVH Tzava'ot)." (Jer. 23:6)

Joshua, the High Priest (Cohen Hagadol) was clothed with filthy garments, and was standing before the Angel of the Lord as Hasatan, the accuser of the Brethren, opposed him. (Zech. 3:3) Did God pay any attention to all Satan's accusations? No, He rebuked him and spoke to those who stood before Him saying, **"Take away the filthy garments from him."**

To Joshua, He said, **"See, I have removed your iniquity from you, and I will clothe you with rich robes."** (Zechariah 3:4)

I believe the Lord would say the same words to us, standing before him in filthy garments, hearing the voices of accusation, of why we are never 'good enough' to be considered righteous, to wear the white robes of purity and holiness.

If we have received Yeshua and the gift of His robe of righteousness in exchange for our filthy garments, then we need not be anxious about the day we will go to pick up our robes. On that day, we will not find any little *"We're sorry, but...'* notes pinned to them explaining why they couldn't quite get that last stubborn stain out.

We will join the great multitude of people from all nations, tribes and tongues, standing before the throne and before the Lamb, clothed in white robes with palm branches in our hands, shouting,

"Salvation (Yeshuah) to our God (Elohim) who sits on the throne and to the Lamb!" (Rev. 7:9-10)

Let's walk in the confidence of knowing that our pure, clean, shining robes are waiting for us; they have been washed and made white in the blood of the Lamb. Halleluyah!

Prayer: Thank you God for forgiving my sins and cleansing me from all unrighteousness. Thank you, Yeshua, for exchanging my sins for Your righteousness, so that I may stand before God totally clean, pure, and holy - a glorious Bride without spot or stain.

Wash and sanctify me with the water and the Word. Thank you that I am completely and totally cleansed from any and all past sins and unrighteousness because Your word says so.

Now help me to believe it by the convincing power of your Holy Spirit, that I may walk with boldness and confidence from this day forward.

In Yeshua's name I pray, Amen.

Hannah in her white parka coat in the Old City Jerusalem

CHAPTER THIRTY-SEVEN

YOU ARE MINE

I love you and you are mine

A Devotional on Belonging

"I have called you by your name; you are Mine." (Isaiah 43:1)

This Scripture from the Prophet Isaiah has always been a meaningful one to me, since it was from this Hebrew verse that we chose our youngest daughter's name, Liat. It was a company of women – prayer warriors – who helped bring Liat to birth.

Several of my previous pregnancies had ended in miscarriage; but these Israeli women from my weekly Ladies' prayer group in Ariel, Israel, bathed the child in my womb with their saving intercession.

At one meeting, someone read this verse from Isaiah and mentioned that this phrase, *"You are Mine"*, is a

462

beautiful Hebrew name. The name stuck. In Hebrew, it reads, Lee-atah, לִי-אָתָה which we feminized to Lee-at (Liat). Literally, it translates, *"You are - to Me"*.

Whenever we asked Liat to tell someone what her Hebrew name means, she puffed up proudly and boasted, *"I belong to God"*. What a wonderful thing for a child to know that this wonderful truth is contained in her very name.

In 2015, we travelled to California for a whirlwind speaking tour and a 'family fun trip' which included a stay aboard the Queen Mary ship on Liat's 'sweet sixteen' birthday. At her birthday dinner celebration that evening, my ears suddenly picked up the lyrics to an old song being played over the restaurant's speakers: "You're sixteen." [1]

Liat at her sweet sixteen birthday dinner on board the Queen Mary ship, Long Beach, California

---

[1] **"You're Sixteen"** is a song written by the Sherman Brothers (Robert B. Sherman and Richard M. Sherman). It was first performed by American rockabilly singer Johnny Burnette,

Johnny Burnette crooned out the lyrics, *"You're sixteen, you're beautiful, and you're mine."* I sat in total shock! The Almighty Himself had arranged to serenade His beautiful daughter, Liat, on her sixteenth birthday – to remind her once again that she is beautiful – and that she belongs to Him.

Perhaps most of us have never had the privilege of being serenaded by the God of the Universe; so I wonder how many of us know this truth deep in our spirits – God says to each of His sons and daughters, *"You are Mine."*

The White Wolf - Dog

I have been pondering this issue ever since a large, white dog showed up one day at our gate[2].   I had been praying, as had others, for our physical protection here in this violent and turbulent land of Israel; and shortly thereafter, 'she' showed up. This pure-white, wolf-dog had been following me around ever since.

She walked by my side everywhere I went and shadowed my every step I take. She guarded our house, alerting us to any intruders or invaders such as stray cats trying to sneak into the porch. She greeted me happily every morning, wagging her tail in anticipation of my greeting in return.

---

[2] In Neve Oved, Galilee, Israel, 2005

It seemed to be no matter to her that she often came to me cold, wet, and bedraggled from spending a wet and rainy night under the neighbor's porch. She was always happy to see me. I could not resist such unconditional love!

I began feeding this stray dog, but found that it was the touch of my hand, my affection and attention that she craved even more than the food. Still, she always stayed outside the fence around our yard and was never allowed to enter. It was because the rest of the family did not seem as accepting of this stray dog hanging around. You see, they already had 'THEIR DOG'.

Someone had showed up at our doorstep holding the cutest little puppy we had ever seen in our life. Abandoned at the garbage dump, covered with fleas, dirty and hungry – just a baby – how could we resist the instinctive impulse to take the puppy in and care for him?

Liat called me the Good Samaritan and expected me to take in every lost or hurting animal we found (and Israel seems to have so many of them). Because of my background training in animal science, some of the villagers thought I was a veterinarian and began bringing me abandoned animals as well.

LITTLE RUFFI

Thus began the process of adopting this cute puppy and making him part of our family. First some mushy food, warm milk, a flea bath; and then a collar, a warm blanket to sleep on, and of course we had to choose a name. We called him Ruffi, since Timothy, my middle son, thought he looked like a little ruffian.

Timothy had always wanted a dog of his very own and now his dream had come true. This puppy not only had permission to enter our yard, we even brought him into our house and let him sleep in the front closed-in porch. We fed him, gave him water, cleaned up after his messes, cuddled him, laughed at his silly puppy antics, and loved him absolutely.

But this big, white dog – she was something else. Timothy found her an annoyance; in fact a nuisance. It became a point of contention between us. *"Why do you keep feeding her, Mom?!"*, he would complain. Over and over again, he would proclaim, "SHE'S NOT OUR DOG!!"

My husband had forbidden me to feed this stray, but how could I let her go hungry? Me – a Jewish mother – let someone go hungry? Unthinkable! That day, after praying about this situation, I read the verse about doing our good deeds in secret. Aha! I had my answer – I would just feed her secretly.

But soon I was found out to my dismay. She had obviously been abandoned in this village, which is a place well-known to be a dumping ground for people who no longer want their pets.

A woman who went for a walk every morning noticed us together and asked,

"Is she your dog?" "NO!", I would answer. *"She's a stray. I just feed her."*

But secretly, I had already given her a name. Ruffi and the white dog were the best of friends. She acted as the Imma (Mommy) that this playful pup needed – always patient, letting him climb all over her back, wrestling and playing with him; but also able to give a sharp nip if he began to chew on her ear a little too hard.

WHY GOD?

Only once did I see Sheba administer serious discipline to her little charge - when Ruffi ran onto the road in front of a car. Obviously Imma[3] dog was trying to teach her baby to be careful of cars. One night, however, despite the white dog's best efforts, we received the terrible news that Ruffi had been hit by a car on the road in front of our house.

The next door neighbor girl phoned, and said, *"I just saw Ruffi on the street and there's blood coming out of his mouth!"* *"Oh, no!"*, I cried. I ran outside to find that our little pup, once a rumbling, tumbling ball of fluff, now lay in a pool of his own blood - his life cut off in an instant by a passing vehicle. How ironic that just the day before, as I walked with my other neighbor, he happened to say that should a dog ever be hit by a car, it seemed more merciful that the animal be killed instantly rather than suffer in agony. Now his prophetic words rang in my ears.

---

[3] Imma means Mommy in Hebrew

The white dog stood guard over Ruffi, not allowing any other animals to come near. As she defended him in life, so did she in death. I carried his body off the road, but it was totally limp; it felt like all of his bones were crushed. I knelt down, buried my face in my hands and wept. Heart-wrenching sobs welled up within me and spilled out, shattering the stillness of the darkness. I didn't care who heard or what they thought; I just knew that we had lost someone we loved forever and would never have him back.

I cried for a long time outside. Then I noticed little pairs of eyes peering out at me from the slits in the window shutters. I went inside, embraced my children and we all cried together. Days later, whenever someone mentioned Ruffi, the tears flowed again. The white dog also seemed lost without her little buddy to tussle with.

As always, when terrible things like this happen, something inside of us asks of God, "*Why?*" That night, as we sat together with our children to read our evening family devotion, I was amazed to discover that for this particular day, the message was about a boy whose dog had died. The boy was also grieving, questioning, "*Why God, why?*"

The point of the devotion brought forth the hard truth that although we don't always understand why some 'bad' things happen, we can still trust in God's goodness. It brought some comfort to my soul to know that our God, who knew exactly what we were going through at this moment in time, would arrange that we would read this devotion to our children. It showed me that He is still in control and on the Throne in heaven, no matter what happens here on earth. I knew that, despite the enemy's announcement that his intention towards us is death and destruction, greater is the One within us than he who is in the world.

In my own devotions, God also spoke to me, saying *"Hannah, no one is too young to die."* I knew in my heart that the Lord was warning me of the death and destruction that will come to this Land through His judgment; that even innocents will suffer. We witnessed this through Tsunamis, earthquakes, terrorist attacks and other disasters that even young children are not immune from the sting of death. But in Yeshua, *"death is swallowed up in victory."*

Time is short and we must be about our Father's business to share with people the Way of Salvation through Jesus (Yeshua).

"He who believes in the Son has everlasting life; and he who does not believe the Son shall not see life, but the wrath of God abides on him."(John 3:36)

The Lord knows those who are truly His and will save us from the coming wrath. But how do we know when we truly belong to Him, Almighty God, Creator of the Universe? Yeshua said,

"All that the Father gives Me will come to Me, and the one who comes to Me I will by no means cast out."(John 6:37)

When we come to Yeshua, we truly find a place of belonging and acceptance. We are not left, like the white dog, an abandoned stray without a master. We have been set free from serving the Kingdom of darkness and have now a new master to love, worship, praise and serve with loyalty.

"But now having been set free from sin, and having become slaves of God, you have your fruit to holiness, and the end, everlasting life." (Romans 6:22)

Ownership is a tricky issue but it's important to settle the matter once and for all. We will never really understand our true identity unless we can forever settle in our heart that we are a true son or daughter of God.

I'M JEWISH.... SO?

We see people in Messianic communities who want to find their identity in being Jewish. But is this of ultimate significance? Does this really matter when the Word of God says of Yeshua that, **"as many as received Him, to them He gave the right to become children of God, to those who believe in His name."**(John 1:12)

Some Christians begin searching for their 'Israelite or Jewish Identity'. I have a friend who came to me excitedly shouting, *"I knew it! I knew it! I just found out that I am part Jewish!"* As it turns out, she had a DNA test done which showed her to be 1 percent Jewish. She was so proud of this 1 %; but lineage, blood-line or genealogy is not what gives us the right to claim God as our Father.

"For they are not all Israel who are of Israel , nor are they all children because they are the seed of Abraham; but, "In Isaac your seed shall be called." That is those who are the children of the flesh, these are not the children of God; but the children of the promise are counted as the seed." (Romans 9:6-8)

Blasphemy? Some may think so; but Yeshua said the same thing to the religious Jewish leadership who attempted to offer up their bloodline as their ticket to membership in the family of God. They said,

"We are Abraham's descendants, and have never been in bondage to anyone. How can You say, "You will be made free?" Yeshua answered them, "Amen, Amen, I say to you, whoever commits sin is a slave of sin. And a slave does not abide in the house forever, but the son abides forever." (John 8:33-36)

The son abides forever; but they still didn't get it. They still kept appealing to their status as Abraham's descendants. This in-house debate continued on and became quite heated. Yeshua went so far as to say to their face, **"You are of your father the devil, and the desires of your father you want to do."**(John 8:44).

We must always keep in mind, He was not speaking this to the common people, but to the elite, religious leadership who thought that simply being born into the right earthly family gave them access to our Heavenly Father and being born into the wrong family (ie. Gentile) kept them out of the club. Any natural privilege or status in this world pales in comparison with the wonderful privilege of knowing the Messiah and the power of His resurrection!

SHEBA THE QUEEN

Left now with only 'white dog', I began to wonder, "Is she mine?" I began to call her by the name I had chosen – Sheba – because to me she looked as beautiful as a queen. For a while after Ruffi died, sorrow seemed to have become my daily companion. It was as if his death signaled the start of a burden of intercession and lamenting for my brethren in the flesh, Israel, of whom God has said, "You are Mine."

"I will be the God of all the families of Israel, and they shall be My people." (Jeremiah 31:1)

Despite their sin, God has not completely rejected Israel as His people, nor will He – ever! **"For You have made Your people, Israel, Your very own people forever; and You, Lord, have become their God."** (2 Samuel 7:24)

Everything in my life was being shaken and I sometimes fell into despair. At times like these, I often went for a walk in the village with Sheba at my side. Sometimes I just sat on the curb of the sidewalk or on my steps, buried my face in my arms, and wept. It was then that I felt her moist muzzle, nuzzling me gently, as if to say, "Don't be sad; I'm still here with you."

And so I would throw my arms around her neck and she would wait patiently until I could stop crying. We would then sit quietly together for awhile until I felt ready to get up and walk some more. She always waited patiently for me with her definite regal dignity. It was clear that she considered herself mine and me hers, but what would it take for me to take ownership of Sheba?

Did I own her because I fed her? Because I gave her a name? Was it when I applied flea drops to the back of her neck? No, even after all of this, I still couldn't bring myself to call Sheba 'mine'. She was still not allowed inside the yard and certainly not inside our house, as was Ruffi!

What about God? Do we belong to Him just because He takes care of us? What about when He cleans us up a bit so that we look a bit better to the world? How about when He delivers us from some of those pesky demons that had been tormenting us? No, God indeed does all these things for us but He only gives one requirement to receive His mercy – to know that we desperately need it, to ask for it, and to receive it through the sacrifice of Yeshua.

The New Covenant Welcomes All

God not only allows us into the 'yard', He even calls us into the house, even into the Holy of Holies – the place of intimacy. Through a new and living way, the veil that was torn in His flesh, we may now boldly approach His throne to find help and mercy in time of need. Jewish people might call this 'chutzpah' (nerve), but I call it amazing grace.

Watching Sheba lying on the driveway outside our yard, separated by a fence, I thought about the outer court of the Goyim (Gentiles) that kept non-Jews from entering into the inner sanctuary of the temple. Peter knew that is was unlawful for a Jewish man to keep company with or go to one of these Gentiles' homes. But after he received a vision and the Holy Spirit gave him revelation, he finally understood, **"God has shown me that I should not call any man common or unclean."** (Acts 10:28)

The vision was not about food but about people. This was truly a momentous occasion! Up until this point, Gentiles had been excluded from the New Covenant, until God showed the Jews that the New Covenant is inclusive – it is for everyone – from every tongue and tribe and race of people. There is no longer Jew nor Greek for we are one in Messiah. Elohim the Creator of the Universe has created One new Man out of the two – Jews and Gentiles and brought us into complete unity and equity before Him through the Messiah.

Peter said, **"In truth I perceive that God shows no partiality. But in every nation whoever fears Him and works righteousness is accepted by Him."** (Acts 10:34-35)

"And those of the circumcision (the Jews) were astonished, because the gift of the Holy Spirit had been poured out on the Gentiles also." (Acts 10:45)

In Yeshua's day, the Mosaic covenant was exclusive. In fact, when a Canaanite woman came to Him, pleading for deliverance for her daughter, Yeshua answered that He was sent to the lost sheep of the house of Israel.[4] And yet she persisted, begging for his help and mercy. Yeshua answered, **"It is not good to take the children's bread and throw it to the little dogs." And she said, "Yes, Lord, yet even the little dogs eat the crumbs which fall from their masters' table."** (Matt. 15:26-27)

Yeshua honored her great faith and her daughter was healed that very hour. I sometimes wonder, especially when attending Messianic Congregations, if some of the non-Jewish Believers ever feel like they are being treated like this woman – just accepting any of the crumbs from the children's bread that may fall from the table? It seems that the number one question asked of new people is, *"Are you Jewish?"* Should this really matter so much?

Does not the word of God say that **"as many as received Him (Yeshua), to them He gave the right to become children of God, to those who believe in His name."** (John 1:12)

Through the Messiah, those who were once far away have been brought near and given an equal inheritance, an equal portion, an equal position in the family of God, an equal birthright to every promise of God given to the Jews.

"Therefore remember that you, once Gentiles in the flesh (note that this Gentile status is past tense) ...that at that time you were without Messiah, being aliens from the commonwealth of Israel and strangers from the covenants of promise, having no hope and without God in the world. But

---

[4] Matthew 15:24

now in Messiah Yeshua you who once were far off have been brought near by the blood of Messiah." (Ephesians 2:11-13)

This dividing wall, called a machitzah in Hebrew, that kept non-Jews relegated to the outer court has been broken down in Messiah Yeshua. **"For He Himself is our peace, who has made both one, and has broken down the middle wall of hostility (machitzat Ha'eivah)...so as to create in Himself one new man from the two..."** (Ephesians 2:14-15)

Asking, "Are you Jewish?" is no longer the appropriate question. Rather, it should be, *"Are you a member of God's family through the Messiah?"* It is only through Yeshua that we both (Jew and Gentile) have access by one Spirit to the Father. Those who were Gentiles in the flesh should not be made to feel that they are somehow 'less than' as the 'adopted' siblings to the natural born children. For we all have to be adopted into the family through Yeshua.

Even the natural branches must be grafted back into our own native olive tree by faith. **"And they also, if they do not continue in unbelief, will be grafted in, for God is able to graft them in again."** (Romans 11:23)

If we are being led by the Spirit of God, then we can legitimately call ourselves sons and daughters of our Heavenly Father (Abba). We have **"received the spirit of adoption by whom we cry out, Abba! (Father)."** (Romans 8:14-15)

This wonderful inclusion into the family of God was predestined before the foundations of the world.

"Just as He chose us in Him before the foundation of the world, that we should be holy and without blame before Him in love, having predestined us to adoption as sons (and daughters) by Yeshua the Messiah to Himself, according to the good pleasure of His will, to the praise of the glory of His grace, by which He made us accepted in the Beloved." (Ephesians 1:4-6)

We are accepted in the Beloved; we don't need to wonder if we belong. We are all fellow citizens and members of the household of God. "Now, therefore, you are no longer strangers and foreigners, but fellow citizens with the saints and members of the household of God, having been built on the foundation of the apostles and prophets, Yeshua Hamashiach Himself being the chief cornerstone..." (Eph. 2:19-20)

Yes, Yeshua's mission on earth was first to the Jew, but it was never meant to remain exclusively a 'Jewish club'. The gospel was first offered to the Jewish people, but was then given equally to anyone who would believe.

"For I am not ashamed of the gospel of Messiah, for it is the power of God to salvation for everyone who believes, for the Jew first and also for the Greek." (Romans 1:16)

Even the ancient Hebrew prophets knew that for the Messiah to come only for Israel would be way too small of a mission. For God's heart is to reach the ends of the earth with His saving grace. It is not His will that even one should perish.

Isaiah prophesied of the Messiah, **"It is too small a thing that You should be My Servant to raise up the tribes of Jacob, and to restore the preserved ones of Israel; I will also give You as a light to the Gentiles, that You should be My salvation to the ends of the earth."** (Isaiah 49:6)

ONE FLOCK & ONE SHEPHERD

Other prophets also foretold of the gathering of many nations into one united people of God. Hosea said, **"In the place where it was said to them, 'You are not My people,' there it shall be said to them, You are the sons of the living God."** (Hosea 1:10,11)

This will happen as the children of Judah (Yehudim – Jews) and of Israel – those who have been assimilated amongst the Gentiles – gather together under the lordship of the Messiah, son of David.

Yeshua, in speaking of Himself as the Good Shepherd, said, **"And other sheep I have which are not of this fold; them also I must bring, and they will hear My voice; and there will be one flock and one shepherd."** (John 10:16)

Ezekiel spoke the same prophecy – of the joining of Yehudah and the other tribes of Israel into one flock under one shepherd. **"Surely I will take the children of Israel from among the nations, wherever they have gone, and will gather them from every side and bring them into their own land; and I will make them one nation in the land...and one king shall be king over them all...Then they shall be My people, and I will be their God. David My servant shall be king over them, and they shall all have one shepherd,..."** (Ezekiel 37:21-24)

This is the united flock that will dwell in the Land when Yeshua returns and re-gathers the exiles. Yes, the New Covenant is definitely inclusive. It is a covenant that simply says, 'come as you are' and I'll find a place for you where you fit perfectly - where you belong - where you can be useful, productive, and fruitful.

Healing from the Root of Rejection

Most of us have had the painful and humiliating experience of being rejected or left out of the group. Unless we allow the Lord to heal us with His love and unconditional acceptance; - unless we find our place of belonging in the Body of Messiah - this sense of rejection can follow us for a lifetime.

I used to be a chubby little girl. Formerly, I would have labeled myself as 'fat'; now perhaps I have grown in mercy, even towards myself. Because of my 'chubbiness', physical awkwardness and shyness, other children often rejected me in school. Being the last picked for the team, publicly ridiculed, told to 'go away' when trying to join the in-group, spending recess times at school alone and lonely – these linger as painful memories – not just for me but I know for many others as well.

But God in Messiah accepts us and does not reject us. It is often the rejects and outcasts whom He chooses to use, that we may not glory in ourselves. There is nothing that can separate us from His love.

Max Lucado wrote a beautiful story that touched my heart about a crippled lamb. This 'reject' had to stay behind when the whole flock moved to the higher, greener pastures because his crippled condition wouldn't allow him to travel with them. The little lamb was lying in a barn, alone and abandoned, when he saw a young couple enter and the woman gave birth to a baby. Of course this was Miriam and Yoseph – and the baby born was Yeshua, the Son given to us who will rule the nations – the Messiah.

This lamb, rejected by all, was used in the end to keep this very special child warm with his soft fleece. And so we all have hope that God has a good plan for each of us – even if we are rejected, and abandoned, even if we are crippled. God has not forgotten us. **"Coming to Him as to a living stone, rejected indeed by men, but chosen by God and precious..."** (1 Peter 2:4)

Dead Dogs and Cripples

We have such a beautiful picture of this amazing grace also in the biblical story of David and Mephiboshet (2 Samuel 9). Crippled shortly after birth in a tragic accident, this surviving son of Jonathan suffered from a serious case of low self-esteem. He lived in a place called 'Loh Davar', which means 'nothing' in Hebrew. He was a 'nothing from nowhere' who called himself a 'dead dog'.

David wanted to show kindness to someone from the house of Saul for Jonathan's sake, but Mephiboshet did not consider himself worthy of receiving King David's grace and mercy. Still, David persisted,

"So Mephiboshet dwelt in Jerusalem , for he ate continually at the king's table. And he was lame in both his feet." (2 Samuel 9:13)

The King's kindness lifted a rejected, crippled, nobody from nowhere, to live in the Holy City of God and to eat at the royal table. Why? For Jonathan's sake – because they had made a covenant together and because King David remained faithful to this covenant. We are also lifted from our own ash heap, from our own sense of futility and insignificance to dine at the King's table. Why? For Yeshua's sake. Because of the New Covenant sealed in His very blood.

None of us need sit under the master's table any longer, hoping to catch any stray crumb that perchance falls from his children's bread. We are sons and daughters of the King because of Yeshua and will one day dine with Him at the marriage supper of the Lamb.

"Behold, I stand at the door and knock. If anyone hears My voice and opens the door, I will come in to him and dine with him, and he with Me." (Rev. 3:20)

YOUR PEOPLE!

I realized that we, however, had still not accepted Sheba as a true member of our family. What would it take for her to truly belong to us? One day, a young Israeli girl stopped Sheba and I on the street and asked, *"Is this your dog?"* I was somewhat taken aback, not knowing why she wanted to know, and struggling with my less than fluent Hebrew, I tried to communicate our complex relationship.

Now Israelis are not generally known for their sensitivity and patience with people who are less than sure of themselves. And so, true to her Israeli nature, this teenage girl gave me a look of ultimate disgust, turned on her heels and stomped away.

Often, Sheba followed us to the park where the children played after school and usually was very well behaved, but one day, her exuberance got the best of her. She chased after a little boy, only wanting to play with him, but the child was terrified of this big white wolf-dog and the mother screamed in fury, *"Whose dog is this*?!"*

I was relieved to be able to say, *"She's not mine. Nope, not my dog. She just hangs around."* Afterwards, I felt ashamed. I thought, "Does God disown us when we misbehave?" If we act up a little (or even a lot), does He look the other way and pretend He doesn't know us? If questioned about our relationship, does He evade responsibility by saying, *"No, this rascal is not really Mine; she just hangs around Me a lot and so I feed her."* ?

Often, a dog is dumped or abandoned because of some nasty habit that becomes too much of an annoyance to deal with anymore – like jumping up, barking excessively, or chewing up every shoe in sight. Sheba seems to indulge in all three vices. The other day, she got into the garbage and scattered soiled diapers all over the neighbor's yard. Oye!

I asked Timothy to clean it up, saying, *"Look what our dog has done!"* Tim looked at me glumly saying, *"It's THE dog, Mom, not OUR dog."* Sigh... But God does not dump us in some isolated Israeli village when we persist in some bad habits. He is incredibly long-suffering and patient with us, not wanting that even one of His children should perish.

Actually, I think God did come close to disowning the people of Israel . When they made a golden calf and worshipped it, The Lord said to Moses, **"Go, get down! For YOUR PEOPLE whom YOU brought out of the land of Egypt have corrupted themselves."** (Exodus 32:7)

Poor Moses could not carry this burden, and so he turned it back on the Lord, pleading with him to take back ownership of His people: **"Lord, why does Your wrath burn hot against YOUR PEOPLE whom You have brought out of the land of Egypt with great power and with a mighty hand?"** (Exodus 32:11)

The people of Israel became like a 'hot potato' between Moses and God – neither of whom wanted to take responsibility for the unruly lot. We who are parents have probably all had days like this too when we'd love to simply run away from all the frustrations, demands and responsibilities of raising our children.

Sometimes we say to our spouse, "Do you know what YOUR child did today?!" Perhaps even God sometimes grows weary of the shenanigans of His children and has the urge to just rent them out to someone else for awhile – to let someone else, Moses maybe - anyone - take the responsibility for a change. But no, God is faithful, long-suffering, perfectly just and perfectly merciful. He pities us as a Father pities His children. He knows that we are but dust.

I AM YOURS & YOU ARE MINE

My neighbor threatened to call the dogcatcher because her children are afraid of Sheba. Alex, my Russian neighbor on the other side, who himself just got a puppy suggested I put a collar on Sheba so they wouldn't take her away. Alex is doing it right – he's out there putting up a fence to build a kennel for his pup so she won't be in danger from the road. Thanks to Alex's faithfulness, the puppy sported a fancy collar, got all her immunizations, worm pills, and slept in her own custom-made doghouse.

We donated Ruffi's old blanket to Alex's new pup. Sheba and the little schnauzer are starting to chum around together quite a bit. It does my heart good to see them playing together. Imma has another little rascal to keep out of trouble now.

Alex's schnauzer puppy & Sheba

I finally broke down and bought Sheba a collar and eventually let her into the yard despite the protests of other vocal members of the family (I won't mention names...☺).

I ran into the same woman out walking the other day in the village. When she saw Sheba still trotting faithfully at my side, she smiled and asked, "So, is she registered in your teudat zehut yet?" What she was referring to is our Israeli identity papers that officially list all of our children.

O.K., she got her little jab in. The other day, some people came to visit and, seeing the white dog lounging on our sidewalk, they asked, *Is this your dog?*"

Quite easily and naturally, I simply answered, "*Yes*'. I think I saw Sheba smile. I am now able to say to her, " *Sheba , I have called you by name; you are mine. And I love you.*"

Prayer: Thank you God that You are mine and I am Yours. It makes no difference if we are Jew or Gentile; we are all sheep of Your pasture and the flock under Your gentle care. Our identity is not in our lineage; but in You. It is so comforting to know that we belong to You – in a world that can be so rejecting, cold and cruel – we have a place of acceptance where we can feel at home.

Help us to accept one another; and to love one another. Thank you that we don't have to strive and struggle to earn Your love; because we are saved by Your grace and accepted in the beloved. Thank you You chose us and will never let us go. Amen.

CHAPTER THIRTY-EIGHT

Wilson the Therapy Dog

A Devotional on Emotional Healing

"He heals the brokenhearted and binds up their wounds."
(Psalm 147:3)

I would like to end this collection of assorted devotionals, stories and general ramblings with a deeply personal story about my eldest son, Clayton, and his *'therapy dog'*, Wilson. The last time we left Israel[1] (I know... you've probably lost count of our comings and goings – so have I ☺) we did not realize that one of the primary reasons God directed us to return to Canada was for the sake of my beloved eldest son, Clayton. I received permission to share his story; and I hope & pray it will be a special blessing to you.

---

[1] November 2015

Being so far away in Israel, I had not realized how desperate Clayton's situation had become. Communication tended to be limited and sporadic over the years. I knew that he had been ill; but I just assumed (in my negligence) that he was coping with his condition; and that people were helping him. Such was not the case.

Friends of mine in the United States sent me some tragic news – their adult son had taken his own life. He had become deeply depressed and unfortunately, suicidal thoughts were one of the recognized side effects of the medications upon which he had been placed. These grieving parents had been so far away that they did not realize it had come to this point. I felt the Holy Spirit warning me that if I did not do something about it, Clayton could possibly share the same horrible end – without hope and without God.

So... we headed back to Canada (again)....

What exactly was Clayton's condition? Well, as most of us know, our physical health is closely connected with our emotional and spiritual states of being. Clayton's problems with his stomach became an issue in his teens when a whole host of circumstances led him down a dark and dangerous path of rebellion, drugs, and addiction. This led to him turning away from God; and leaving home at a very early age. Anything I tried, from indulgence to 'tough love' only seemed to make things go from bad to worse.

Our home life became disturbing and chaotic. Clayton began to do bizarre things like insisting on going to school wrapped in a towel instead of wearing jeans. One morning I awoke to find the bathroom garbage full of his beautiful curly locks of long hair. He had totally shaved his head.

He began to steal money from my purse to support his drug habit. When he stole my credit card to make purchases, I decided that I had to do something drastic. I called the police. They actually came and took him away to jail in handcuffs, using 'scare tactics' to try and dissuade him from the path he was choosing.

I will never forget, as the police were leading him out of our home, the look in his eyes as he turned to me and said in a low, menacing voice, "*I hope you die a slow and painful death.*" I felt completely devastated; like I had lost my firstborn son.

Later (much later), God showed me that the pain I had experienced in that moment had been but a small taste of the excruciating pain God felt in His heart when His firstborn son, Israel, turned away from Him to serve other gods. And yet, how could He give them up?

"How can I give you up, O Ephraim?
How can I surrender you, O Israel?...
My heart is turned over within Me,
All My compassions are kindled." (Hosea 11:8)

One night, in the early hours of the morning the doorbell rang and there stood some young men holding the unconscious body of my son. He had been beaten up by some Lebanese thugs at a party. As I laid him upstairs in his old bed, I sat beside him and wept, remembering that this bruised and bloodied face used to be that of my sweet, tender, funny, innocent little boy. This was the son that I had given birth to with agony and tears; the one I had nursed with milk from my own breasts; the precious child I had watched grow and learn to walk.

Clayton around 5 years old with his little sister Courtney (age 2)

"I taught Ephraim to walk, taking them by their arms; but they did not know that I healed them. I drew them with gentle cords, with bands of love, and I was to them as those who take the yoke from their neck. I stooped *and* fed them." (Hosea 11:3-4)

As Clayton grew it became apparent that he was a very special boy – so bright and inquisitive. He was speaking in full sentences from such an early age and had an amazing sense of humor. Once, as just a toddler, we took him to the hot springs in Banff. When I turned my head for a moment, Clayton slipped off the ledge and sank into the hot water (not yet knowing how to swim). I dived in to rescue him and, not wanting him to be traumatized by the incident, tried to make light of it.

I said, *"Did you see any sharks down there Clayton?"* He answered, *"No Mommy, just bubbles. I was drownding."* ☺

Clayton struggled in school. He attended Talmud Torah Hebrew Elementary but hated the structured environment and resulting boredom. Often I would come home from university (where I was taking an education degree) to find him waiting for me at the bus stop. He had run away from school (again). When the school had him tested, the results showed him at the 99.9 percentile in IQ. We just didn't know how to help him in his giftedness.

By the time Clayton was in his early teens, I had come to faith in Yeshua as my Messiah.[2] Not yet knowing of the path of Messianic Judaism, we attended a Christian church and Clayton went to their Christian school. However, when Clayton's teenage rebellion began with him smoking, the

Christian parents instructed their kids to stay away from him because he was, in their eyes, a 'bad influence.' I understand. I have myself told my kids to stay away from certain 'friends' that I felt would lead them down a wrong path. I forgave them; but it didn't help Clayton to be rejected and alienated at a time when he most needed love and acceptance. The school eventually asked us to withdraw Clayton from their program.

By the time Clayton reached high school, he simply refused to attend; and so my 'genuis boy' never even completed grade 10 level of education. When we made aliyah (immigrated to Israel), Clayton refused to join us. I had re-married and he did not get along

---

[2] For Hannah's personal testimony, read her book: 'Grafted in Again' or watch DVD 'Because He Lives' available through website: www.voiceforisrael.net

with my new husband. Sometimes I think, if we could only turn back the hands of time, how many things we would do differently. But this is impossible - in life there are no 'do-overs' - and often it is our children who suffer the brunt of our foolish choices.

"And your sons shall be shepherds in the wilderness forty years, and bear the brunt of your infidelity, until your carcasses are consumed in the wilderness." (Numbers 14:33)

Clayton went on to have his own children. He eventually had a daughter, Zoe Rachel; but for many years, had no contact with her whatsoever.[3]

Clayton had a second daughter, Amelia Madison, with a woman he was living with at the time. Eventually this woman left them also, leaving Clayton a single Dad. Although heartbroken over the breakup, Clayton proved to be a wonderful father. [4]

---

[3] Zoe Rachel is now a beautiful young woman who, while in her teens, initiated personal contact with Clayton.
[4] Amelia is now a sweet, bright young lady who lives with her mother & granny & and attends an arts high school

All of this emotional upheaval caused further devastation in Clayton's life. He continued to use drugs as a way of coping; but as we know this only leads a person further down the path of destruction. Clayton began to suffer from stomach pain, which the doctors treated as a symptom of anxiety. Now, not only was he on street drugs, but also began to become addicted to prescription drugs as well.

Eventually, after many years of suffering, Clayton was diagnosed with an uncommon and not well understood illness called gastroparesis. It is a condition in which the stomach is paralyzed, with delayed gastric emptying, causing nausea and vomiting. In some, the condition is mild and can be treated with special diets and other remedies; however some cases are so severe that there is no effective treatment. Such was Clayton's condition. The doctors told him that there is no cure; and that there is nothing more they could do for him. They tried a feeding tube but it failed; and so Clayton was slowly starving to death. His own words were coming back to him: he seemed to be *dying a slow and painful death*.[5]

By the time we returned to Canada[6], Clayton was just a living skeleton. It broke my heart to see him in such a terrible condition – almost resembling a holocaust victim. He looked like a homeless junkie

[5] We have prayed fervently for this word curse to be broken and for deliverance from any resulting spirit of death.
[6] December 2015

with long, stringy, greasy hair; torn, dirty jeans; and a long, unkempt beard. Worse than his physical condition, however, (if that was even possible) was his emotional, mental and spiritual state. Never in my life have I seen someone so hopeless, so angry and so broken. If I tried to speak any words of life or encouragement, it sent him into a rage. He swore, yelled and cursed constantly - hating God, hating life, hating everyone in his life, and most of all perhaps - hating himself.

I took him from doctor to doctor and tried all kinds of alternative health treatments but all to no avail. It only seemed to make things worse. Because of his negative state, few people wanted to visit him (I can't blame them), which meant that Clayton would sit in his gloomy apartment day after meaningless day, alone and isolated. He felt betrayed and abandoned by his former 'friends'. As he became worse physically, he just stopped going out at all. Any kind of family get-togethers always involved food, and were therefore torture for him, since he could not eat. It was awful for him to watch others enjoy food that he simply couldn't 'stomach'.

Sometimes on the way home from yet another futile doctor's appointment, Clayton would begin to sob - gut-wrenching sobbing that broke my heart. Even his psychiatrist, who kept prescribing more and more medication to keep him sedated, said *"There is no hope for you."* The few so-called 'friends' that he spoke to occasionally told him that he would be better off just killing himself than continuing to live like this. It is a miracle that he did not take the legalized euthanasia route.

On more than one occasion, Clayton called me saying he was going to take his own life. I tried to talk him out of it. I called the suicide hotline and crisis lines. Once they sent a team to break into his apartment and take him to the hospital. After seeing a psychiatrist there, the 'powers that be' apparently deemed him as no threat to himself or others and simply let him go. I was so angry, I was shaking! Why could I find no help for my son?

Meanwhile, we were praying. And praying... and praying... and praying..... but it all seemed so utterly hopeless. Have you ever been in a similar situation – where something seemed so dark that you could not detect even a glimmer of light – no matter how much you fasted and prayed?

We tried deliverance prayer – casting out demons and breaking curses - but even this seemed to make no difference. I prayed fervently for forgiveness of all our sins and a breaking of the remnants of any lingering curses. There seemed to be absolutely no change whatsoever – or if anything, it only got worse. And yet God told me to keep praying and stay in faith no matter what!

I tried to obey; but so often I got discouraged and wanted to give up completely. I had surrendered my home in Israel and my life there with my daughter and four grandchildren and our rightful place in the land to try and help my son; but I felt like it had all been in vain. It was difficult not to give in to despair; but this is where other believers – my brothers and sisters in Messiah - helped to keep my arms lifted high for victory.

The first breakthrough came like a tiny cloud the size of a man's fist. I had taken Clayton to another appointment to get a refill on his medication. God had led Clayton to a Christian clinic where his doctor was a 'born again' believer who often prayed for Clayton right there in the office. He also prayed with me on occasion, asking for God's help and merciful intervention.

On this particular time, Clayton seemed much worse than usual – bent over, unable to even talk. I found out later he was going through withdrawal (something I had never witnessed before). I didn't try to say anything to him. I just sat with him silently, like Job's friends (in the beginning before they messed up by trying to talk).

Later that day, he sent me a text message expressing his first words of love and appreciation. He said, "*I'm sorry that it seems I always express only anger to you. It comes out of my pain. I do love you and care about you. And I appreciate you too.*" How I treasured those words.

One evening, I took my youngest two children, Liat & Avi, to a movie called, "*A Dog's Purpose*." It reminded me of what a good, loyal friend that a dog can be. One of my greatest sorrows in leaving Israel was the loss of my dog, Pepper. Because we didn't know where we'd be staying and because we'd be traveling extensively and not knowing how long we'd be away, we decided to leave Pepper in Israel with a loving, caring foster Mom named Esther.

 I know she absolutely adores Pepper and dotes on him; but I still miss the little fellow who had been my faithful furry friend for so many years through all our ups and downs. When I was in pain, he would just silently sit beside me – his presence always such a comfort.

I began to wonder about the possibility of getting a dog for Clayton. Although he is allergic to fur, I know that some breeds are hypoallergenic. The next time I saw Clayton, I asked him if he had ever thought about getting a dog and he replied that he would like to have a dog but didn't think he could afford it. I said that if he thought he could care for a dog, I would be willing to help pay for its food and vet bills. Clayton said he would think about it.

I really didn't know if Clayton would be capable of looking after a dog; he didn't seem even able to move off his couch – how would he care for another living being? But it seemed worth a try if he was willing. Clayton confessed his doubts – he didn't think that anything good could ever happen to him — but if I was willing to look for a dog for him then he was open to consider it.

Together, Liat & Avi & I prayed fervently to find just the right dog for Clayton. We looked and looked — shocked to find that most small breed, hypo-allergenic dogs in the area (even of mixed breed) cost over $1000! How would I ever pay for this? The idea came to me to ask all the family to chip in.

I sent out a secret e-mail, telling everyone in our family about Clayton's condition and how I hoped that a dog would be a good companion for him and help bring healing. Most of the family responded favorably and together we gathered up enough funds to purchase a dog for Clayton.

In this e-mail, I wrote about the many benefits of having a dog for a faithful companion.

1. Dogs Boost Your Mood

Research has shown that it only takes a mere 15–30 minutes with your pet to feel more relaxed and calm.

Playing with your dog also raises your brain's levels of dopamine and serotonin, which are neurotransmitters that are associated with pleasure and tranquility.

Psychologists from Miami and St. Louis Universities found that the benefits of having a canine companion can be equivalent to having a human companion.

2. Dogs Are Better Than Medicine

In addition to boosting your mood, your dog is also great for your health.

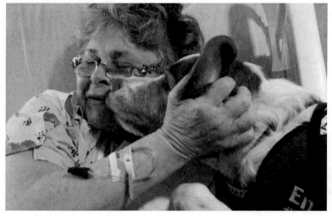

Dog owners have been found to have lower cholesterol, lower blood pressure, fewer heart attacks, and according to a study by the British Journal of Health (2004), dog owners also have the added benefit of having fewer medical problems than those without pets.

Clearly, dogs are extremely helpful in helping people deal with medical issues. Dogs help people to move more often and encourage play as well as helping them get their mind off of their condition. Dogs are great motivators to get moving and they sure are good at distracting us from things!

3. Dogs Help You Stay Active

An added unexpected benefit of having a dog is that he encourages you to exercise more! Taking your dog on walks and throwing the ball around makes for good exercise.

4. Dogs Help You Be More Social

Doing activities with your dog such as going to pet stores, dog parks, or special events is great for both you and your furry friend, as it is a great way to meet new people and mingle with other dogs and dog lovers.

A study by Britain's Warwick University fo und that 40% of people reported making friends much easier as a result of owning a dog.

5. Dogs Help Relieve Stress

Another great yet unexpected benefit of owning a dog is that they are masters at helping us relieve stress and feel calm.

10. Dogs Can Make You a Better Person

Having a dog teaches us patience, commitment and selflessness. Caring for a dog teaches us to be more patient and less selfish. We also learn to be less focused on ourselves and more patient.

At the same time that I understood all these benefits of having a dog, I was also reminded (warned) by some family members that getting a puppy can be like having a baby and can be downright overwhelming! And yet we pressed on in faith, trusting God to show us just the right dog for Clayton.

It became almost an obsession as we poured over the ads and scoured the internet. Clayton and I talked and messaged back and forth for several days. Finally we found an ad for a *'monkey dog'* [7] which Clayton thought looked a bit scraggly; but was willing to look at it. First, he wanted to see a little 'Shorkie' – a cross between a Shih-tzu and a Yorkie.

We met at Starbucks, everyone practically vibrating

---

[7] Affenpincer is a German breed of dog often called a monkey dog. This one was mixed with a Yorkie, producing a smaller dog with the loyalty of the affenpincer and its good nature with the spunk and playfulness of the Yorkie.

with excitement. This tiny, six-week old female Shorkie puppy was adorable; but she seemed so utterly fragile. I was worried that Clayton might roll over in bed and accidentally suffocate her; or that she may hurt herself falling off the couch. I didn't have peace that this was the right dog for Clayton even though he fell in love with her.

We asked him to just have a look at the monkey dog before making a decision which he did. At first he didn't quite like them. They were a bit older... and smelled like the horse farm they came from which set off Clayton's allergies. But there was this one little black male pup that had the most intelligent look on his face.

He would cock his head when we talked to him as if he understood every word we were saying. He seemed gentle and good-natured, not as 'hyper' as his brothers and sisters from the litter.

It seems that we didn't choose Wilson - he chose us - or rather, he chose Clayton. He snuggled up in his arms and fell fast asleep. But the most amazing thing to see has been the incredible transformation that has taken place before my very eyes because of the unconditional love & companionship of this funny fellow.

The same man who could barely move himself from his couch was now literally leaping over the back of his sofa to catch Wilson & stop him from peeing on the carpet. The one who was totally isolated and often didn't even hear a single human voice all week, who had to call tech support just to talk to someone, was now meeting other dog owners at the park and chatting it up with them (yes, Wilson turned out to be quite the "chick magnet" ☺)

Clayton said he talked to more people in one week than he had all the past year. Suddenly, Clayton was being friendly; initiating conversations with people in the elevator who stopped to pet Wilson. The apartment which had been silent as a tomb before was now filled with happy laughter, as visitors who came to see the new puppy chuckled at his antics.

The invalid who at one time could barely walk to the bathroom and back, and who breathed in only stale, tobacco-poisoned air, was now walking a couple of hours per day outside in the fresh air getting plenty of exercise with Wilson.

We had Wilson registered as an emotional-therapy dog and he looked so cute with his little service jacket. One week, we took Wilson to the veterinary clinic. The once angry, hopeless, mentally disturbed person was now having a congenial conversation with the vet, asking intelligent questions and apologizing for his attention to detail, saying he felt like a new father taking his first child to the pediatrician.

How we laughed. How good it felt to hear him laugh. His hair was washed, his eyes clear, and his beard trimmed. He was wearing new jeans and a nice, clean jacket. He looked great. He was smiling, laughing, and carrying on whole conversations that no longer centered only on himself and his illness. It was all about Wilson now.

The two of them were totally devoted to one another. It was amazing to see! Wilson snuggled beside Clayton on the couch, licked his face (and his socks), and kept his feet warm in bed. He stuck to Clayton like crazy glue (or rather concrete)!

Clayton took the training of Wilson so seriously and enjoyed it so much that he even enrolled in a dog training course. For years, Clayton's life had no purpose or meaning. One long dreary day dragged on after another.

I prayed that Clayton would find something to interest him again, but none of my suggestions were received. He no longer had any interest whatsoever in the computer (he had previously tried writing a blog), or reading (couldn't concentrate), or tropical fish (the aquarium lay dry and empty).

He was no longer able to work (he had received his diploma as a registered nurse before he became too ill to work and went on disability).

There seemed to be nothing that could fill his dull days with meaningful activities. But since he got Wilson, Clayton not only enrolled in the on-line course to become a certified, professional dog trainer; but also started his own on-line business. He had hoped that this might even become a means to a viable livelihood.

Then, tragedy struck when, in a freak accident, Clayton collided with Wilson and broke his skinny leg bone so severely that he either had to have his leg amputated, or undergo complex surgery with an experienced canine orthopedic surgeon that would cost thousands of dollars, or be put down. We agonized over the decision; but in the end (not having the funds) Clayton signed over his rights to Wilson to the veterinarian, and went home to end his life as well.

But God.... This wonderful veterinarian (knowing Clayton's story) refused to euthanize Wilson until he gave it his best shot to find someone to pay for the surgery and adopt him. Instead, a couple of beautiful souls, friends of Clayton's, Chelsea and Kelsey, set up a 'go-fund me' campaign, asking people to contribute towards Wilson's surgery.

In their "Our boy Wilson needs surgery" campaign, they wrote, *"Wilson saved the life of our friend, Clayton; now please help us save Wilson's life."*

People came out of the woodwork – people we didn't even know from all over the country contributed generously. A good Samaritan offered to finance the entire operation before he even knew if we could pay him back. Thank you Adas. Thank you Chelsea and Kelsey. Thank you Crestwood Veterinary Clinic. Thank you everyone ! Todah rabah! God bless you!

Finally, they raised the full amount for Wilson's surgery which was a complete success. Wilson was running and jumping and playing again like a happy puppy in no time.

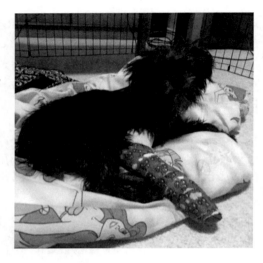

Although Wilson's recovery was complete, Clayton's journey to wholeness began to falter. His doctor changed his medication, which sent him on a steep, downward, dangerous spiral. As anyone who has ever had to deal with addictions as well as physical and mental illness can testify, the path to freedom and healing is usually neither smooth nor easy.

Clayton became physically unable to continue caring for Wilson; and others (including myself) needed to temporarily look after him. But without Wilson, Clayton completely lost all hope and seemingly any remaining wil to survive.

On December 6th, 2017, I went to deliver a Chanukah card to Clayton; and instead was met by Shawn, his building manager who insisted I come upstairs. Rather than taking me to Clayton's apartment, he took me to the upper level where the police were waiting. They informed me that Clayton had been found deceased in his apartment. He seemed to have passed away peacefully on his sofa where he spent so much time laying together with Wilson.

It is not easy sometimes to understand the ways of God, for His ways are not our ways and His thoughts so much higher than ours. In these times, our faith is sorely tested. Will we continue to trust God when we don't understand?

So many prayed for Clayton's healing, salvation, and freedom from the terrible suffering and torment he had been living under for far too long. God didn't answer these prayers as we would have chosen; but in my heart I have to trust that God, in His mercy, did hear our prayers and answered them in His way.

I will always remember that when the shofars were blown at the last Feast of Trumpets, Clayton said, "*I believe that this year my name has been written in the Book of Life.*" My hope is that today , Clayton is healed and whole. safe in Abba's arms: that somehow he made peace with His heavenly Father before he passed from this world.

I hope he is enjoying the great feast at the '*all*

you can eat buffet' at the King's table.

Rest in Shalom my beloved son....

"*Weeping may endure for a night but joy comes in the morning.*" (Psalm 30:5)

I am so thankful to Wilson for the love and joy he brought into my son's life, even if for a brief period. You may be wondering what has happened to Wilson? Shawn (who called Clayton his adopted brother and who was the one who found him at his death), chose to keep Wilson in their loving home where he continues to act as an emotional therapy dog to others with emotional issues such as fear and anxiety.

Huge thanks to Shawn and Miranda for making room in your hearts and home for Wilson (along with your other dog and tortoise and children). I know that Clayton would be happy to know that he is being so well cared for.

I have come to the conclusion that there may be some broken souls who cannot be reached by our imperfect human love. Neither can they receive the love of God, for they feel too unworthy. These individuals may only be reached through the unconditional love of a devoted animal companion.

Perhaps their 'puppy love' may also act as a bridge to bring the lost, broken and hopeless of this world into a realization of how deep the Father's love for us.

For ultimately, it is the perfect love of God that will never fail.   Love always trusts, always hopes and always perseveres. [8]

So let us never grow weary or give up in praying for our loved ones who are wounded; and have strayed far from God. His arm is not too short to save. [9]

There is nowhere we can go that could take us out of the presence of the living God. No matter how far we wander away from Him - even if we make our bed in sheol (hell) — we are still under God's watchful care.

Where can I go from Your Spirit?
Or where can I flee from Your presence?
 If I ascend into heaven, You *are* there;
If I make my bed in hell, behold, You *are there*.
If I take the wings of the morning,
And dwell in the uttermost parts of the sea,

[8] 1 Corinthians 13:7-8
[9] Isaiah 59:1

Even there Your hand shall lead me,
And Your right hand shall hold me."

(Psalms 139:7-10)

Thank you Wilson.   You're a good dog.

Hannah, with Clayton, and Wilson the Therapy dog, March 2017

Shalom to all. Thank you for listening to my stories – the good, the bad and the ugly. Thank you to all the animals who bless us with their love, affection, and devotion.

Prayer: Thank you God that with You there is always hope. No matter what happens in this life, You are always with us. You will never leave us nor forsake us. Nothing can separate us from Your love in Messiah Yeshua. Help us to stand in faith – whether on the mountaintops or in the valley of the shadow of death – in the dry, desert wilderness or swimming in deep waters.

Yeshua, you are the author and finisher of our faith.

Lift up our hands that sometimes hang down in discouragement; grant us a garment of praise instead of a spirit of heaviness. We so often look down at our circumstances instead of looking up to You – our glory and the lifter of our heads.

Thank you for Your promise that you are close to those who are brokenhearted and save those crushed in spirit. (Psalm 34:18)

Help us to remember all You have done for us in the past; and to trust You with our present and our future. Cause us to know that, even when we don't see You at work in the darkness, You are faithfully completing the work You have started in each one of us.

Halleluyah! Amen v'Amen.

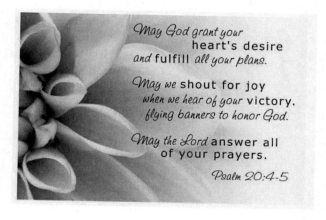

May God grant your heart's desire and fulfill all your plans.

May we shout for joy when we hear of your victory, flying banners to honor God.

May the Lord answer all of your prayers.

Psalm 20:4-5

---

[10] Psalm 108:13

About the Author

Hannah Nesher was born and raised in an Orthodox Jewish home in Canada, and educated at a private Hebrew school. She has always been an animal lover and as a child, Hannah used to bring every stray cat she could find into the house (even though her sister had serious allergies).

Hannah studied Animal Health Technology after high school, and later went on to receive a Bachelor's degree in Intercultural Education at the University of Alberta.

Through a crisis pregnancy, Hannah came to know Yeshua (Jesus) as her Messiah. She and her family made aliyah (immigrated to Israel) where they lived for several years.

Hannah now shares in the nations about the Jewish roots of the Christian faith, Israel, and matters of the heart.

Other Materials by Hannah Nesher:

A Messianic Jewish Commentary
New Insights on the weekly Parashah and Haftarah portions & festival readings from the Torah, Prophets and New Covenant writings. A complete curriculum of Torah studies for the year.

Hebrew Courses (DVD or Digital Viewing):
Shalom Morah I - Hebrew Names of God
Shalom Morah II - Wisdom in Hebrew

DVDs or Digital Viewing:
- Exploring the Jewish Roots of the Christian Faith
- There is a God in Israel
- Walking through the Wilderness
- Shalom Jerusalem
- Esther's Last Call to the Church
- Because He Lives
- Passover Lamb or Easter Ham?
- Messianic Jewish Passover
- Ruth: A Righteous Gentile
- Unity In The Messiah
- Where is Your Brother Jacob?
- Messiah in Chanukah
- Blow The Shofar for Zion

Books or eBooks:
- Grafted in Again
- Journey to Jerusalem
- Come out of Her My People
- Messiah Revealed in the Sabbath
- Messiah Revealed in Passover
- Messiah Revealed in Shavuot
- Messiah Revealed in The Fall Feasts
- Messiah Revealed in Chanukah
- Messiah Revealed in Purim
- Kashrut: The Biblical Dietary Laws

Order Form

QTY	BOOKS	
QTY	**DESCRIPTION**	**PRICE**
	Messiah Revealed in the Fall Feasts	*$20*
	Grafted in Again (Testimony)	*$20*
	Journey to Jerusalem	*$20*
	Come out of Her My People	*$20*
	Messiah Revealed in Purim	*$20*
	Messiah Revealed in Passover	*$20*
	Messiah Revealed in the Sabbath	*$15*
	Messiah Revealed in Chanukah	*$15*
	Kashrut: The Biblical Dietary Laws	*$15*
	Messiah Revealed in Shavuot	*$15*

QTY	COURSES	
QTY	**DESCRIPTION**	**PRICE**
	**NEW CURRICULUM! A Messianic Jewish Commentary: *New Insights on the weekly Parashah and Haftarah portions & festival readings from the Torah, Prophets and new covenant writings.*	*$300*
	Complete Volume (including Feast and Festival readings) 1299 pages !	
	Shalom Morah I (+ Hebrew names of God study) DVD set + workbook	*$120*
	Shalom Morah II + Wisdom in the Hebrew Aleph Bet & workbook	*$120*
	Shalom Morah Workbook only	*$20*

☐ I would like to become a *chaver* (friend/member) of Voice for Israel with a monthly donation of
  ☐ $25 ☐ $50 ☐ $100 or ☐ other $_____
    ☐ I am enclosing post dated cheques **OR**
    ☐ I will donate online through paypal or credit card

☐ I would like to make a one-time donation to the ministry of Voice for Israel in the amount of $_____

☐ I am interested in having Hannah speak at our congregation/fellowship.

☐ Please add me to the VFI mailing list and/or e-mail group.

☐ I am interested in ☐ Hebrew ☐ Feasts of the Lord
  ☐ Tour to Israel

Note: Please inquire about wholesale discounts for congregations, libraries, bookstores or group Bible studies.

Comments:_____
_____
_____

Order Form (Continued)

QTY	TEACHING DVDs ($20 each or 3 for $50)	
	DESCRIPTION	
	Exploring the Jewish Roots of the Christian Faith (*Bestseller – introduction)	
	Unity in Messiah	
	Because He Lives (Pro-life testimony)	
	There is a God in Israel	
	Messianic Jewish Passover	
	Passover Lamb or Easter Ham?	
	Where is Your Brother Jacob – Holocaust Rememberace	
	Walking Through the Wilderness	
	Ruth: A Righteous Gentile	
	Chanukah (Festival of Lights)	
	Shalom Jerusalem (Israel's Independence Day)	
	Esther's Last Call to the Church (Purim)	
	Blow the Shofar for Zion (Fall Feasts)	

QTY	OTHER	
	DESCRIPTION	**PRICE**
	NEW! Messianic Jewish Calendar With scenic photography from the Land of Israel	*$15*
	NEW! AV HARACHAMIM (Father of Mercies) Heb.-Eng. worship music CD	*$15*

ITEMS Subtotal	
Monthly donation	
One-time donation	
Shipping & Handling*	
TOTAL ENCLOSED	

*Orders up to $40, add **$9.50**. Orders $41-$100, add **$14.50**. Orders over $100, add **$17.00**. Outside North America add an additional **$2.50** for each item ordered.

SURNAME   GIVEN NAME

ADDRESS

CITY   STATE/PROVINCE

COUNTRY   ZIP/POSTAL CODE

(   )

TELEPHONE   E-MAIL

Please send form along with cheque or money order to:

**Voice for Israel #313 - 11007 Jasper Ave.
Edmonton, Alberta, T5K 0K6 Canada**

E-mail: nesher.hannah@gmail.com
Items can also be purchased online at **www.voiceforisrael.net**